The (Un)governable City

New Perspectives in South Asian History

The New Perspectives in South Asian History series publishes monographs and other writings on early modern, modern and contemporary history. The volumes in the series cover new ground across a broad spectrum of subjects such as cultural, environmental, medical, military and political history, and the histories of 'marginalised' groups. It includes fresh perspectives on more familiar fields as well as interdisciplinary and original work from all parts of South Asia. It welcomes historical contributions from sociology, anthropology and cultural studies.

The (Un)governable City

Productive Failure in the Making of Colonial Delhi,
1858–1911

RAGHAV KISHORE

Orient BlackSwan

THE (UN)GOVERNABLE CITY: PRODUCTIVE FAILURE IN THE MAKING OF COLONIAL DELHI, 1858–1911

ORIENT BLACKSWAN PRIVATE LIMITED

Registered Office
3-6-752 Himayatnagar, Hyderabad 500 029, Telangana, India
e-mail: centraloffice@orientblackswan.com

Other Offices
Bengaluru, Bhopal, Chennai, Guwahati, Hyderabad, Jaipur, Kolkata,
Lucknow, Mumbai, New Delhi, Noida, Patna, Visakhapatnam

© Orient Blackswan Pvt. Ltd 2020
First Published by Orient Blackswan Pvt. Ltd 2020

Series cover and book design
© Orient Blackswan Pvt. Ltd. 2011

ISBN 978-93-90122-98-1

032457

Typeset in Minion Pro 10/13 by
Jojy Philip, New Delhi 110 015

Printed in India at
Glorious Printers, Delhi

Published by
Orient Blackswan Private Limited
3-6-752 Himayatnagar, Hyderabad 500 029, Telangana, India
e-mail: info@orientblackswan.com

Contents

Figures

Abbreviations

ADC	Agra–Delhi Chord
BJP	Bharatiya Janata Party
CC	Chandni Chowk Clearances
CCO	Chief Commissions Office
CO	Commissioner's Office
DCO	Deputy Commissioner's Office
DDA	Delhi Development Authority
DIT	Delhi Improvement Trust
DMC	Delhi Municipal Corporation
DSA	Delhi State Archives
ETC	Ellenborough Tank Clearances
HAC	Hamid Ali Khan's Clearances
MCD	Municipal Corporation of Delhi
NCR	National Capital Region
NDMC	New Delhi Municipal Corporation
NNR	Native Newspaper Reports
PWD	Public Works Department
RR	Residency Records
SOAS	School of Oriental and African Studies

Glossary

*Bagh*s	gardens
*bazaar*s	markets
Begum	princess
bela	a local term used for the riverine lands running on both sides of the Yamuna River
*bigha*s	a unit of measurement
*burj*s	towers
chabutra	a masonry or wooden platforms used for various purposes in shops and houses
chahar bagh	quadrilateral garden
*chowk*s	squares
*dalal*s	brokers
*doli*s	carriages
Durbar	ceremonial court
Dussehra	a major Hindu festival
*ekka*s	two-wheeled horse carts
Faiz Nahar	the canal that brought water into the city
Feel Khana	elephant stables
ganj	neighbourhood
*ghat*s	river banks usually accompanied by a flight of steps
gur	jaggery
*halwaie*s	confectioners
Id-ul-Fitr	a ceremony of the Muslims

ilakas	wards
Jagirdar	an official of the king acting given rights to collected revenue of the land allotted to him
jamaadars	sweepers
Jati	endogamous units
Jharokha Darshan	the trellis window
Kaghazi Mohalla	paper-makers' neighbourhood
karkhanas	workshops
Kashmiri Darwaza bazaar	a marketplace
Katra Dhobi	washer-men's quarters
Kikar	Prosopis Juliflora
kotwal	magistrate
kuchas	areas or corners leading to a cluster of houses and shops
Lal Diggi	a water reservoir commissioned by Lord Ellenborough
Lal Qila	Red Fort
Lebkhana	Mughal offices
maalis	gardeners
mahzur	a certificate
Mandi	market
maund	an Indian unit of measuring weight
mohalla	an area resembling a neighbourhood
Muharram	a procession of the Muslims
Naya Mandir	new temple
nazul	land escheated to the state government
panchayats	village councils (with possible reference to those in the larger Delhi district)
Parasnath	the Saraogi idol
patri	pavement
Pirs	spiritual leaders
police *thana*	police station
Qila e Mubarak	exalted fort

Raises	influential native gentlemen
rath yatra	chariot procession
Sabzi Mandi	the main vegetable market of the city
Sarai	literally translated as a tavern or an inn; however, in the contemporary sense, a municipality, area or junction
Sardarakhti	a type of entitlement to land and trees
Sardarakhtidar	cultivator
Shaikhs	holy men
shakkar	sugar
Sisu	Dalbergia Sissoo
takhts	seating plinths
teh-bazari	ground rents
zamindars	landlords

Acknowledgements

This book would not have been possible without the support of a number of friends and colleagues over the years.

I began working on the project from which this book originates as a doctoral student at the School of Oriental and African Studies (SOAS). As a supervisor, Shabnum Tejani enthusiastically supported my research and has been a source of great encouragement ever since. I was fortunate to gain from intellectual exchanges with Peter Robb, Daud Ali, Ravi Ahuja, Eleanor Newbigin and Ahmad Azhar. Early on at a workshop, Nikhil Rao and Will Glover provided helpful comments on a draft chapter. Upal Chakrabarty was a sounding board for ideas, and our lively discussions piqued my intellectual curiosity. I am indebted to all these individuals as their input shaped the direction of the project in its early days. I am also thankful for thought-provoking conversations (interspersed with plentiful banter) with Stefan Tetzlaff, Tom Alberts, Shazia Ahmad, Francesca Fuoli, Martyn Smith, Matt Phillips, Sultonbek Aksakalov and Riyad Koya during our studies.

In Delhi, I must begin by thanking Sunil Kumar, whose friendship, encouragement and passion inspired my academic interests, and without whom I would not have taken up any research on Delhi. Narayani Gupta's helpful advice early on was indispensible as I went scouring for archival material. Research trips to the Delhi Archives were made extremely enriching through interactions with Tarangini Sriraman, Devika Shankar, Rotem Geva Halperlin and Anish Vanaik. Anish and I were baffled when we realised that we worked in two different archives in the Town Hall that existed without the knowledge of their custodians! I am also grateful to him for some memorable conversations on Delhi's urban history. My

Urdu *Ustad*, Ghulam Haider Sahib, helped with the translation of archival material, some of which has made its way into this book.

My erstwhile dissertation examiners, Prashant Kidambi and Stephen Legg, are probably as relieved as I am to see this book come to fruition. Their close engagement and critical comments on my work have helped sharpen its arguments, and I remain indebted to them for their counsel. Taylor Sherman's friendship, her encouragement to keep pushing on with chapter drafts and help with revising the book's title into something more meaningful has been brilliant. Anna Cant painstakingly read through chapter drafts, for which I am truly grateful. I am indebted to several others for their encouragement with the project: Sanjoy Bhattacharya, Ed Simpson, Navtej Purewal, Miles Taylor, Laura Almagor, Monica Saveedra and Alex Medcalf. Conversations with others at workshops and conferences in London and elsewhere have influenced my ideas and arguments and my apologies to anyone who I have unintentionally left out.

The assistance of staff and archivists was indispensible in the completion of this project. I would like to thank the staff of the Delhi Archives, National Archives of India, Delhi Municipal Corporation (DMC), Chandigarh State Archives and The British Library. Special thanks are due to Sanjay Garg and Geetika Singh of the Delhi Archives for prompt permission to reproduce archival images.

I am grateful to the series editors of the New Perspectives in South Asian History at Orient BlackSwan for commissioning this book. Two anonymous reviewers provided valuable comments on the manuscript, which I have taken on board. Veenu Luthria and Pooja Sanyal have made the publication process a breeze and I sincerely appreciate all their time, effort and patience.

I am incredibly lucky to have the support of a close network of old friends and relatives who have remained steadfast with encouragement over the years. Aditya, Shagun, Varsha, Saurabh and Jaclyn, Shruti, Smriti, Victoria, Ashutosh, Sanjay, Govind, Manjima and Kapil, Jessy, Mayank and Kabeeir—thanks for always being there.

Life has been challenging as an early-career academic, and the greatest of gratitude goes to my family for their forbearance and faith in my abilities. Grete and Farid, my in-laws in Austria, have been unwavering cheerleaders and will be relieved that I finally put this book to bed. From an early age, my parents Neelu and Arvind have been supportive of my endeavours, academic and otherwise. I have them to thank for their love and guidance, especially when self-doubt has plagued my mind. I also thank my brother Madhav for always being there with a helping hand.

Finally, thanks to my wife, Schirin, who has had to test her endurance; words cannot express my gratitude and love. If it were not for her balancing childcare with work, I would not have had the time to finish this book. Our sons, Dariush and Kayvan, growing up in a brave new world, have provided welcome distractions during the completion of this book. I am grateful to them for the love, laughter and happiness in my life.

Introduction

Mirza Ghalib, the poet laureate of Delhi, wrote with a profound sense of grief in 1861 when he lamented the transformation of the city into a cantonment in the aftermath of the Great Rebellion of 1857.[1] By this time, the Mughal regime was long gone, and Ghalib would claim that with one sweep, there remained no vestiges of old, 'no fort, no city, no bazaars, no watercourses'.[2] No more the Mughal imperial capital, Delhi was stripped of its political status and incorporated within the province of Punjab as punishment by its colonial masters. For its residents, this process represented an unimaginable assault on the senses. Huge sections of Delhi were being cleared on grounds of security; the city had been divided into civil and military jurisdictions, with the latter operating out of the erstwhile Mughal palace, now simply called the 'Fort'. Canons mounted on the ramparts of the Fort were meant to overawe those re-allowed in Delhi. Moreover, armed troops, housed in depopulated quarters such as Daryaganj, and the Fort itself, became visible manifestations of colonial order and control. In the midst of such tumult, one aspect that gave the everyday life in the city a familiar consistency was the writ of colonial officialdom. Ghalib's own account in his twilight years recounts the various ways in which permissions were sought: first, to enter the city, particularly for Muslims who were suspected as the instigators of the rebellion, and second, to restore erstwhile entitlements to property. The 'Delhi authorities' became a ubiquitous feature in Ghalib's life throughout those years.[3] Indeed, the 'state' had acquired a certain everydayness in urban life after the rebellion, with no action or undertaking escaping its scrutiny. Now, there was a hierarchy of municipal officials who enforced by-laws to regulate 'public' spaces; there were sanitary and medical departments with officials bringing 'insanitary' practices under their watchful gaze, and police and military personnel scrutinising details of proposed processions and festival activities in the interests of public security. Foresters, engineers and Public Works Department (PWD) officials all abounded, drafting and pursuing their various 'improvement' policies. At a time of rapid change, the one seemingly constant factor in the provincial city was the ever-present and ever-expanding world of bureaucracy, with its departments, plans and regulations.

This book uncovers the processes that underpinned the expansion of such bureaucratic worlds by focusing on the transformation of urban governance in colonial Delhi between 1858 and 1911. The period that it covers broadly coincides with what historians have labelled as the 'High Noon' of the Empire (1858–1914)—an era of stability and consolidation of British power in India—a time when perhaps colonial rule felt most secure of its own position.[4] Scholars who have written on the history of the Indian city in the aftermath of the rebellion have extended such insights and have highlighted that this period was marked for the imposition of colonial ideologies of rule and cultural norms over the city and its inhabitants.[5] Indeed, read at face value, Ghalib's much-recounted ruminations, as presented in the introductory paragraph of this book, would support the contention that the colonial government was relatively unconstrained as it consolidated its power after the rebellion of 1857. However, this book complicates such a narrative. It demonstrates how internal tensions and conflicts were a defining feature of colonial governance between 1858 and 1911. Rather than a monolithic colonial state imposing its designs upon the urban space and the local population, this book presents the complexity of interactions between various colonial authorities, departments and officials in Delhi, their contradictory visions and priorities, and suggests that these often clashed with one another, exacerbating a host of urban problems in the colonial city.

The book reveals that as urban agencies intervened to transform the city, their efforts were often scuppered as a result of competing logics of improvement, notions of public order, and understandings of how native rights and customs functioned. Disagreements over protocol and contradictions within urban policy made the execution of projects extremely complicated. Their costs spiralled, the differing opinions of experts stifled the progression of particular schemes, and all this generated a considerable amount of resentment from city-dwellers who objected to what appeared to be poorly thought-through colonial plans. Indeed, this book finds that the 'crises' of urban governance were not simply identifiable in a particular period, but were present straight from the establishment of colonial rule after the rebellion.[6]

Yet, a key argument I present is that if there were tensions, conflicting agendas, crises and clashes between government authorities and agencies, many of which resulted in the failure of particular efforts, schemes or urban plans, these were also productive, inasmuch as they provided new opportunities for the extension of bureaucratic and regulatory capabilities of the government, they legitimated particular strands of colonial knowledge and scientific expertise, and drove urban planning in new directions.[7] Then, Ghalib's account of the ins and outs of bureaucracy after the rebellion, and the burgeoning departments and their exhaustive corpus of regulations must not be read as a spontaneous response linked to the imposition of colonial rule, but as a product of the incoherence of colonial power and its inconsistency. This book thus joins a body of literature calling for attention to the unintended effects of 'failed' state interventions and their legacies.[8] As Cunningham Bissell states in his study of urban planning in colonial Zanzibar, failed colonial plans often 'served as justification for the reformist claims of British rule, consumed inordinate amounts of energy, promoted an expansive administrative apparatus and inserted colonial subjects within an arbitrary legal and bureaucratic order'.[9] In a similar manner, I reveal that the contradictions, ambiguity and the ultimate 'failure' of urban policies in colonial Delhi provided new directions in which the state could expand and which allowed for its self-renewal.[10] The chapters highlight several examples: the development of new and eventually permanent establishments that grew as a result of investigative committees meant to understand why and how plans went wrong or failed; the ways in which new medical and sanitary theories were legitimised out of controversial improvement schemes; the corpus of complex legislations and orders that were drafted even when the removal of encroachments resulted in failure; or when local authorities found themselves grappling with problems of public order that resulted from previous contentious government rulings. These arbitrary, contingent and unintended outcomes provided a wealth of resources for the augmentation of the state's powers and promoted the longevity of its agencies.[11]

However, where this book departs from much of the literature on the relationship between state failures, and its unintended gains is that it does not see the state as the sole beneficiary of such *productive* tensions and ultimate failures. This was not some zero-sum game. Indeed, I suggest here that the unintended consequences of colonial interventions, the contradictions within, and failures of, urban policy, should not simply be seen as a one-sided affair for the entrenchment of colonial agencies, but also as a process through which opportunities were presented and used by different sections of the population for their own ends. Delhi's residents, as I show in the subsequent chapters, used the contradictions of colonial policy to assert their claims to their entitlements and spaces of the city. As rules and regulations proliferated, enterprising individuals found in them a considerable amount of ambiguity and inconsistency with which to obtain concessions from governing bodies and urban authorities.

This book and its arguments are situated within what has become a vibrant field of South Asian colonial urban history over the last decade or so. Historically grounded works now abound on subjects including, but not restricted to, the relationship between the built environment and urban identity, and thereby, the nature of 'modernity' in South Asia. Such works also study the distinctiveness of urban planning and the development of governance under colonial rule, as well as the place of indigenous agency and contestation within the colonial city.[12] This body of literature is perhaps indicative of a broader conceptual shift suggested by scholars, that the 'rural' has been displaced as the 'authentic' site of Indian tradition, and that identity and the Indian city is coming into its own as an object of study.[13] Another welcome departure has been the acknowledgement of Indian voices in urban transformations, a move away from earlier readings that relied too narrowly on imperial ideologies and initiatives in reconstructing the history of the Indian city.[14] Yet, the foregrounding of the question of Indian agency, I feel, has meant that some recent works have tended to locate colonial power and the colonial state more generally, on different ends of a spectrum: from characterising it in a linear manner and with a singular purpose, as a coercive symbol of domination, to suggesting its eventual redundancy in the public landscape of the city.[15] However, other studies on colonial urbanism have shifted their emphasis to the messiness and incoherence of an overstretched colonial state whose urban plans constantly failed to materialise.[16] These alert us to the cacophony of voices in the colonial government, their multiple agendas, as well as 'contending logics', which resulted in the eventual collapse of urban projects and plans. While building on such insights, this book goes beyond exposing the failures of urban renewal and the limitations of the colonial government to explore the unintended effects of such 'failed' interventions and contradictory clashes. By suggesting that failure was inextricably linked to the reconstitution of colonial governance, it reiterates the significance and distinctiveness of the latter in shaping the urban landscape of the Indian city. Yet, in making this point, it does not relegate the question of agency. Indeed, the book highlights various forms of Indian agency, from cooperation and collaboration to resistance; but it does so within the context of changing 'political rationalities' of power.[17] In other words, even as it provides evidence of the multiple ways in which the colonial encounter was negotiated in the city, the book does not lose sight of the altered political landscape brought on by colonialism.[18]

SITUATING COLONIAL DELHI: THE CITY AND ITS HISTORIOGRAPHY

Delhi was a seat of power long before the British Empire in India. Located at a strategic juncture between the north-west frontier of India and the rich alluvial plains of the Doab to its east, the region of Delhi remained an important political and commercial centre in India for centuries. Comprising walled habitable settlements, several 'old' cities known as Delhi assumed the status of political capitals under the Delhi Sultanate between the thirteenth and the sixteenth centuries.[19] Beyond its political importance, the region of Delhi was a centre of pilgrimage associated with the most important Muslim religious shrines in the subcontinent.[20] As an act of piety, devotees of *Pirs* (spiritual leaders) and *Shaikhs* (holy men) made their way to the numerous shrines and tombs that dotted the landscape, from neighbouring regions and beyond.[21] Much of this influenced the Mughal emperor Shah Jahan's decision to build his eponymous capital Shahjahanabad in the seventeenth century. On the banks of the Yamuna

River, navigable for trade the whole year round, with convenient access to arterial highways and a rich agricultural hinterland, Shah Jahan's chosen site was extremely well-situated.[22] Various notables and members of the Mughal household domesticated the landscape outside the city walls, creating sumptuous gardens replete with cypress and fruit trees.[23] As a city meant to rival the Safavid capital of Isfahan, Shahjahanabad was renowned for its famed *Qila e Mubarak* (exalted fort), its mosques, gardens and *chowks* (squares), and it emerged as a beacon of urbane culture and economic importance.[24] Scholars have shown how, even during the politically tumultuous long-eighteenth century that saw the decline of Mughal power, there is no evidence to speak of an absolute decline of Indian cities like Delhi or Shahjahanabad (hereafter simply addressed as Delhi), which remained economically and culturally resilient.[25]

The Mughal emperors of Delhi continued to remain a source of symbolic power even as the East India Company took control of the city's administration after 1803.[26] For this 'Company Raj' (1803–57) period, there is a rich body of work highlighting the nature of political, economic and cultural transformations in Delhi. Scholars have examined the ways in which the Company's administration was run, and how its power was projected and negotiated by different groups in Delhi, including the role of the Muslim intelligentsia.[27] With topics including confrontations between citizens and the government, education and elections, and the strains of urban expansion, Narayani Gupta's landmark book on Delhi remains the most comprehensive work on the city, covering a long dureé from 1803–1931.[28] Gupta's book highlights the challenges of urban development in a colonial context, demonstrating how changing racial attitudes impacted Delhi's economic and institutional growth after a period of relative 'peace' under the East India Company. The destruction wrought by the British forces during the rebellion of 1857, the socio-economic changes under 'Crown Rule' post-1858, and finally, the shift of the capital from Calcutta and creation of a 'New' Delhi after 1911, are all accounted for in her narrative.[29] More recently, Gupta's work has been followed by historically informed studies, many of which extend their examination into the postcolonial period, on subjects such as Delhi's architectural and spatial history, middle-class identity, social geography, environmental change, and the relationship between memory and archaeological heritage.[30]

A significant aspect of this literature has been that it has complicated older colonial representations of Delhi as an 'exotic' and 'traditional' order in decline, bringing to the fore its contested relationship with modernity.[31] As Jyoti Hosagrahar points out, colonial narratives of Delhi as a relic of the past or as an 'un-modern' city were used to justify the British imperial presence and colonial reforms.[32] Hosagrahar, an architectural historian who works on the post-rebellion period after 1857, reclaims the category of modernity for Delhi by suggesting that its residents resisted and subverted colonial designs and spatial plans to carve out an alternative modernity for the city.[33] What prompted such a response was the 'difference' of colonial governmental rationality or 'governmentality' in Delhi, a divergence from Western norms.[34] As geographer Stephen Legg writes in his study of colonial Delhi between 1911 and 1947, this difference manifested itself through a series of 'excesses' and 'neglects' in the urban environment, underpinned by a hyper-regulated colonised society and economy without the provision of democratic rights.[35] Much of this resulted in the delayed execution of urban schemes, the failure of planning in the city, and therefore, resistance to colonial intransigence. Both Legg and Hosagrahar thus point out how urban plans in Delhi remained incomplete, as the exercise of creating maps, plans and surveys was directed towards 'representing technological superiority' instead of aiding sanitary improvement, and bio-political 'improvement' plans failed due to financial conservatism.[36] This book, while indebted to such scholars and their insights, places 'contradiction' and 'failure' not as the endpoint, but as the mainstay of its analysis in thinking about the afterlife of 'failed' and 'incomplete' schemes in Delhi. It argues that while project mishaps or tensions between different authorities may have prevented originally stated planning goals, they could also be productive. Contradictions and rivalries among government departments, for example, could drive local agencies to push forward their 'improvement' practices, legitimise or reinforce certain strands of sanitary expertise, and stimulate long-term colonial urban planning in the city. Moreover, as much as civic agencies of the state, such as the Delhi Municipal Corporation (hereafter referred to as DMC and/or Delhi municipality), failed to provide urban renewal, these were accompanied by an expansion of their bureaucratic and technical capabilities, which carried long-term effects for the city's development.

At one level, we may follow Gwendolyn Wright and Paul Rabinow and agree that Delhi was, just as other parts of the colonial world, a 'laboratory' of modernity—a site of experimentation where new ideas and practices of governance were organised and developed with an intention to order and regulate colonial society.[37] However, this book shows that far from achieving 'controlled' conditions on the ground, the policies and processes that enabled such transformations were never uniform or crisis-free. Indeed, much of colonial policy in Delhi actually exacerbated urban problems such as sanitation and disease instead of ameliorating them. Yet, it is significant that this also sowed the seeds that enabled the realisation of the colonial project. Delhi's example will demonstrate how new modes of bureaucratic governance, new procedures and forms of knowledge arose out of a seemingly inchoate practice.

Second, whereas studies on Delhi have focused on a long dureé or on the period after the shift of the capital from Calcutta to Delhi post-1911, in this book, I bring a shorter time frame into sharp relief. I concentrate exclusively on the period when Delhi's political status was that of a provincial city of Punjab from 1858–1911, and I suggest that this was a formative period in the urban transformation of the city. Thus, it was during this period that the city's hinterland, including its famed Mughal gardens, became enmeshed within various 'improvement' programmes, indelibly altering its relationship with the city. Moreover, although the Mughal empire had ended, the memory of the Mughal city functioned as a powerful symbol of contestation, particularly as new economically powerful groups wished to assert their dominance through rituals and processional activities in Delhi. Further, Delhi's transformation as a transport node, evinced in urban plans from the 1880s, was a product of contestations between different scales of the state in which the railways became central to the city's planning imaginary. Such examples, along with the creation of an urban property market, the restructuring of 'public' spaces and the management of traffic, and significantly, the diverse ways in which these changes were negotiated, underline the significance of this provincial era in Delhi's history.[38]

Finally, a focus on Delhi allows the book to recover relatively unused archival material on the city's provincial era, offer fresh theoretical insights on the nature of 'expertise' in the colonial context, and contribute to the development of the historiography of South Asian cities. Thus, in the chapters, I present materials on how the priorities of different levels—local, regional and imperial—of the colonial government intersected in Delhi. An analysis of 'scale' in this manner is particularly helpful in problematising the notion of 'scientific expertise'. As I suggest, 'experts' in various guises, from sanitary specialists to forest authorities, were inclined to favour the imperial (government of India) or provincial (government of Punjab) proposals at the expense of municipal or local government demands in Delhi. This was therefore not what is commonly understood as 'disinterested' or 'neutral' expertise at work, but a distinctly colonial project in the making. The DMC would indeed respond to such changes by expanding and augmenting its regulatory and bureaucratic capabilities; but it is necessary to understand its rootedness in a distinct colonial framework.

Fresh material presented in this book includes executive committee proceedings and general proceedings of the activities of the municipality found in the Municipal Corporation of Delhi (MCD) office in the Town Hall in Delhi. These fragmented but rich pieces of information are exceptionally useful when attempting to understand the everyday operations of the Delhi municipality during the period under consideration. Their analysis has been integral to the book's arguments on the tense exchanges between officials, the reversal of decisions, and conflicting priories of government departments in the city. Included in Chapter 4 is material from local police reports, primarily in English, but some also translated from Urdu. This is related to the processions of the Jain Saraogis between the 1860s and 70s and their confrontations with Hindu residents. This focus on the Jain Saraogis in Delhi brings to light the social history of this group, but it also underscores how new claims by marginal actors in a city can reflect back on and expose the relationships of power and space in the city.[39] Along with material on the relatively well-documented Mughal *Baghs* (gardens) of Delhi, the book also presents fresh material on colonial arboriculture initiatives and plantation projects in the city.[40] This is part of a broader attempt to explore colonial interventions in the natural landscape in India and think about how nature is remade in urban contexts.[41] Focusing on understudied spaces such as riverine lands and forested areas in the vicinity of Delhi, I use such examples to expose power relationships, just as in the case of marginal figures like the Jain Saraogis.

THE CHAPTERS

Chapter 1 reveals how urban property relations were transformed by the event of the rebellion of 1857. Historians have chronicled the widespread destruction and devastation brought on by colonial reprisals on Delhi in the aftermath of 1857. Yet, just as symbolic as this retributive justice was the question of compensation of 'loyal' natives who had sided with the colonial authorities during the rebellion. A range of officials, including military personnel and Lord Canning, the Viceroy, debated over the extent to which native elites who did not participate in the rebellion could be co-opted into the imperial fold by compensating them for their losses. Thus, compensation was to become a mechanism for the re-establishment of colonial power and the reins of the government. However, the chapter suggests that imperial debates over compensation and the process it took were far from straightforward. The prospect of, first, identifying loyal supporters as demanded by higher-level authorities, and then, providing them some form of compensation, was to bear heavily on an incipient local government, which was simultaneously being pressured by military demands for strategic clearances in the city. The answer to such tensions and pressures was found through the redistribution by auction of confiscated urban property belonging to rebels. This became the mechanism through which the scheme of compensation was elaborated. This chapter further demonstrates that such a compensation scheme had to be continually modified to suit local conditions. This meant satisfying the demands of loyal native elites by selecting what they felt were the most valuable properties before auctions, as well as managing an unwieldy system of speculation in promissory notes, which the authorities had devised for property transactions. The constitution of a market in urban property was the result of such accommodations by the local administration; and the chapter thus sheds light on the fraught nature of urban governance in the colonial context.

Chapter 2 considers the everyday operations of the DMC to promote urban renewal in the city from the 1860s. Like many others instituted across India after 1858, the DMC was a civic agency responsible for checking sanitary offences, regulating building construction, and the overall management of what were defined as 'public' spaces—a novel concept brought to India by the British. This chapter examines a wealth of fresh material in the form of municipal committee reports in Delhi, applications to construct platforms, disputes over 'encroachments', and the creation and establishment of commercial markets to examine the DMC's role in the governance of the city. It suggests that the DMC was able to adopt a sophisticated set of by-laws and create a large administrative apparatus, with cutting-edge 'expertise' in its employment. From sanitary experts and engineers, advising it on ways to ameliorate disease through the construction of new surface drains for the city's salubrity, the support of codified laws to punish offenders for their encroachments, to a hierarchical administration with European and Indian representatives, the DMC was able to centralise and expand its powers tremendously. However, this very process created severe challenges for its functions, as the complexity of its operations, recommendations by its experts, costs of ambitious projects, and local resistance constantly subverted municipal intentions. Yet, as this chapter shows, from these very problems, or what might be termed 'failures', arose 'opportunities' for the DMC's longevity, which allowed it to move into different directions from its originally stated intentions, giving it new bureaucratic and regulatory powers in the city. The chapter also points out that far from this being a one-sided affair, different sections of the population were also able to redefine and reinterpret municipal by-laws, taking advantage of the ambiguity of its ordinances and using it for their own ends. Therefore, unintended opportunities did not exist simply for the benefit of municipal power.

Chapter 3 examines colonial improvement initiatives in Delhi's outlying or 'suburban' lands.[42] As part of a political project meant to civilise Indians and reshape their urban environment, a wide range of agencies and authorities in the city were entrusted to carry out improvement projects. Sanitary professionals, engineers of the PWD, medical officers, the forest department, military authorities and the DMC, all flexed their muscles when it came to 'improving' Delhi, particularly its extensive erstwhile Mughal garden lands and retreats, which existed to the north-west of the city. From strictly economic concerns, the improvement of the health of the city and its agricultural population, the moral upliftment of natives, to aesthetic prerogatives, many of the agencies mentioned above championed multiple, diverse, and sometimes a contradictory number of aims in their improvement drives. This chapter focuses on the designs to improve garden lands, such as the famed Roshanara *Bagh*, and create plantations out of the riverine lands of the River Yamuna, and shows how such interventions brought with them a host of complications. It demonstrates how clashes over turf and jurisdictions among different professional bodies, disputes over the nature and direction of improvements, and accusations of dilettantism and profligacy levelled by officials at one-another, often marred improvement projects, increased their operational costs, and exacerbated sanitary problems. Not least, they created difficulties over determining entitlements with regard to soil, land and trees in the suburban areas by different social groups, who were themselves quick to exploit any lapses in government policy. Piecing together sections of disparate archival records, this chapter suggests that such contradictions and tensions among different agencies could actually serve to promote distinct strands of colonial knowledge and practice, thereby legitimising the notion of improvement.

Chapter 4 explores the relationship between ritual precedence and public order in Delhi after the rebellion. The street posed a particular problem for colonial governance after 1857, especially in cities like Delhi, which although now relegated in political status, carried a symbolic attachment as former centres of Mughal power. On the one hand, streets were now 'public', and therefore subject to strict rules of 'public order' and discipline at a time when the need for security was acute. On the other hand, when it came to street processions, the responses of officials remained tentative. For fear of intruding over what were framed as 'religious rites', conflicting opinions prevailed among administrative officials at different levels of the government. Thus, while city commissioners were reluctant to allow any 'novel' processions on grounds of public security, their superiors in the government of Punjab were more willing to make concessions on grounds of non-interference in religious observances. This in turn led to contradictory sets of orders and notices over time. This chapter explores the ambiguities of colonial governance over the question of street processions in Delhi and the ways in which new understandings of the city were mobilised to challenge the claims of the local government by social groups like the Saraogi Jains. As wealthy but ritually insignificant actors in the public arena prior to the rebellion of 1857, the Saraogis wished to express their growing wealth and influence via grand processions in the Chandni Chowk, the largest thoroughfare in Delhi, after 1857. However, the chapter shows how contradictory practices of governance led to the ban of their *rath yatra* (chariot procession) on grounds of public security, and reduced them to a minor entity in Delhi's post-Rebellion public-arena activities. This context, the chapter highlights, was crucial in shaping the Saraogis' demand for access to the Chandni Chowk, their skilful translations of notions of public conduct, and the way they challenged the rights of their rivals and appraised different levels of government authority.

Chapter 5 reveals how the management of traffic, and particularly, railway traffic, gained a new resonance in colonial urban plans after the 1880s. Although founded in Delhi in the 1860s, the growth of the railways and its commercial traffic from the 1880s onwards was profound, inducing concerns about how the city itself was to be made conducive to flows of people, goods and commerce in future. With goods carts and passengers competing with other modes of transport for road space when trying to get to the Delhi Central Station or from there to other markets, a perceptible need for the management of traffic flows in the city was felt by senior municipal officials. In new gardens and localities, city extensions and re-designed neighbourhoods, through overbridges and high-level pavements, all intended to encourage quick access to the central station while minimising bottlenecks and congestion, answers were found for re-invigorating the city in what has been called the 'second stage' of its railway history.[43] However, as new plans were created to enable smooth flows of traffic and generate a commercially healthy city, they were 'colonial' in their orientation. This was not only because they continued to voice policing anxieties, but also because they were based on distinct imaginaries of what constituted the 'natural' features of the urban environment in Indian cities. Hence, mosques and Mughal *burjs* (towers) were strategically fit into plans since they were deemed necessary for the success of traffic schemes and urban projects. Finally, and quite significantly, the chapter also highlights how the process of railway-inspired urban planning was itself driven by a clash between different levels of government. If plans were drafted by urban agencies like the DMC to promote commercial growth and enhance circulation within the city, then there is a larger context within which such actions should be understood, particularly the demands made by the central government for the absorption of the city into larger rail networks—a representation of its desire to territorialise and inscribe its power. It was therefore the tension between authorities at different scales of government that could fuel planning in the city and its suburban lands.

The final chapter concludes by thinking about the book's arguments in relation to the legacies of urban governance in Delhi after 1911. It examines in brief the literature on the history of colonial and postcolonial Delhi to situate its arguments, and suggests that parallels can be found even today in the way urban agencies such as the MCD reproduce their power despite the 'failure' to provide urban renewal in the city.

NOTES

1. Ralph Russell and Khurshidul Islam, 'Ghalib: Life and Letters', in *The Oxford India Ghalib: Life, Letters and Ghalzals*, ed. Ralph Russell (Oxford: New Delhi, 2003), 188.

2. Russel and Islam, 'Ghalib: Life and Letters', 188.

3. Russel and Islam, 'Ghalib: Life and Letters', 188; Ghalib writes in 1864: '... I've given up calling upon the Delhi authorities—the commissioner, the deputy commissioner and so on—but I *have* to meet the deputy commissioner once a month because he has charge of the treasury and if I didn't meet him he wouldn't issue my pay to my agent. Now the deputy commissioner, Mr Decrowther (?) has taken six months' leave and gone to the hills. Mr Rattigan has been appointed in his place. Of course I had to meet him ...' (italicised emphasis in original).

4. This is the norm for teaching texts that periodise the study of colonial rule in South Asia. See, for example, S. Bose and A. Jalal, *Modern South Asia: History, Culture, Political Economy* (New York: Routledge, 2004), 78.

5. The seminal text here is Veena Oldenburg's study of colonial Lucknow. See Veena Oldenburg, *The Making of Colonial Lucknow: 1856–77* (Princeton: Princeton University Press, 1984).

6. This is in contradistinction to studies that have identified a specific historical urban 'moment', taking the late-nineteenth century to the first quarter of the twentieth century, in which urban crises gave rise to specific governmental interventions and responses. See Prashant Kidambi, *The Making of an Indian Metropolis: Colonial Governance and Public Culture in Bombay, 1890–1920* (Aldershot: Ashgate, 2007), and Sandip Hazareesingh, *The Colonial City and the Challenge of Modernity: Urban Hegemonies and Civic Contestations in Bombay City 1900–25* (New Delhi: Orient BlackSwan, 2007).

7. To use the words of Timothy Mitchell, it was these very practices that produced a 'state effect' and enabled the state to be seen as a reified object. Timothy Mitchell, 'The Limits of the State: Beyond Statist Approaches and their Critics', *The American Political Science Review* 85, no. 1, 1991, 77–96.

8. See, for instance, James Ferguson, *The Anti-politics Machine: 'Development', Depoliticisation and Bureaucratic Power in Lesotho* (Cambridge: Cambridge University Press, 1990); W. C. Bissell, *Urban Design, Chaos and Colonial Power in Zanzibar* (Indiana: Indiana University Press, 2011); Timothy Mitchell, *Rule of Experts: Egypt, Techno-politics, Modernity* (Berkeley: University of California Press, 2002); James S. Duncan, *In the Shadows of the Tropics: Climate, Race and Biopower in Nineteenth Century Ceylon* (Aldershot: Ashgate, 2007) and Kidambi, *The Making of an Indian Metropolis*, 71–114.

9. Bissell, *Urban Design, Chaos and Colonial Power*, 3.

10. In this manner, the book develops sociologists Peter Miller and Nicholas Rose's provocative suggestion that while the government is a 'congenitally failing operation', governmentality in the Foucauldian sense—ways of governing around distinct rationalities—is always 'optimistic'. Peter Miller and Nikolas Rose, *Governing the Present: Administering Economic, Social and Personal Life* (Cambridge: Polity Press, 2008), 35. On Michel Foucault's notion of governmentality more generally, see Mitchell Dean, *Governmentality: Power and Rule in Modern Society*, Second Edition (London: SAGE Publications, 2010); Michel Foucault, 'Governmentality', in *The Foucault Effect: Studies in Governmentality with Two Lectures and an Interview with Michel Foucault*, ed. Graham Burchell, Colin Gordon and Peter Miller (Chicago: University of Chicago Press, 1991), 87–104; Michel Foucault, *Security, Territory, Population: Lectures at the College de France 1977–78*, ed. M. Senellart, trans. Graham Burchell (London: Palgrave Macmillan, 2007); and Michel Foucault, *The Birth of Biopolitics: Lectures at the Collège de France, 1978–79*, ed. M. Senellart (New York: Palgrave Macmillan, 2008).

11. My understanding of arbitrary responses to internal tensions and resistance comes close to Akhil Gupta's formulation in the context of welfare programmes in postcolonial India. Gupta identifies bureaucratic arbitrariness and contingency; he terms this the 'production of arbitrariness', which is constitutive of state-formation. In his account, Gupta uses the notion of contingency slightly differently—as agentive in producing structural violence against the poor. Akhil Gupta, *Red Tape: Bureaucracy, Structural Violence and Poverty in India* (Durham: Duke University Press, 2012), 13–14 and 44–47.

12. This body of literature is growing, the canvas is broad, and in some cases, the works bridge the colonial–postcolonial divide. See, for example, Swati

Chattopadhyay, *Representing Calcutta: Modernity, Nationalism and the Colonial Uncanny* (London: Routledge, 2005); Jyoti Hosagrahar, *Indigenous Modernities: Negotiating Architecture and Urbanism* (London: Routledge, 2005); Hazareesingh, *The Colonial City*; William J. Glover, *Making Lahore Modern: Constructing and Imagining a Colonial City* (Minneapolis: University of Minnesota Press, 2007); Kidambi, *The Making of an Indian Metropolis*; Stephen Legg, *Spaces of Colonialism: Delhi's Urban Governmentalities* (New Delhi: Wiley-Blackwell, 2007); Vikramaditya Prakash and Peter Scriver (eds), *Colonial Modernities: Building, Dwelling, Architecture in British India and Ceylon* (London: Routledge, 2007); Gyan Prakash, *Mumbai Fables* (Princeton: Princeton University Press, 2011); Preeti Chopra, *A Joint Enterprise: Indian Elites and the Making of a British Bombay* (Minneapolis: University of Minnesota Press, 2011); Partho Dutta, *Planning the City: Urbanisation and Reform in Calcutta, c. 1800–1940* (New Delhi: Tulika Books, 2012); Janaki Nair, *The Promise of the Metropolis: Bangalore's Twentieth Century* (New Delhi: Oxford University Press, 2005); Nikhil Rao, *House But No Garden: Apartment Living in Bombay's Suburbs, 1898–1964* (Minneapolis: University of Minnesota Press, 2012); Howard Spodek, *Ahmedabad: Shock City of the Twentieth-Century India* (New Delhi: Orient BlackSwan, 2012); and David Andrew Johnson, *New Delhi: The Last Imperial City (Britain and the World)* (Basingstoke: Palgrave Macmillan, 2015).

13. Gyan Prakash, 'The Urban Turn', in *The Cities of Everyday Life*, Sarai Reader II (New Delhi: Centre for the Study of Developing Societies [CSDS] 2002), 2–7; Nair, *The Promise of the Metropolis*, 2–5; and Kidambi, *The Making of an Indian Metropolis*, 2–8.

14. This early body of work includes, among others, Anthony King, *Colonial Urban Development: Culture Social Power and Environment* (London: Routledge, 1976); Jan Morris, *Stones of Empire: Buildings of the Raj* (Oxford: Oxford University Press, 1983); Phillip Davies, *Splendours of the Raj: British Architecture in India, 1660–1947* (London: John Murray Publishers, 1985); Robert Grant Irving, *Indian Summer: Lutyens, Baker and Imperial Delhi* (New York: Yale University Press, 1982); Mariam Dossal, *Imperial Designs and Indian Realities: The Planning of Bombay City, 1845–1875* (New Delhi: Oxford University Press, 1991); and Thomas Metcalf, *An Imperial Vision: Indian Architecture and Britain's Raj* (California: University of California Press, 1992).

15. See Hosagrahar, *Indigenous Modernities*; and Chopra, *A Joint Enterprise*. These two monographs take such opposing views.

16. As exemplified in Kidambi, *The Making of an Indian Metropolis*; and Legg, *Spaces of Colonialism*.

17. This is David Scott's formulation—the beginnings of a new political *project* concerned with the redefinition and transformation of the everyday lives of the colonised population; David Scott, 'Colonial Governmentality', *Social Text*, no. 43, 1995, 191–220. Yet, as Tania Murray Li suggests, we must remember that colonial objectives were not singular; rather, they were 'combined in awkward amalgams' with others; from permanent deferral (the insistence or political tutelage over racialised subjects), to division (on the basis of class logics), and even obliging (inducing) natives to pursue their own 'authentic' traditions; Tania Murray Li, *The Will to Improve: Governmentality, Development and the Practice of Politics* (Durham: Duke University Press, 2007), 13–15.

18. Janaki Nair has pointed out that we must always be aware of the political rupture caused by colonialism in response to the newer wave of writings on the colonial city. See Janaki Nair, 'Beyond Nationalism: Modernity, Governance and a New Urban History for India', *Urban History* 36, no. 2, 2009, 327–41.

19. See M. Athar Ali, 'Capital of the Sultans: Delhi during the Thirteenth and Fourteenth Centuries', in *Delhi Through the Ages: Selected Essays in Urban History,* ed. R. E. Frykenberg (New Delhi: Oxford University Press, 1994), 21–31; and C. B. Asher, 'Delhi Walled: Changing Boundaries', in *The Urban Enceinte in Global Perspective*, ed. J. Tracy (Cambridge: Cambridge University Press, 2000), 247–81.

20. Stephen Blake, 'Cityscape of an Imperial Capital: Shahjahanabad in 1739', in *Delhi Through the Ages*, ed. Frykenberg, 154.

21. Blake, 'Cityscape of an Imperial Capital', in *Delhi Through the Ages*, ed. Frykenberg, 154.

22. Hamida Khatoon Naqvi, 'Shahjahanabad, The Mughal Delhi, 1638–1803: An Introduction', in *Delhi Through the Ages*, ed. Frykenberg, 144.

23. Blake, 'Cityscape of an Imperial Capital', in *Delhi Through the Ages,* ed. Frykenberg, 161.

24. For architectural and morphological studies of the imperial capital, see Shama Mitra Chenoy, *Shahjahanabad: A City of Delhi 1638–1857* (New Delhi: Munshiram Manoharlal Publishers, 1998); and Stephen Blake, *Shahjahanabad: The Sovereign City in Mughal India, 1639–1739* (Cambridge: Cambridge University Press, 1991).

25. For studies that counter the narrative of the general 'decline' of urban cities in the eighteenth century and show how Delhi witnessed a major growth in the development of Urdu literature and in artistic production, see Khurshidul Islam and Ralph Russell, *Three Mughal Poets: Mir, Sauda, Mir Hasan* (New Delhi: Oxford University Press, 2012), and William Dalrymple and Yuthika Sharma (eds), *Princes and Painters in Mughal Delhi, 1707–1857* (New York:

Yale University Press, 2012). On Delhi's economic resilience, see Christopher Bayly, 'Delhi and Other Cities of North India During the "Twilight"', in *Delhi Through the Ages*, ed. Frykenberg, 121–36.

26. Rather than seeing the later Mughals as ineffectual in contrast to their earlier forebears, Amar Farooqui has recently suggested that the role of the Mughal emperor was actually redefined under the rule of Shah Alam II (1728–1806), who devised a new conception of Mughal sovereignty in cognisance of the rising power of the East India Company. Fastidiousness with regard to court ceremonials and rituals became the norm under the later emperors as a way of exercising their legitimacy and authority. See Amar Farooqui, *Zafar and the Raj: Anglo-Mughal Delhi, c. 1800–1850* (New Delhi: Primus Books, 2013).

27. See Percival Spear, *Twilight of the Mughals: Studies in Late Mughal Delhi* (Cambridge: Cambridge University Press, 1951); Margrit Pernau (eds), *The Delhi College: Traditional Elites, the Colonial State, and Education before 1857* (Oxford: Oxford University Press, 2006); C. M. Naim, 'Ghalib's Delhi: A Shamelessly Revisionist Look at Two Popular Metaphors', in *Urdu Texts and Contexts: The Selected Essays of C. M. Naim*, ed. C. M. Naim (New Delhi: Permanent Black, 2004), 250–73; Michael Mann, 'Turbulent Delhi: Religious Strife, Social Tension and Political Conflicts, 1803–1857', *Journal of South Asian Studies* XXVIII, no. 1, 2005, 5–34; and Sylvia Shorto, *British Houses in Late Mughal Delhi* (London: Boydell and Brewer, 2018). On the rebellion in Delhi and the joint rebel–Mughal administration's command of the city, see William Dalrymple, *The Last Mughal* (New Delhi: Penguin Books, 2006); and Mahmood Farooqui, *Besieged: Voices from Delhi, 1857, With Notes on the Rebellion Papers and Governance in Delhi 1857* (New Delhi: Viking Books, 2010).

28. Narayani Gupta, *Delhi Between Two Empires: 1803–1931: Society, Government and Urban Growth* (New Delhi: Oxford University Press, 1981).

29. Gupta, *Delhi Between Two Empires*.

30. See Margrit Pernau, *Ashraf into Middle Class: Muslims in Nineteenth-Century Delhi* (New Delhi: Oxford University Press, 2013); Hosagrahar, *Indigenous Modernities*; A. Sharan, *In the City, Out of Place: Nuisance, Pollution, and Dwelling in Delhi, c. 1850–2000* (New Delhi: Oxford University Press, 2014); Legg, *Spaces of Colonialism*; Nayantara Pothen, *Glittering Decades: New Delhi in Love and War* (Viking Books: New Delhi, 2012); Andrew Johnson, *New Delhi: The Last Imperial City*; Mrinalni Rajagopalan, *Building Histories: The Archival and Affective Lives of Five Monument in Modern Delhi* (Chicago: University of Chicago Press, 2017); and Anand Taneja, *Jinnealogy: Time, Islam*

and Ecological Thought in the Medieval Ruins of Delhi (California: Stanford University Press, 2017).

31. This colonial exoticism drew heavily on romanticising the tombs and ruins of 'older settlements of Delhi', and continued through the nineteenth century. Such accounts of Delhi can be found in colonial travelogues and archaeological guides, including James Forbes, *Oriental Memoirs: A Narrative of Seventeen Years Residence in India*, Second Edition by his Daughter, the Countess of Montalembert (London: R. Bentley, 1834); Emma Roberts, *Scenes and Characteristics of Hindustan* (London: Allen Lane, 1837), Fredrick C. Cooper, *The Handbook for Delhi: With Index and Two Maps, Illustrating the Historic Remains of Old Delhi And the Position of the British Army Before the Assault in 1857 &c. &c.* (Lahore: T. C. McCarthy, Lahore Chronicle Press, 1865); Carr Stephen, *The Archaeology and Monumental Remains of Delhi* (New Delhi: Aryan Books International, 2002). However, colonial visitors and officials were not the only ones to undertake the process of documentation of Mughal sites, tombs and surveys of the city. Guides on the city were also written in Urdu by Delhi's elites, albeit at the behest of colonial officials. See Mirza Sangin Beg, *Sair ul Manazil* (New Delhi: Ghalib Institute, 1982); and Syed Ahmad Khan, *Aasaar us Sanaadeed* (Delhi: Urdu Academy, 2006).

32. Hosagrahar, *Indigenous Modernities*, 8.

33. Hosagrahar, *Indigenous Modernities*, 8.

34. The notion of 'difference' underscores the ways in which the ideological and institutional frameworks of the colonial state contrasted with those in the metropolis. This literature urges us to think against the inexorable unfolding of 'liberal' governmental practices in colonial India. In light of this, studies have highlighted the enlargement of disciplinary powers of the colonial state, and how these were reflected in arenas such as policing, the work of medical establishments, prisons, legal institutions, and the development of scientific technology in India. For examples on the intersection of classificatory and enumerative technologies, such as statistics and the census with colonial knowledge, see Bernard Cohn, 'The Census, Social Structure and Objectification in South Asia', in *An Anthropologist Among the Historians and Other Essays*, ed. Bernard Cohn (New Delhi: Oxford University Press, 1987), 224-54; and Arjun Appadurai, 'Number in the Colonial Imagination', in *Modernity at Large: Cultural Dimensions of Globalisation* (Minnesota: University of Minnesota Press, 1996), 114-38. On mapping, see Ian J. Barrow, *Making History, Drawing Territory: British Mapping in India c. 1756-1905* (New Delhi: Oxford University Press, 2003). On colonial policing, see David Arnold, *Police Power and Colonial Rule in Madras: Madras 1859-1947* (New

Delhi: Oxford University Press, 1986). Arnold has also examined how the development of state medicine was central to colonial political concerns; David Arnold, *Colonising the Body: State Medicine and Epidemic Disease in Nineteenth-Century India* (Berkeley: University of California Press, 1993). On criminality and the Indian body as a site of colonial power, see Clare Anderson, *Legible Bodies: Race Criminality and Colonialism in South Asia* (Oxford: Berg Publishers, 2004). On how the colonial state drew upon and reworked Indian normative codes in the field of colonial law, see Radhika Singha, *A Despotism of Law: Crime and Justice in Early Colonial India* (New Delhi: Oxford University Press, 1998). On science and technology serving the interests of the colonial state and working in tension with their universalising roles, see Gyan Prakash, *Another Reason: Science and the Imagination of Modern India* (Princeton: Princeton University Press, 1999). On race, liberalism and modernity see Partha Chatterjee, *The Nation and its Fragments: Colonial and Postcolonial Histories* (Princeton: Princeton University Press, 1993); Uday Singh Mehta, *Liberalism and Empire: A Study in Nineteenth-Century British Liberal Thought* (Chicago: University of Chicago Press, 1999); and Dipesh Chakrabarty, *Provincializing Europe: Postcolonial Thought and Historical Difference* (Princeton: Princeton University Press, 2000).

35. Legg, *Spaces of Colonialism*, 20–25.
36. See Legg, *Spaces of Colonialism*, Chapter 4; and Hosagrahar, *Indigenous Modernities*, 140.
37. Gwendolyn Wright, *The Politics of Design in French Colonial Urbanism* (Chicago: University of Chicago Press, 1991), 12; and Paul Rabinow, *French Modern: Norms and Forms of the Social Environment* (Massachusetts: MIT Press, 1989). For more studies on the reordering of colonial urban environments outside of South Asia, see Zeynep Celik, *Urban Forms and Colonial Confrontations: Algiers Under French Rule* (London: University of California Press, 1997); Brenda Yeoh, *Contesting Space: Power Relations and the Urban Built Environment in Colonial Singapore* (Kuala Lampur; Oxford: Oxford University Press, 1996); Garth Andrew Myers, *Verandah's of Power: Colonialism and Space in Urban Africa* (Syracuse: Syracuse University Press, 2003).
38. The book thus consolidates and treats comprehensively the themes that Narayani Gupta raises in her seminal work. See Gupta, *Delhi Between Two Empires*, 28–30, 73–76, 83–86, 90–92, 171–74.
39. This focus on the Saraogi Jains as distinct from others who have worked on the more obvious aspect of the Hindu–Muslim tension in Delhi, see Mann, 'Turbulent Delhi'.

40. Barring Michael Mann and Samiksha Sehrawat's work on the afforestation of the Delhi Ridge, plantations and forestry work have received little interest in Delhi's environmental history. See Michael Mann and Samiksha Sehrawat, 'A City with a View: The Afforestation of the Delhi Ridge, 1883–1913', *Modern Asian Studies* 2, no. 43, 2009, 543–70.

41. In this regard, see Dane Kennedy, *The Magic Mountains: Hill Stations and the British Raj* (Berkeley: University of California Press, 1996); and Nandini Bhattacharya, *Contagion and the Enclaves: Tropical Medicine in Colonial India (Postcolonialism Across the Disciplines)* (Liverpool: Liverpool University Press, 2012).

42. The book takes the term 'suburb' as it was used in the archival records to mean lands outside the city. However, the notion of 'suburbanisation' in South Asia has been problematised recently as a twentieth century phenomenon when examining the relationship among modernity, community-formation and the urban-built environment. See Rao, *House but No Garden*.

43. Gupta, *Delhi Between Two Empires*, 171.

1

Restructuring the City
Property and Compensation in Colonial Delhi

INTRODUCTION

The rebellion of 1857 was a cataclysmic event in the history of Delhi. As the seat of the erstwhile Mughal empire, rebel soldiers from the East India Company's army converged on the city and declared the ailing emperor, Bahadur Shah Zafar, the leader of the rebellion. Subjected to an onslaught by the rebel army as well as by the British forces, Shahjahanabad became a veritable battleground as violence raged in its *mohallas* (an area resembling a neighbourhood), streets and squares.[1] As the tide eventually turned and the British forces subdued the rebels, violence persisted in the form of plunder and pillage of personal property.[2] This chapter highlights how, at this very moment of tumult, a new colonial administration was entrusted to take charge of the city and it faced a myriad political demands, ranging from disciplining the population, to ensuring that 'loyal' supporters of the government were identified and compensated for their support during the rebellion. The result of these demands was the creation of a market in urban property. The redistribution of property, it is suggested, was at the heart of establishing a colonial political economy and creating ties with loyal supporters. Confiscated properties of those who were assumed to be rebels passed through property auctions into the hands of those recognised as 'loyal' men. But rather than a straightforward process, this urban property market was constituted by the means of negotiation of diverse interests by the local administration. This chapter, then, emphasises how tensions within the government and within local politics created an imprint upon a scheme of property transfers, which emerged after British victory in Delhi.[3]

As large swathes of house property came under military demolition operations, the local administration was left to establish a system of credit where tickets were given to 'loyal' inhabitants, whose houses were demolished following military clearances in the city. To save the government from paying from its coffers, it was hoped that the tickets would be used as notes of exchange for the valuable confiscated house properties of individuals in other parts of the city. However, putting this policy into practice became increasingly complicated. A limited supply of confiscated properties meant that officials relied on selling confiscated property through auctions, with the hope that people would bid over the value of their tickets to secure a share of profit after the sales. This policy of compensation had to be continually modified by officials to include requests from local elites, which was to select the most valuable confiscated properties and to tackle the problem of speculation that resulted from assessing the value of demolished property in promissory tickets. The constitution of a 'free market' of property transfers, as a result of these series of accommodations by the local administration, sheds light on the contradictory nature of urban governance in the aftermath of the rebellion.

PROPERTY AND POLITICAL ECONOMY IN PRE-REBELLION DELHI

By the nineteenth century, the idea that land was an economic asset, to be defined, assessed and improved in order to achieve enhanced taxation, was a concern that permeated policies of governments across the world, in metropoles and their colonies.[4] In colonial India, defining property rights in land and establishing a 'rule of property' became a core tenet of state governance.[5] Indeed, as the basis of agricultural production, questions over rural land remained a central concern during the tenure of the colonial state as it moved from deliberating over issues of land control to those of land improvement.[6] However, just as the significance of rural land changed with the change in the nature of colonial political economy, urban property, too, played an important role as an object of colonial governance, particularly after the events of the rebellion.[7] While not a basis of production, urban property could be measured and valued, and eventually, taxed for state revenues. When sold, it was again liable for taxation. For the colonial government, its position as an asset was primarily in its circulation or exchange.[8]

In fact, even prior to British rule, under the Mughals, as William J. Glover discusses in his study of colonial Lahore, urban property was regarded as an asset worth holding on to, and was subsequently transferred to one's dependents as inheritance.[9] When transfers outside the family did take place, they needed the sanction of the community-*mohalla* leaders, and their approval was then re-affirmed by the agencies of the government.[10] And while a community-*mohalla* identity was an important determinant in property transfers, it was by no means the only one. Properties could be sold to people outside the close network of the *mohalla*, and evidence from other parts of India suggests that by the seventeenth and eighteenth centuries, properties were sold readily to buyers from different caste or social backgrounds.[11]

The advent of colonial rule, however, did not mean an instant transformation to a supposed 'free market' in urban property. This was because of competing ideologies of property that existed under the aegis of the early East India Company. Evidence for this in the case of rural land in South India has been put forward by David Washbrook, who has shown how two different schools of thought were competing against each other in the eighteenth and early-nineteenth centuries. Washbrook argues that on the one hand, while Thomas Munro was influential in advocating a system behind the rapid circulation of land through society, another school under F. W. Ellis strove for a return to 'custom', that is, the restoration of a 'Hindu Golden Age' by giving land back to its 'original' owners who were dispossessed of it with the advent of 'Mughal despotism'.[12] The latter endeavoured to create a sense of social stability over matters of commercialisation of land.[13] Significantly, Washbrook's analysis demonstrates how internal tensions shaped the nature of colonial governance in Madras, and how functions of the administration were marked by considerable ambiguity. With respect to transfers of urban property, we also find conflicting ideologies and practices undertaken by the administration in cities. In Delhi, before the rebellion of 1857, for example, we find some administrators espousing the 'preservation' of neighbourhood customs in the transfers of real property, but others advocating the dissolution of the same, and a more systematised approach to the protection of individual property rights.

In 1820, for example, Thomas Fortescue, the Civil Commissioner of Delhi, believed that it was best for colonial policy to ensure that land transactions, including its exchange and sale, were kept within the neighbourhood as a natural extension of 'local' institutional arrangements. He argued:

> When castes and professions get together, they are united in their internal economy and thus become readily managed by the Magistrate, though when all descriptions of persuasions and callings are intermixed we find nothing tangible .... bearing in mind the religious distinctions and prejudices of the natives, we observe how congenial and well calculated these institutions springing therefrom are to preserve them in peace and prosperity.[14]

Fortescue's belief in what he termed the 'native tenacity to neighbourhood' defined his approach and the governance of property transfers.[15] This should be seen as a new dimension to the understanding of urban property. Orientalist discourse represented India as a timeless civilisation characterised by irrational customs and traditional social formations of caste and sect.[16] Fortescue echoed such sentiments and ensured that the authorities 'preserve' those practices that were best suited to native traditions. Under these arrangements, the purchasers or sellers of urban land were not under any obligation to record the cases in the registry or *nazul* (land escheated to the state government) office. Moreover, in the absence of documentary titles, a *mahzur* or certificate signed by the inhabitants, neighbours or friends of the party that was interested in proving rights of pre-emption, was enshrined in the policy and understood as being in line with former Mughal policies.[17] Arguably, at least for some time, local officials like Fortescue perhaps reversed the process of the sale of property outside the confines of the *mohalla*, which had been taking place earlier, as Glover suggests was happening in the seventeenth and eighteenth centuries. However, this process did not continue for long. Unlike Fortescue, there were other officers like H. Middleton, the Acting Resident of Delhi, who believed that an adherence to the *mohalla*-neighbourhood system of property transfers was full of limitations and lacked credibility. In 1822, just two years after Fortescue's report, Middleton lamented the efficacy of the *mahzur* documents, claiming that it was a 'mere thing or form', and in his opinion, was invalid because those who signed it were ignorant of the paper they were attesting. The fact that it was readily obtainable meant that its veracity needed to be investigated thoroughly by government officers.[18] Therefore, the prevailing policy was found wanting when it came to the preservation of individual property rights.

Both these cases reveal that the micro-management of urban property transfers was a matter that greatly concerned local officials, even while there were different political considerations and inconsistencies regarding which policy was best suited to the local conditions. As I show below, the governance of property transactions was influenced by political needs after the rebellion. The political act of 'compensation' was worked out through the redistribution of urban property that belonged to those who were considered to be rebels. However, the direction that this redistribution of property took was based on the acceptance that a market in property was the ideal resolution to a host of administrative pressures. The next section examines how the debate over compensation to those who had suffered from the rebellion originated while sections within the government were debating how the population of towns and cities that took part in the rebellion were to be disciplined or punished.

COMPENSATION, PROPERTY AND IMPERIAL DEMANDS FOR LOYALTY

As the British forces re-took the city in 1857, the army was given a free hand in ransacking houses and *mohalla*s, and 'prize agents' confiscated a huge amount of valuable items, which were later sold in European markets.[19] Along with this, came military orders that the residents of the city were to evacuate their houses so that the city could be made 'safe'. While Hindu residents of the city were allowed to return in 1858, Muslims were kept out for another year, and their houses seized by the army as 'confiscated property'.[20] Presumed to be the real conspirators behind the rebellion, Delhi's Muslim residents faced the full wrath of the colonial government by virtue of having their places of worship and other symbols of power seized and occupied as barracks by British troops. This capture and desecration was, as one historian described it, an 'intentional desacralisation' project where symbols of the rebellion like the Jama Masjid and the palace were metamorphosed by the victors.[21]

However, significant to note here is that the pillage of Delhi was not condoned by all sections of the imperial administration. Indeed, the question of compensation to both English and native subjects emerged almost as immediately as that of retribution. John Lawrence, the Lieutenant Governor of Punjab, and later, Viceroy of India, was particularly opposed to the presence of military forces in the city and condemned the acts of plunder that were taking place in north India. For Lawrence, the restoration of property rights needed to be at the heart of any reconstruction of British authority in India. As a senior administrator with several years of experience governing areas like the Punjab and Delhi, he was of the opinion that natives had to be compensated for the losses they suffered.[22] He argued in his correspondence to Viceroy Canning that unless there was 'some security to lives and property of the natives', tranquillity in cities like Delhi was not possible.[23] Yet, such liberal behaviour of officials like Lawrence was contingent on the question of 'loyalty'. Compensation, after all, could not be separated from the political exigencies of the government, and in Lawrence's mind, the rationale of compensation was to favour those 'influential men' who were needed to re-establish the reins of the empire. In a letter to the Commissioner of Hissar, E. Brandreth, a man who would later oversee the compensation process in Delhi, Lawrence wrote about how 'influential' men (even Muslims) were to be given every consideration for the restoration of their lands and properties:

It is in my mind very impolitic being very severe in such cases [of confiscations]. General confiscations are to be deplored, and only endorsed in great and exceptional cases. If we deprive large number of influential men of their proprietary rights, we give them the strongest inducements to resist.[24]

In concurrence, Viceroy Canning also declared, 'A loyal native is the last man who should go uncompensated if there is compensation as such', and he agreed with the thrust of Lawrence's argument that 'loyalty' should be a prerequisite for compensation.[25] Like Lawrence's views, this was a tacit indication that political expediency would guide the liberality of the government in matters of compensation. Canning also favoured a discrete method of compensation to save the government from doling out large sums of money. He felt that the best way to avoid numerous 'loyal' claimants from approaching the government with a litany of their complaints and losses was to allow local officials to decide cases on the ground. When a dispatch was released in December 1857, which suggested that a commission of enquiry was to be formed in the disturbed districts to settle the question of compensation, Canning expressed his dismay to the Secretary of State:

> I am now inclined to think that the instructions can be executed in a quieter way and by means less ostentatious and at the same time more effective than a commission—and that is by the officers of each Division and District. There will be some little gain in this. It will have less of the appearance of a deliberate determination to compensate.[26]

This policy of local arbitration was based on Canning's faith that the 'liberal' impulses of the officials would guide them through the compensation process, but with strict adherence to the economy. Thus, any mode of compensation at the level of the bureaucracy had to negotiate such demands made by the government of India: the need to identify loyal residents of cities who had sided with the government during the rebellion, to make concessions for influential men who would then be relied upon as intermediaries, to create a mechanism of compensation that would be cost-effective, and thus, reduce the financial liabilities of the government.

MILITARY CLEARANCE, FINANCES AND BUREAUCRATIC RESPONSIBILITIES

As the likes of Canning and Lawrence deliberated over the nature of compensation, both civil and military authorities had control over the city of Delhi.[27] It has been suggested that this joint civil and military control in the immediate aftermath of the rebellion gave a fillip to the commodification and exchange of urban property in Delhi.[28] This argument is elucidated to explain that while the domains of the two authorities were demarcated eventually, the fear and threat of insurrection resulted in an absolute space of power, that is, in the fusion of the military and civil domains. With the ability to use violence on its side, the state was able to have a much freer role in the eventual commodification of property.[29] It is right to suggest that the military and civil authorities were indeed working together at that time, but the implied fusion of the two domains gives too much direction and linearity to the operations of the government. This cooperation also needs to be contextualised in the context of the government of India's own involvement in the matter, and its intervention in the development of a compensation scheme. The development of a market in property, which was the eventual result of this process, was thus not an inevitable outcome of state dominance, but became by default, a way of responding to the many tensions that were accommodated in the scheme of compensation in Delhi.

In order to create a visible line of control from the palace, where the troops were being stationed, it was decided by the military that an area of 400 yards needed to be cleared free from habitation.[30] As mentioned earlier, by 1858, the Hindu residents of Delhi had been allowed to re-enter the city, and in the following year, re-entry permission was granted to those Muslims who could prove that they had not participated in the rebellion. The order by the military authorities for a 400-yard clearance meant that a densely populated area dotted with houses, *bazaars* (markets), mansions, reservoirs and offices was to be cleared by the PWD through a series of systematic demolitions.[31] Sources suggest that the area in question was densely populated; locations such as *Katra Dhobi* (washer men's quarters) near the Jama Masjid and *Kaghazi Mohalla* (paper makers' neighbourhod) in the eastern half of the city meant that along with valuable houses of nobles and their retinues, *karkhanas* (workshops) and gardens, the area also contained occupational or caste quarters.[32] Moreover, by the seventeenth and eighteenth centuries, properties began to be sold to buyers from different caste or social backgrounds, and the name of the *mohalla* may not have necessarily reflected a homogenous caste or an occupational group in residence.[33] Thus, the line of demolitions engulfed a heterogeneous mix of houses and buildings either owned by individuals or perhaps containing different rights to land.

Two issues confronted the local authorities, both military and civil, if these demolitions were to be carried out. The fact that individuals, largely Hindus but including some Muslim notables, had already been allowed to re-enter the city, meant that they had been deemed 'loyal' by the government. Moreover, they had also been allowed possession of their house property. Any clearances within the 400-yard area would comprise the properties or landed rights of such loyal individuals who would have to be ejected again. Therefore, this opened up the question of how these individuals were to be brought under the process of compensation. The second issue was related to the cost of the demolitions. How were the demolitions to be financed when the imperial government was fixated on spending the least possible amount on financial outlays?

The question of the loyal claimants as well as finances dovetailed into a plan for compensation, which was voiced by the likes of Lieutenant Newmarch, the Executive Engineer of the PWD in 1859. For Newmarch, the solution for economising the cost of the demolitions was through the disposal of the confiscated property of individuals. He presented his case to the authorities in the following manner:

> With a view to reducing as much as possible the cost of this clearance, the buildings materials of the confiscated houses may be sold and the amount realized or profitable amount that will be realized deducted from the total value of houses if any, for which compensation may have to be paid, so as to reduce as much as possible the cost for which the sanction of government will have to be solicited.[34]

Newmarch's proposal struck a chord with the military authorities, who were required to pay a part of the expenditure; and soon after, the Officiating Military Secretary of Punjab agreed that instead of giving cash payments to the claimants, it was better to grant 'forfeited houses' in other areas of the town.[35] For military officials, since Muslims who were guilty of treason by virtue of siding with the rebels formerly owned the forfeited houses, these could be used to settle the bill for the compensation to the claimants and would reduce the cost that the government had to pay. Compensation was thus largely concerned with the question of 'Mahommedan' houses and their re-allocation. While the debate over the treatment of Muslim properties led to intense discussions among sections of the government, the Hindu residents of the city who would suffer from the clearances were automatically considered for compensation, and their property fell under the de-facto classification of loyal houses. This tendency to favour Hindus over Muslims was all the more telling as directives were soon passed to save Hindu temples in the areas of the clearances from being demolished.[36]

But the allocation of forfeited or 'confiscated' property in Delhi was not as straightforward as the military authorities desired it to be. To negotiate the demands of the imperial government for a system of compensation that was 'liberal' and flexible on the ground and, the civil authorities in Delhi had decided to differentiate the properties of Muslims who were actually implicated in the rebellion from those of Muslims who were innocent but had been kept out of the city by the authorities. In other words, the civil administration had created different categories: 'confiscated', 'attached' or belonging to owners who were innocent but who had been excluded from the city as a result of the rebellion, and lastly, those that were occupied by owners.[37] This measure implied not only the reduction of the pool of confiscated properties available for compensation, but also the potential increase of claimants under the excluded or 'attached' categories. Brandreth, who was now the Commissioner of Delhi, wrote about the policy followed by the civil authorities to Captain Newmarch, when the latter asked about the mode of compensation that could be paid in lieu of the clearances around the Ellenborough tank, a water reservoir outside the palace:

> Many of the Mahommedans who owned houses in this locality have doubtless either absconded or perished and in all probability will never be heard of again, but the greater proportion doubtless come under the denomination of excluded rather than absconded Mahommedans and will as soon as the prohibition of their admission into the city is removed doubtless come forward and lay claims to their houses.[38]

Thus, there are a host of factors that had begun to influence the local administration's compensation scheme. The need to create a 'liberal' scheme of compensation, with property at the heart of urban restructuring, to ensure that political expediency prevailed when it was being judged as to who would receive compensation, to find a solution to keep financial liabilities of the government low, and last, to balance the demands of the military authorities for clearances so as to keep the city 'safe'. These were worked out by the local administration through the provision of 'credit' via a process of ticketing.

LAW, CREDIT AND PLANNING COMPENSATION

We have seen that the nature of demands on the administrative apparatus in the city and the needs of the military authorities for security created tensions, which had to be accommodated within the system of compensation that was being formulated. However, what was the legal framework through which confiscation and compensation rights were understood? We know that the policy was not to look equally upon the claimants of compensation, and that while Hindus under the scheme were automatic recipients of any scheme, Muslim-owned or -held properties were extensively scrutinised into 'attached' or 'excluded' properties. This method, however, did reveal tensions between the civil and military authorities when the latter opened the question of clearances in the city and how the individuals in the 400-yard area were to be compensated. But how far did the writ of colonial law guide the seemingly arbitrary actions of the local administration?

Prior to the rebellion, the government of India had passed an all-India land acquisition act called Act VI of 1857 in order to deal with the confiscation of properties. This lay the terms for the 'public' ownership of previously 'private' lands and houses, and it was to provide guidelines for officials in their respective areas.[39] Compensation, according to the principles of the act, was to be given at the time of the possession of properties, and if not, the government was liable for an amount of six per cent interest from the particular date.[40] Only in exceptional circumstances could payment be deferred, for instance, if a court order was pending.[41] The act gave also a significant amount of autonomy to local administrations to seize land from indigenous inhabitants if it was required for state purposes from. In Awadh, which fell under the jurisdiction of the government of the North-West Provinces, the act was used to consider the nature of land reclamation and compensation after the event of the rebellion. In Delhi, however, the manner in which the administration carried out its 'liberal' measures of property confiscation, as well as the discussions over demolitions and compensation, reveal a more complicated story vis-à-vis the legal precedent of the act.

Officials like Brandreth contrasted the situation of Delhi to Lucknow, where the government was also responsible for demolitions, and where *all* property had been labelled 'confiscated' under the provisions of Act VI. Brandreth stressed that Delhi's case was different since arrangements had been made to identify and separate the 'attached' properties of Muslim owners.[42] The category of 'confiscated houses' or absconded property included the property of the rebels who had fled the city. However, this category had been kept separate from house property of 'innocent Muslims' who were evicted by British forces after the rebellion. Labelling Delhi's case as an exception in light of the exceedingly liberal policies, Brandreth argued that he was in favour of all owners of house property receiving suitable compensation, other than those whose houses were actually confiscated.[43] He felt that his position was helped by the fact that the demolitions in Delhi were delayed because of the government's indecision and deliberation over whether the city was to be completely destroyed or not.[44] It seems as if the government eventually agreed to a newer method of compensation, but to one that was not completely different from the Act of 1857, inasmuch as the powers of local authorities to act with autonomy in matters of compensation were preserved. It can also be suggested that the tacit approval that Brandreth and the local authorities eventually received for a deviation from the law enshrined in the act of 1857 was due to the heavy rate of interest that the government would have to pay in light of delays, if it followed the course of its legal rulings. Therefore, colonial law did not work through its unitary imposition by the state, but as the case of compensations in Delhi suggests, it was also a product of internal negotiations and modifications. The law had to be modified to suit the many requirements that went into the logic of compensation.

In these circumstances, Brandreth suggested to his superiors that a viable way of creating a mechanism for compensation was to have a system of credit that would be the engine behind property transfers at auctions. He wrote that the best option was

> To put up a sufficient number of them (confiscated houses) to auction, giving as much publicity as possible to the sale in order to secure the full market value being bid: and, further, to allow all the owners of demolished houses to bid up to the estimated value of their own houses for those thus put up to auction without requiring any payment from them to that extent.[45]

Brandreth's plan was thus to use the system of compensation and gear it towards investment in property. His complex scheme would allow the cash-strapped colonial government to sidestep the question of payment for the demolitions in cash, administer a liberal compensation process, and ultimately enable the market to settle the values of houses. This scheme would, in Brandreth's opinion, also solve the problem of excessive dependence on Indian native officials, who he deemed would otherwise resort to 'bribery or favouritism'.[46]

Brandreth's seniors eventually agreed upon the system of compensation, and he was given the go-ahead to ensure that the owners of would-be demolished houses were given credit equal to the value of their properties. Listing the help of the Deputy Commissioner of Delhi, Mr Cooper, Brandreth gave an order to prepare 'tickets' that would be issued to householders with the value of their houses. The idea of 'ticketing' was not entirely alien to the administration in Delhi, as a similar system of granting 'passes' had been used immediately after the rebellion to regulate the entry of residents into the city.[47] While previously, this had proved to be complicated,[48] Brandreth's faith in the process was unwavering. Along with tickets, a list of confiscated houses, with details of where they stood, was prepared for auctions.[49] Taking a cue from James C. Scott, such administrative practices of standardised measurement (in this case, sheets with numbers, value, locality and description of houses used as units) were tools used by modern states for the purposes of 'legibility' of the landscape.[50] Through these lists and tickets containing the value of demolished properties, we can see how local administrators like Brandreth were creating strategies to ensure the governance of a market in property.[51] To manage the problem of scarcity of confiscated properties, the market was envisaged as an arena of exchange, where those given an amount of credit could buy house property. Inflated values were given to the houses (to the tune of 10–15 per cent), which ensured that the government did not have to pay from its own pocket.

Another dimension of the compensation process was the promise of 'profit'. If bidding could ensure that the properties were sold for higher than their estimated values, then the ticket-holders would benefit from the increased sales proceeds. Bidding high would also allow the government to keep its liabilities down since if bids fell short of the estimates, the government would have to pay the difference. It was thus in the financial interests of the local authorities to encourage the ticket-holders to either buy houses at par value with their tickets or push the bids up. In a proclamation, Brandreth elaborated his new compensation procedure by giving examples of how the auctioning process would take place:

> Your house is valued at so much, but you will not get compensation at that valuation. An estimate has been made of demolished and confiscated property (land and houses); on the same principles confiscated houses of equal amount with the demolished houses will be sold by auction. If the sale proceeds equal the estimate for the demolished houses, you will get full compensation; if more, more; if less, less: you can buy any houses at auction in lieu of your house, and in that case you will not have to pay cash ...

He further continued:

> ... but if you buy a house of a greater price than your own, you will have to pay the difference; if at a less price, you will get the difference from Government; but in either case, the account of compensation will be adjusted proportionately: attend the auction according to a Proclamation of Auction which is to be issued, and endeavour to raise the bids, because the greater the sale proceeds, the greater the profits to the recipients of compensation.[52]

In this manner, officials in Delhi created a link between compensation, property and profitability. However, such confident assertions by the likes of Brandreth belie just how complicated the compensation procedure was in reality. Indeed, the very process of 'valuation' itself, as will be seen in the next section, was marked by disagreements between government officials on the one hand, and on the other, brought local actors to negotiate with the government over what constituted the 'value' of their property.

THE CREATION OF 'VALUE'

As Brandreth laid out the basics of his compensation scheme, a joint task force of military and civil officials in the local administration began the process of estimating the value of property to be demolished and confiscated. This was to be done judiciously in order to estimate the 'probable selling price as it then stood.'[53] The desire of the administration to value accurately the personal property of individuals meant that orders were given for tickets to be created, showing the 'ownership, value, size and description of the part or tenement' that was to be demolished.[54] The ticket was, in effect, to bind the individual in the form of a contract with the state and to act as a promissory note of payment. Unlike the neighbourhood-based system that the East India Company had championed at one time, the desire to procure precise information meant that the state officials needed to interfere directly in urban matters and record data. However, as the conversion of property rights or holdings into abstract measurements was undertaken, there was a scope for individuals to negotiate the value attributed to particular properties. It should be made clear that the fragmented nature of the archival record does not provide voluminous instances of such negotiations, and neither is it implied that the terms of the negotiation were on an equal footing. Indeed, we are aware that the government's desire for, and identification of, loyal men were the very preconditions for any engagement with the populace. What we will see then are the ways in which residents used categories employed by the government in order to secure better terms of compensation.

One example of the assessment and valuation of property of which there exists some detail is that of Nawab Hamid Ali Khan's houses. The Nawab had once been a wealthy man who owned a substantial amount of property near the Kashmiri gate, an area in the north-east of the city. In the course of the time leading up to the rebellion, his fortunes dwindled and he was in debt to several creditors who paid for his lifestyle and to whom he owed a large amount of money, a sum of Rs 95,000.[55] In the aftermath of 1857, the military authorities in Delhi decided to clear the area under which his property fell, and to his dismay, the question of his compensation was sidelined. In the rush to clear properties for the construction of regimental barracks, the military authorities in Delhi failed to communicate their decision to the civil agencies that were still discussing how the process of compensation would be conducted. After some time had passed, and when the authorities were bombarded with repeated complaints, the Nawab's property was finally considered as 'attached', and he was declared liable for compensation. As an influential Muslim nobleman whose services were deemed important by the local authorities and the government of India, the Nawab became, albeit belatedly, a 'loyal' subject, and therefore, worthy of compensation.

The destruction of his buildings meant that their value had to be assessed by making enquiries and examining the sites that the Nawab remonstrated, were 'summarily dismantled'.[56] After an inspection had been made, the surveyor declared that an amount of Rs 100 was sufficient, as the prevailing property prices were lower than before the rebellion and the Nawab's houses were made of 'bricks and mud'. The Nawab challenged this assessment by claiming that the houses were made of 'pucca bricks and mortar', two of them being mortgaged for Rs 3,000 and the whole lot worth Rs 7,000. The situation proved to be an embarrassment for the local administration in Delhi since proper records went missing, and without any 'neighbourhood' basis for mediation, the claims of the Nawab had to be dealt with directly. A settlement was made, where the Nawab agreed to claim Rs 3,500 as the value of his demolished property.[57]

The question of whether the Nawab's claim was an accurate representation of the loss he suffered is perhaps not as important here as the new categories he used to validate this claim. He was eager that the local administration value his properties and agreed that the modalities of valuation, that is, the cost of materials, quantity of land, the price of the materials of removed buildings, and the price of cost of damage to nearby buildings, were as per the colonial administrative protocol.[58] Even when it came to his disagreement, it was to do with the 'buildings materials' not being valued at the rate he felt they were supposed to be valued. In his opinion, the houses being made of bricks and mortar were more than the estimated value. At a time when there was no universal consensus on the part of the authorities on how 'buildings materials' were to be valued (even as it was listed as a modality of valuation), the Nawab's claim and ability to negotiate with the authorities becomes more significant.[59] Thus, far from the imposition of a unitary value of property, the government's scheme of assessment was a process that allowed some scope for negotiation by the residents of the demolished areas. While the archive is silent over how subalterns or ordinary residents negotiated these claims, and it renders the case of the Nawab visible because of his status as an elite Muslim, it still provides us with evidence of how messy the demolition and valuation process was, and how the indeterminacy of administrative practices provided an opportunity to negotiate terms with the local government in the valuation process.

The valuation process also constituted confusion and retrospective 'corrections'. The civil–military nexus only exacerbated the problems as the military authorities, pressed by demands of securing the city, were more than eager to demolish buildings quickly and create a clear firing line between the fort and the city. Moreover, the negotiations and bickering did not end at the question of valuation, but even extended to whether the demolitions were 'public' works at all. The Executive Engineer, a military officer called Captain Skyes, was responsible for keeping an account of the sales proceeds (of the materials sold when the clearances were being carried out) and was under the assumption that the clearances were a 'civil' responsibility; and thus, he disbursed money from his accounts towards the clearances.[60] When this was found out, the civil authorities claimed that the proceeds were to be kept in the PWD accounts for compensation purposes and gave instructions to not foot the bill for clearances. The Deputy Commissioner, P. Egerton, was of the opinion that since the clearances were 'entirely a military affair', they could not be financed by the PWD funds.[61] He immediately requested that if money was needed for the clearances, then there was some available in the local *nazul* funds.[62] The ad-hoc manner of keeping multiple accounts of disbursement was deemed irregular, with calls for closure. The recommendation was that one main PWD account be credited with the arrears of the missing transactions.[63] Even the Chief Engineer of Punjab needed clarity over the nature of the clearances, and he had received complaints over the fact that his subordinates were keeping irregular accounts to settle bills.[64]

Such examples illustrate the ways in which the assessment and valuation process was an outcome of internal tensions between different departments, and how the joint control of the city by the military and civil authorities led to confusion and a degree of indeterminacy in the administration. In this context, different branches and officers of the government conducted what they felt were 'proper' means to settle assessments, disbursements and valuations, and thus, were pursuing their own imperial agenda when undertaking the clearances. This caused unnecessary delays and financial losses, and instead of appearing as an example of order and rationality, the valuation and demolition process tended to look the exact opposite.

LOCAL ELITES AND SPECULATION

To resolve the shortage of supply in house properties, the compensation plan relied on giving credit to the owners of demolished houses to procure confiscated houses, and thus, limit the liabilities of the government for compensation in cash. Theoretically, once the valuation process was finished and tickets were created, the auctions could finally get underway. Yet, between the valuation process and auctions, the local authorities attempted to enshrine in the policy a settlement for local elites to select properties of their choice as well as address the tricky question of speculation. The negotiation of these interests entailed inconsistency in decisions and actions, and revealed further tensions in the scheme of compensation.

Through the ticketing system, individuals became a body of 'ticket-holders' so that they could participate in property purchases. Yet this, too, had complications, as tickets changed hands rather quickly. The ticket-holders included owners of attached property (some Muslims who had proved that they did not participate in the rebellion) and other owners (Hindus) of property whose houses were in the 400-yard clearance zone. Moreover, since owners of properties of all valuations were given tickets, men of different social standing were grouped together as ticket-holders and primed for the auctions. For example, a neighbourhood of paper-makers in Daryaganj (*ganj* literally means neighbourhood), that is, the *Kaghazi Mohalla* was included in the demolitions.[65] The property in the area was first marked as 'attached' or 'confiscated' on the basis of whether the residents could prove that they had not participated in the rebellion (thus loyal), and then valued.[66] The members of this neighbourhood, among others, were included as 'ticket-holders' along with wealthier men who threw their lot in with the colonial forces during the rebellion, and were promised 'every consideration' and compensation at a 'very liberal scale' for their support.[67] Immediately after the auctioning process was announced, the ticket-holders who were suffering from pecuniary difficulties sold their tickets at heavily discounted prices, some at a rate of 75 per cent.[68] This exchange was perhaps all the more significant as the residents of the city had been hard hit by famine, and subsequently, an epidemic of cholera in 1860–61.[69] In short, since the government had decided that the tickets were promissory notes to pay, those who had the purchasing power, including merchants and traders with liquid currency, bought the tickets from those who were suffering from hardship.

As instruments of exchange, the fact that tickets changed hands would not have surprised the authorities, at least initially. One could suggest that since the idea behind the creation of a market in urban property developed because of the scarcity of confiscated properties, the authorities preferred to let things take their course based on what were understood to be 'natural' economic forces.[70] If there were people who had to sell their tickets because of the famine, and thus could not bid, to the local authorities this was simply the effect of market forces playing their part. In principle, therefore, the market was a site of 'veridiction' of government practices.[71] In other words, the local authorities in Delhi set limits on their own interference—on what they should or should not do upon the belief that the market functioned on the basis of certain 'truths'. In the process, the creation of a property market in the city and the insistence on giving credit, not cash, ultimately resulted in the exclusion of those who were perhaps most in need of 'compensation' after the rebellion. The hurried exchange of heavily discounted tickets for money was a clear evidence of this.

While the authorities were not perturbed by the fact that some lost out because of the prevailing distress, their attention was quickly stirred by demands made by a group of influential merchants in the city who had lost their house properties in the demolitions. In 1860, soon after the stamp of approval was given to the new ticket-holders, 48 *Raises*, or in the words of the colonial government, the most 'influential native gentlemen', met the Deputy Commissioner of Delhi requesting that they be given first preference in terms of 'selecting' properties before they went to auction.[72] Archival records state that these men included 'Lallas Choonna Mull and Salig Ram, Nawab Hamid Alee Khan and Monshee Tafuzzul Hossein'.[73] The mention of names like Salig Ram and Hamid Ali Khan (who we have encountered before) indicates that these were the individuals who were promised generous compensation by the government on the basis of their loyalty. Although a minority within the body of ticket-holders, these men saw an opportunity within the scheme of compensation to not only recover their losses, but also gain from acquiring a profit from prized confiscated properties whose value was less than what it would have been if the city was fully populated. It is also possible that these *Raises* themselves bought and accumulated more tickets when they were being sold at a discounted rate. Taking advantage of the scheme of compensation, these individuals requested that out of the government valuations of confiscated properties that amounted to Rs 13 lakh, they would 'select' around Rs 7 lakh worth from the total value.[74] Eager to retain strong ties with those who had either supported them during the rebellion or were deemed men of great influence, the local authorities agreed to the demands and issued an agreement with the *Raises*. Thus, not only had colonial governance laid the framework for certain colonial subjects, that is, the *Raises*, to engage with the authorities as economic agents, but the latter also used their new positions to negotiate favourable terms with the authorities.[75]

In line with these new developments, the Deputy Commissioner, Mr Cooper, addressed the question of profit and loss by issuing orders that the ticket-holders as a body were to bear the loss or profit from the sale of these properties.[76] However, just as Cooper delivered his statement, two more demands were made by the ticket-holders. The first was that if the ticket-holders were to bear the losses from sales, what would be the minimum rate at which the government would receive their tickets? The second question linked to this was: how would money be collected if some individuals held on to their tickets until the end?[77] Both were pressing issues for the ticket-holders seeking to save themselves from any perceived losses. The latter question, however, was one that touched upon speculation in tickets, something that was also accommodated in the compensation process.

The ticket-holders, as we have seen, were individuals who had liquid currency; but they also included the *Raises*, or men who were 'influential' in the eyes of the government. The body of ticket-holders were keen to ensure that they would not suffer losses from the auctions, and some began enquiring whether keeping the tickets in hand was possible and if the government would sanction the profits to be distributed to those who did. From the administration's point of view, however, the question of speculation brought a certain amount of hesitation in the responses of the local authorities because of the potential of speculation to disrupt the real demand and supply principles of the 'market'. What happened next was a process of negotiation by the authorities in Delhi to ensure that speculation was regulated officially, but at the same time, that the ticket-holders remained placated through the auctioning process.

Upon hearing of the demands of the ticket-holders, Cooper altered his original decision to declare that if there was profit after the sales, it would be rateably divided, but only those who retained their tickets were to bear the losses from the sales.[78] This was different from his first declaration that all ticket-holders were entitled to a share of the profits, but also to bear the losses. In the second instance, the question of speculation in tickets, while not addressed explicitly, was seen from the perspective of who was to bear the losses from the sales.[79] Again, in line with the original recommendations, all ticket-holders were instructed to buy houses. From the authorities' point of view, the latter was imperative and had to be re-enforced so that cash compensation would not have to be paid, and many who were in need of houses were provided for. As both officers suggested, profits were to be distributed rateably. This needs to be understood as a balancing act being performed by the officials. The promise of profit was to ensure that people bid for houses; but the risk of losses would deter them from holding on to their tickets. Cooper and Brandreth did not address speculation but from the point of view of losses to those who held on to their tickets. Those who would receive rateably divided profit were never mentioned in the address, and this was perhaps evaded as a deliberate attempt to avoid the question of speculation in the official proclamation without dismissing it.

But why was this so? There was the issue of the *Raises*. Some were interested in knowing if they could hold on to their tickets, and who had been promised that their selected property would be added to the auctioning process to gain profits. There is evidence of this from Brandreth's discussions with a group of ticket-holders (including the *Raises*) over the 'depressed state of the market'.[80] Since many ticket-holders, and even Brandreth himself, were still unsure about whether there would be profit after the sales because of the city being half-empty, Brandreth consented 'as a matter of course' that only those who held on to their tickets till the end would receive a share of profits, if and when it arose. Alternatively, any loss would fall on the shoulders of those who wished for compensation in cash.[81] It would seem that through these policies, the administration was attempting to balance multiple demands in the scheme of compensation through property, such as the provision of 'selected' property (ensuring that those who wanted it made a profit if they held on to their tickets), and even encouraging collective ownership to save itself from paying in cash. As we have seen, the compensation scheme became a means of regulating speculation without banning it.

If it were hoped that compensation matters were finally being put to bed, a new intervention by the military authorities would complicate matters further. Just as the question of speculation was being discussed, orders were issued that more land was required under the clearance measures and that the line of demolitions be extended from 400 to 480 yards in order to secure the palace, which now housed British troops, from any external threats. As another political act of concession to their loyal supporters, the local authorities lobbied to spare the Dariba, a prosperous neighbourhood inhabited by the rich Hindu merchants of the city, from demolitions. The line of military demolitions ultimately stopped just short of the area.[82] However, as the military establishment needed land, once again, the question of compensation was brought before the civil authorities. In the manner as the previous lot, properties falling within the second wave of demolitions were demarcated, surveyed and assigned a 'value'.[83] Another batch of tickets was issued to a new group of ticket-holders who were promised confiscated properties for their losses and included in what was the original general scheme of compensation.[84] The property demolished within the second line of demolitions was valued at around Rs 1,98,000, and tickets to this amount were created.[85]

The second round of demolitions and Brandreth's approval of reserving profit for those who held on to their tickets created a unique situation which would, as we will see, result in the scheme of compensation being modified extensively. Just as with the first set of tickets, tickets from second lot changed hands and were bought by other individuals. What we find after Brandreth's implicit consent over speculation is an increased interest by individuals from across British India to buy tickets with the hope of receiving profit at the end of the auctions.[86] The composition of the body of ticket-holders became increasingly diverse as 'European and Eurasian' ticket-holders entered Brandreth's compensation scheme with a desire for their share of profit.[87] Along with these people, we also hear of 'some native gentlemen of high position', perhaps also from outside the city, buying tickets in Delhi. All these individuals would later be described as 'bona fide speculators' in tickets by the government of India.[88]

The entrance of new individuals into the ticketing process and the compensation scheme at once affected the circulation of tickets. Earlier, because of the pecuniary condition that the original ticket-holders found themselves in, tickets were sold at heavily discounted rates. During the second round of demolitions, however, the area under valuation was much lesser, and fewer tickets were produced. This situation, coupled with the fact that there was an increased interest in attaining profit at the end of the auctions, and thus, competition for tickets, eventually affected the price of tickets.[89] Interestingly, unlike earlier, neither were promises made to the ticket-holders from the second round of demolitions for the inclusion of any 'selected' property, and nor were lists of property created.[90] All this meant that with the rise in the value of tickets, the stakes were higher, and the hope for profit even more so. This motley group of people, all of whose interests were tied to the sale of landed property, were soon informed by Brandreth's successor Major Browne that all ticket-holders in both rounds of demolitions were to be treated equally in the eyes of the government.[91] Ultimately, inclusive of both the batches of demolitions, 2,761 tickets were issued, which held a collective value of Rs 8,08,927, 6 Paisa and 4 Annas.[92]

But why, at this point we should ask, did the local authorities remain dogged in carrying out a single and unified scheme of compensation? The protection of property was the cornerstone of the imperial project and was vital for its self-legitimation. For the local authorities in the context of Delhi, the redistribution of urban property after the rebellion fulfilled two needs at once. Through the compensation scheme, not only would imperial political needs such as creating ties with its loyal supporters be met, but the experiment would also establish the reins of a colonial political economy in which land was an asset, to be valued and commoditised for circulation. Thus, the victory of a 'market' in property was a modern as well as a colonial project. If the compensation process is understood in this manner, we can also imagine why the authorities envisaged the auctions as the perfect adjunct to it. The auctions produced a certain illusion of distance. Hailing that profit and loss was subject to the forces of economics—the result of 'letting things run their course', and thus, distinct from the domain of politics—the auctions were relied upon as a modern and reliable instrument of governance. Moreover, these techniques were also important for the purposes of self-representation. Through the objective (and benevolent) process of auctions carried out in the name of a liberal government, the local authorities hoped to prevent the perceived chaos of property resettlement at the hands of the population. In the words of the Deputy Commissioner, 'the corruption, the intrigue, the savagery and the dissatisfaction which would have ensued' if property transfers were left with the Indian population, was unthinkable.[93]

Of course, and as we have seen, the constant modification of the compensation process renders the impossibility of the separation of political imperatives from the economic prerogative of the scheme. In fact, how this compensation scheme of creating a market in property was carried out is an altogether different story that reveals many a slip between intent and effect.[94] We know that the authorities could not discharge their scheme without negotiating the demands of the military authorities, and the needs of the 'loyal' *Raises* for 'selected' properties, or without dismissing the question of speculation that the ticket-holders had raised. The auctions were a further process of negotiation and accommodations; and this gives an insight into how complicated the system of compensation became.

THE BATTLE OF NUMBERS: AUCTIONS, NEGOTIATIONS AND PROFIT CLAIMANTS

The much-awaited auctions of confiscated property commenced in October 1860 and closed exactly after a year in October 1861. Run under the aegis of the local administration, the auctions were initially conducted daily in the presence of the Deputy Commissioner or one of his assistants, but with the passage of time, they were held by lower level administrative officials such as the head clerk and a European bailiff. Amounts for each sale were noted in a Sale Book, with details of each house that was sold and also details of to whom it was sold. An officer as a witness to the proceedings then signed the entry.[95] As Arjun Appadurai has suggested, numbers and statistics were important for colonial governments as they helped create an 'illusion of bureaucratic control', and were able to render indigenous reality into abstractions that could be assessed.[96] In the auctions at Delhi, we see a similar obsession with noting facts, and classifying information into figures and numbers for official scrutiny, which was ultimately meant to showcase bureaucratic control over the redistribution of urban property. But as much as the colonial archive can be represented as a testament to the vision of order that the colonial government wished to project, it carries in it traces of indecision, reversals of directives or alterations revealing the imprint of local negotiations, and internal tensions over government policies. In this context, numbers and figures can themselves be seen as constitutive of tensions and upon which the government had to act repeatedly in an attempt to produce that 'illusion' of control. As we shall see, the auctions of property and the division of profit after the sales were subject to similar accommodations and modifications as with the valuation or ticketing practices. The indecision of local authorities over 'correct' protocol, the demands of local actors, and the variety of interests that needed to be satisfied through the compensation process, all impacted the auctions and profit distribution, and revealed how the administration had to constantly modify its policies.

Once the auctions started, a great amount of profit was realised, and from the communications of authorities over the subject much later, we learn that many who had held on to their discounted tickets from the first set of demolitions, exchanged their tickets for houses at par value. Moreover, as there was a great demand for house property, the profit margins increased rapidly.[97] But from December 1860, the levels of profit started falling owing to a problem with the disposal of some of the most valuable and desired properties that belonged to the Nawab of Awadh.[98] Although Awadh was annexed by the British in 1856 and its Nawabi dynasty reduced to the status of pensioners under the colonial government, the city had seen intense fighting during the rebellion.[99] As a result, the colonial government severely punished the residents after the rebellion by seizing and disposing all 'rebel' property in the city.[100] In Delhi, the other major flashpoint during the rebellion was that the Nawabi household also had property, which had been seized and kept aside for the auctions as confiscated property. The extensive area under auction had generated immense interest in English-language newspapers like *The Mofussilite*, which boasted of the fact that the Nawabi properties would secure two–three lakh rupees after the sales.[101] Thus, the atmosphere was abuzz with the hope of a windfall profit once the compensation accounts were assessed. However, just as soon as certain sections of the property had been sold, the authorities faced a stumbling block as the descendants of the Nawab filed a suit against the government. This meant that the sales of the Nawabi property had to be stopped until further notice from the government of India.[102]

The removal of the Nawabi properties caused a hue and cry among the body of ticket-holders, and since they formed a part of the 'selected' properties that had been demanded by the *Raises*, we can understand the anxiety that protests caused in the administration. As a way out of the conundrum, the authorities in Delhi made the choice of 'substituting' property for that which was withdrawn through the addition of Rs 1,05,853 in cash from the sale of confiscated villages outside the city, along with Rs 1,24,000 worth of forfeited compensation tickets from the 'railway clearances'.[103] The alteration of figures and the inclusion of 'substituted' property in the accounts was a move to ensure that the protests over profit would subside, and that control could be asserted over the auctions. Changing numbers thus ensured that the multiple interests that were present in the compensation scheme would be satisfied and the auctions could be left to continue. The new replacement properties, however, failed to generate the same interest as the Nawabi ones, as the ticket-holders deemed them less desirable.[104] As the sales re-started, the profits from the sales became less, and ultimately, a loss was made on the original estimates of profit.[105]

In this situation, the *Raises*, who had requested for the 'selected' properties to be included in the auctions, objected to Deputy Commissioner Cooper and suggested that since inferior properties had been substituted for the Nawabi ones, they were misled regarding the amount of profit they were to receive. In order to manage the disappointment of the selected property owners, Cooper and Commissioner Browne resorted to artificially decreasing the original estimates of the value of the selected property actually sold. This numerical alteration and interference in the 'market' was to give the closest political allies a larger share of the profit on their selected properties. It can be seen next that from Rs 3,41,116, the estimates were reduced to Rs 3,12,336, 12 Paisa and 0 Annas. Thus, a profit of 28,779, 4 Paisa and 0 Annas, in excess to what was entitled to the ticket-holders, was credited to them through the administration.[106] As a further concession, the authorities added more extra-mural property to the list of 'selected property'. This had not been included in the original lists of sales, but had realised a large sum of profit through the sales. This process increased the profit on the selected property actually sold from five-and-a-half per cent to 19.77 per cent![107] What we see again is a clear indication that in the management of the market in the colonial context, political priorities like the need for 'loyal' subjects were embedded within market economics. Numbers were, as we have seen, subject to alteration, but this was because of the protests made by influential men over the share of their profit. Repeated alterations were required to produce the illusion of control over the auctioning process and to re-assert the control of the local administration. While in this instance, the authorities had been able to negotiate the demands of their political confidants, the cracks within the compensation scheme ripped open when the accounts were being settled.

In 1862, the accounts of the sales were tallied, and a payment of Re 1 and 2 Annas per Rupee were declared in favour of those who had retained their tickets.[108] This was based on Brandreth and Cooper's second proclamation to suggest that if there was profit, it would be divided rateably. As mentioned earlier, the question of speculation was not directly discussed in the official proclamations, but was tackled from the point of view of those who would suffer losses if they hung on to their tickets. Not only had the auction sales resulted in a profit, but its rate was modified by the local authorities. With the inclusion of substituted property to compensate for the removal of the Nawabi properties, Cooper had increased the profit that was due to the ticket-holders by 19.77 per cent. Now those who had held on to their tickets were paid a 12 per cent premium on their unredeemed tickets. We can assume that the intent of this measure was to fulfil the requests of the *Raises* who had consistently asked for better terms of engagement. Many of them had accumulated or held on to their tickets and awaited the profit that was due to them.

However, once again as Cooper paid the unredeemed ticket-holders Re 1 and 2 Annas per Rupee, some of those ticket-holders who bought houses at the auctions protested that they, too, deserved a share of the profits. Cooper, and now the new Commissioner, Mr Melville, rejected the demands at first by suggesting that only those who had held on to their tickets and risked suffering from losses were entitled to the profits.[109] This was again a tacit approval of the fact that those who had speculated in the auctions were the recipients of the profits. As we have seen, however, speculation was never openly espoused, but neither was it dismissed because of the ambiguity over whether the compensation claimants simply wanted to reduce their losses (and thus, hang on to their tickets) or actually engage in risky profiteering. This ambiguity represented itself in two separate proclamations, both made with the intent to satisfy the demands of the ticket-holders as they arose, while in all cases limiting the risks borne by the government. Yet, two separate proclamations meant that two policies and could be read as inconsistent or irregular by the ticket-holders who bought houses. This became the Achilles's heel for the authorities, who resorted once again to modify the accounts and change the assessment of profit as pressure mounted on them.

In June 1862, three months after Cooper had dismissed the claims of the house owners, he agreed to adhere to the original proclamation, guaranteeing a profit to all ticket-holders, irrespective of those who had unredeemed tickets and received Re 1 and 2 Annas per Rupee.[110] He modified the accounts to suggest that the profit of 19.77 per cent, which was made on the original property sold, was to be given on all property substituted in lieu of the Nawabi property, which had been withdrawn from the sales.[111] Cooper's alteration of the balance sheet was a work of fiction. Through fictitious profits that were generated by a series of alterations, the administration hoped to remain in command of the compensation scheme, and thereby produce the illusion of being in control.

However, Cooper's intervention, itself a way of concealing the ambiguities of the compensation scheme and the tensions within it, burst open at its seams when a legal suit was filed by a set of ticket-holders who were dissatisfied with the fact that their percentage of profit had fallen since the house-owners were being allowed a share of the profits. This suit was made by a combination of European/Eurasian and some rich Indian merchants who had speculated heavily in the tickets that had been in circulation. Appointing a lawyer, Mr Fenwick, the ticket-holders challenged the conduct of the authorities at Delhi as irregular, and mounted a charge to suggest that the government of India appoint independent legal arbitrators to assess the case.[112] Their dispute was to last years and brought the actions of the local government to scrutiny. Questions were raised over the legality of the auctions, that is, to suggest that the compensation scheme was not in line with Act VI of 1857, and the fact that the government had become an agent selling specific property after agreeing with the ticket-holders over the question of selected property.[113]

ESCAPING IRREGULARITIES AND 'CUTTING THE KNOT'

The system of compensation that the authorities had carried out in Delhi was, in effect, a balancing act where the interests of different actors, including political necessities and colonial law, were negotiated and accommodated. It was through the provision of credit and property re-allocation that the local authorities wished to establish new reins of governance, with the ultimate aim of freeing themselves from any risk of cash payments. By ensuring that the 'natural' forces of demand and supply were left to take their course, it was hoped that the market would iron out inconsistencies and enable a smooth transfer of properties. However, as we have seen, the question of loyalty complicated this scenario. Many loyal supporters, including some of the *Raises*, wished to hold on to their tickets at a time of crisis. But was this a question of preventing themselves from suffering losses, or the desire to speculate for profit? There was a thin line separating the two, and this ambiguity was built into the subsequent responses of the authorities.

Speculation was never openly espoused in policy due to its dubious distinction as an 'improper' form of market exchange. However, the demands from the ticket-holders and the ambiguity over speculation resulted in two different policies being passed, and this created havoc for the authorities when the demands for profit from the sales came to the fore. The situation was not helped by the fact that the local officials, who had promised sections of the ticket-holders a good rate of profit, changed the balance sheets from time to time. By 1864, the government of India found itself trying to salvage the situation and put an end to the constant debates over compensation. J. Graham, the Advocate General of India, was forced to admit that the messy conduct of the authorities over the case of profits was a cause for concern, and that matters needed to be settled urgently so as to avoid more government entanglements:

It is scarcely comprehensible how so simple a matter can have become so entangled. The concessions and new arrangements from time to time present a series of irregularities from which his Honor Lieutenant Governor of the Punjab appears to think there is no escape for the government without a breach of faith.[114]

In order to clarify the arbitrary decisions taken by the authorities in Delhi, the government of India justified their actions as the fallout of an excessively liberal compensation scheme.[115] The Deputy Commissioner, Mr Thornton, also concurred over the fact that the officers had been fair and liberal in their actions, and even if they had erred in their discretion, in any court of law the compensation claims would be considered 'very liberal'.[116] Colonial law, as mentioned earlier, was not simply imposed by local authorities, but was also re-negotiated as a result of internal tensions. It was modified in policy to make it suit the local demands for compensation.

Both colonial law and policy, however, were committed to the preservation of the sovereignty of the 'market'. If the veneer of liberalism was used by law to legitimise the complex negotiations undertaken by the local authorities in Delhi, speculation proved a tougher matter to eradicate, even though it was associated with unhealthy market practices. Although it was argued that 'speculators' had taken advantage of the ordinary proceedings of an extremely liberal compensation process and had exploited the principles of a free market, the Advocate General decided that it was better to 'cut the knot' and divide the entire profit between those who bought houses and those who withheld their tickets.[117] However, to distance the role of law from policy meant that the government would not only need to redeem those who had bought houses from the sales (as in Brandreth's original proclamation), but would also have to identify the original ticket-holders in the case of the speculators and prevent them from making claims in future.[118] This retrospective move was no easy task since a simple seal of approval was used to exchange tickets, and tracing the original holders became inordinately difficult. In the end, the authorities in the city, particularly the Commissioner, felt that the government was not bound to pay anyone except the person who produced or had produced tickets. The ball was thrown back once again by the local authorities to suggest that the matter of original owners or transferees was for the courts to decide and settle.[119]

CONCLUSION

One could suggest that Brandreth's plans of giving credit for the purchase of houses worked only too well in Delhi. With the end result being commoditisation, urban property was measured, valued and sold for the highest price that it could fetch. The desire for profit had fuelled purchases, and the ticket-holders had stimulated market transactions. In fact, by 1868, English-language newspapers would argue quite strongly against the 'depressed state of the market' to suggest that property values had risen spectacularly, and concomitantly, the growing number of landlords had become negligent in maintaining their properties. *The Mofussilite*, speaking about the lack of facilities for dignitaries and colonial officials in a quarter to the north of the city, wrote:

> No station in upper provinces of India is so badly off for dwelling houses as Delhi .... This is the case inside as well as outside the city walls, so that we can easily imagine the annoyances those uncomfortable individuals, who are unable to live outside and enjoy the pure free air, are subjected to. There is not a vacant house to be found, and in spite of bending, cracked, and ant-eaten beams, which threaten to let down the heavy mud and masonry roofs at any moment, such dwelling places are readily taken at risks which no respectable insurance office would undertake, no matter what the amount of premium offered.

It continued in a similar strain:

> It is therefore impossible for any native chieftain on his travels to obtain suitable temporary lodgings even at a most exorbitant rent; and unless they return to the old and more independent mode of travelling by marches, with large camps, we do not see what can be done to avert the inconveniences to which they are subjected.[120]

However, only viewing the balance sheet of the compensation scheme would mean obscuring the many tensions that shaped the nature of the government's plans for compensation. As argued in this chapter, the compensation scheme was used as a means of responding to many different and at times competing demands placed on the administration. Local officials had to negotiate demands placed by the imperial authorities to identify 'loyal' supporters after the rebellion, which meant that legal acts such as Act VI of 1857 had to be circumvented to suit local circumstances. The military demands for a clear space outside of the fort, and pressures at the level of the bureaucracy led to further modifications where 'attached' property owners were identified as future compensation claimants. Unwilling to give cash payments, Brandreth and others resorted to dispensing credit for the purchase of rebel confiscated properties and relying on the seemingly natural market forces to settle compensation matters. Property, that keystone of colonial rule, became, by default, the mechanism through which the compensation scheme was elaborated.

Market transactions were seen as the panacea for all problems, and thus, the compensation scheme was made to accommodate ambiguities such as the lack of a clear-cut distinction between the speculation of profit and avoiding losses. The latter was a matter thrown open by the 'loyal' *Raises*, and as we have seen, it was never completely reconciled. Market management became invasive and accounts were modified, numbers changed, and statistics amended to ensure that a good rate of profit was available in line with new political requirements, such as the need for loyal subjects in the aftermath of the rebellion. Thus, the victory of the market was not only a practice in political economy, but also a colonial project. While the rebellion of 1857 was a watershed event that marked the end of the Mughal regime and established in its place a new colonial administration, this transition was a process fraught with complications, which resulted from balancing political needs and market governance. The answer in the re-distribution of urban property bore the imprint of such negotiations and was constitutive of a 'free market' in property that began in Delhi.

NOTES

1. For personal accounts documenting the chaos unleashed by the event, see Charles Theophilus Metcalfe, *Two Native Narratives of the Rebellion in Delhi, Translated from the Originals by the Late Charles Theophilus Metcalfe, C. S. I* (London: Archibald Constable & Co., 1898), and Rai Jeewan Lal Bahadur, *A*

Short Account of the Life and Family of Rai Jeewan Lal Bahadur Late Honorary Magistrate Delhi, with Extracts from his Diary Relating to the Time of Rebellion, 1857 (Lahore: The Tribune Steam Press, 1911), 26–48. For two contemporary studies that shed light on the social history of Delhi during the rebellion, see William Dalrymple, *The Last Mughal* (New Delhi: Penguin Books, 2006), and Mahmood Farooqui, *Besieged: Voices from Delhi, 1857, With Notes on the Rebellion Papers and Governance in Delhi 1857* (New Delhi: Viking Books, 2010).

2. Dalrymple, *The Last Mughal.*

3. In one sense, my understanding of the 'constitutive' nature of property transfers in Delhi comes close to Ottoman historian Huri Islamoglu-Inan's formulation, which suggests that governmental practices should be viewed as a field of power where multiple actors such as state departments or different groups of people create their imprint on social reality. These kinds of politics, she argues, go into the making of property and market relations. However, differing from Islamoglu-Inan's work, this chapter suggests that there were limits to which natives could negotiate, and their involvement through a loyalist compensation scheme was very much orchestrated by the colonial government. For her study, see Huri Islamoglu-Inan (ed.), *Constituting Modernity: Private Property in the East and West* (New York: I. B. Tauris, 2004), 10–11.

4. Islamoglu-Inan (ed.), *Constituting Modernity,* 13.

5. See, for example, the pioneering work of Ranajit Guha on this subject. Ranajit Guha, *A Rule of Property for Bengal: An Essay on the Idea of the Permanent Settlement* (Paris: Mouton & Co., 1963).

6. This point has been made by P. G. Robb. See P. G. Robb, *Ancient Rights and Future Comforts: Bihar, The Bengal Tenancy Act of 1885 and British Rule in India* (London: Curzon Press, 1997), xvi.

7. While studies on the transformation of landed property rights in colonial India have overwhelmingly been on agrarian land relations, recent works are beginning to buck the trend with an urban focus. See, for example, Anish Vanaik, 'Representing Commodified Space: Maps, Leases, Auctions and "Narrations" of Property in Delhi, c. 1900–47', *Historical Research* 88, no. 240, 2014, 314–32, and Nikhil Rao, 'Uncertain Ground: "Ownership Flat" and Urban Property in Twentieth Century Bombay', *South Asian History and Culture* 3, no. 1, 2013, 1–25.

8. Indeed, the context of these developments is important, and they did not all occur at once, but the point has to be made about the significance of urban property as an object of colonial governance.

9. William J. Glover, *Making Lahore Modern: Constructing and Imagining a Colonial City* (Minneapolis: University of Minnesota Press, 2007), 15–16.

10. See Farhat Hasan, *State and Locality in Mughal India: Power Relations in Western India, 1572–1730* (Cambridge: Cambridge University Press, 2004), 91–109; and and Chris Bayly, *Rulers ,Townsmen and Bazaars: North Indian Society in the Age of British Expansion, 1770–1870* (Cambridge: Cambridge University Press, 2004), 309–10.

11. Glover, *Making Lahore Modern*, 16.

12. David Washbrook, 'Sovereignty, Property, Land and Labour in Colonial South India', in *Constituting Modernity,* ed. Islamoglu-Inan, 69–99.

13. Washbrook, 'Sovereignty, Property, Land and Labour', 69–99.

14. Punjab Government Press, *Records of the Delhi Residency and Agency: 1807–1857* (Lahore: Sang-E-Meel Publications, 2006); Letter from T. Fortescue, Civil Commissioner at Delhi to Holt Mackenzie, Secretary to the Government, Territorial Department, Fort William, dated 22 July 1820, 137.

15. Punjab Government Press, *Records of the Delhi Residency*; Letter from T. Fortescue, Civil Commissioner at Delhi to Holt Mackenzie, Secretary to the Government.

16. See, for example, Ronald Inden, *Imagining India* (Oxford: Basil Blackwell, 1990), and Nicholas Dirks, *Castes of Mind: Colonialism and the Making of Modern India* (Princeton: Princeton University Press, 2001).

17. Inden, *Imagining India*; Dirks, *Castes of Mind*. See also Letter from H. Middleton, Esquire, Acting Resident, Delhi to R. Campbell, Esquire, Principal Assistant, Centre Division, Delhi, dated 25 March 1822, 221.

18. Letter from H. Middleton, Esquire, Acting Resident, Delhi to R. Campbell, Esquire, Principal Assistant, Centre Division, Delhi, 221–22

19. Narayani Gupta, *Delhi Between Two Empires: 1803–1931: Society, Government and Urban Growth* (New Delhi: Oxford University Press, 1981), 21–22.

20. Gupta, *Delhi Between Two Empires*, 24.

21. Nayanjot Lahiri, 'Commemorating and Remembering 1857: The Revolt in Delhi and Its Afterlife', *World Archaeology* 35, no. 1, 2003, 40.

22. Letter from John Lawrence to Rt. Hon. Viscount Canning, dated 10 December 1858, F 90/13, OIOC Lawrence Papers MSS EUR.

23. Letter from John Lawrence to Rt. Hon. Viscount Canning, dated 4 December 1857, F 90/12, OIOC Lawrence Papers MSS EUR.

24. Letter from John Lawrence to Mr E. Brandreth, dated 10 October 1858, F 90/13, OIOC Lawrence Papers MSS EUR.

25. Letter from John Lawrence to Mr E. Brandreth, dated 10 October 1858.

26. Letter from John Lawrence to Mr E. Brandreth, dated 10 October 1858.

27. As Narayani Gupta argues, these two competing rationalities, that is, the civil versus military, which began at this point, were to become a pervasive factor in the spatial politics of Delhi until the shift of the capital in 1911. See Narayani Gupta, 'Military Security and Urban Development: A Case Study of Delhi 1857–1912', *Modern Asian Studies* 5, no. 1, 1971, 61–77.

28. Anish Vanaik, *Changing the Plot: Modern Property Relations in Colonial Delhi, 1857–1920*, Unpublished MPhil Thesis, Jawaharlal Nehru University, 2008.

29. Vanaik, *Changing the Plot*.

30. Letter from T. Thornton Esquire, Officiating Deputy Commissioner, Delhi to Colonel G. W Hamilton, Commissioner and Superintendent, Delhi Division, dated 21 August 1863, Box 5, 17/1865 Chandni Chowk Clearances (henceforth CC), Delhi State Archives (henceforth DSA) Residency Records (henceforth RR).

31. Letter from the Officer commanding at Delhi to the Executive Engineer, dated 29 November 1859, Box 5, 24/1859 CC, DSA RR. This particular file, for example, lists several properties falling under the 400-yard clearances, including the house of a Mughal notable named Ahmad Ali Khan, the *Kashmiri Darwaza bazaar* (a marketplace) outside the Lahore and Delhi gates of the fort, the *Lal Diggi* (a water reservoir commissioned by Lord Ellenborough), the *Feel Khana* (elephant stables) and *Lebkhana* (Mughal offices), as well as a post office and a Roman Catholic Church (two British buildings built in the early part of the century).

32. See, for example, the map of Shahjahanabad in 1850 reproduced by Ekart Ehlers and Thomas Krafft in their book, which highlights the density of settlement in the 400-yard area prior to the demolitions of 1857; E. Ehlers and T. Krafft (eds), *Shahjahanabad/Old Delhi: Tradition and Social Change*. New Delhi: Manohar Books, 2003.

33. Glover, *Making Lahore Modern*, 16.

34. Letter from Lt. G. Newmarch, Executive Engineer Delhi Division to Mr P. Egerton, Deputy Commissioner of Delhi, dated 6 January 1859, Box 5, 1/1859 Ellenborough Tank Clearances (henceforth ETC), DSA RR.

35. Letter from the Officiating Military secretary of Punjab to the Chief Engineer Punjab, dated 1 July 1859, Box 5, 16/1859 CC, DSA RR.

36. Letter from C. Campbell Esquire, Executive Engineer, Delhi Division, PWD, to P. Egerton, Deputy Commissioner, Delhi, dated 11 February 1860, Box 5, 30/1860 CC, DSA RR.

37. Letter from the Commissioner of Delhi to the Executive Engineer, Delhi Division, dated 21 May 1859, Box 5, 15/1859 CC, DSA RR.

38. Letter from the Deputy Commissioner, Delhi to the Executive Engineer, PWD, dated 4 March 1859, Box 5, 5/1859 ETC, DSA RR.

39. Memorial of Thomas Cavendish Fenwick, Attorney for Messer's Healy, Rushton, Lalla Mull and Other Dissident Ticket-holders of Delhi to His Excellency, Sir John Lawrence Bart, Viceroy and Governor General of India, dated 10 August 1864, No. 33–34 A: No. 33, NAI Foreign Department, Genl., September 1864.

40. H. Beverley, *The Land Acquisition Acts (Act X of 1870 and Act XVIII of 1885) with Introduction and Notes* (Calcutta: Thacker, Spink and Co., 1888), 5.

41. Beverly, *The Land Acquisition Acts*, 5.

42. Copy of a Letter from the Officiating Deputy Commissioner, Delhi, to the Commissioner, Delhi Division, dated 21 August 1863, No. 15–22 A: No. 16, NAI Foreign Department, Genl., KW, January 1864.

43. Copy of a Letter from the Officiating Deputy Commissioner, Delhi, to the Commissioner, Delhi Division, dated 21 August 1863.

44. Letter from the Officiating Secretary to the Government of India, Foreign Department, with the Governor General, dated 23 September 1863, 1, No. 15, NAI Foreign Department, Genl., KW, January 1864.

45. Letter from the Officiating Secretary to the Government of India, Foreign Department, with the Governor General, dated 23 September 1863.

46. Letter from the Officiating Secretary to the Government of India, Foreign Department, with the Governor General, dated 23 September 1863.

47. Gupta, *Delhi Between Two Empires*, 24.

48. Gupta, *Delhi Between Two Empires*, 24.

49. Cooper's orders were issued to officials in the following words:

> Prepare a notice of the number, estimated value, locality, and description of the confiscated houses to be sold in order to provide compensation: of these you should advertise for sale about 10 or 15 per cent, more in estimated value than the demolished houses, in order to provide for contingencies, & c.

Copy of a Letter from the Officiating Deputy Commissioner, Delhi, to the Commissioner, Delhi Division, dated 21 August 1863, 11, No. 15–22A: No. 16, NAI Foreign Department, Genl., KW, January 1864.

50. See James C. Scott, *Seeing Like a State: How Certain Schemes to Improve the Human Condition Have Failed* (Yale: Yale University Press, 1998).

51. In his lectures on governmentality, philosopher Michel Foucault argues that one of the hallmarks of 'modern' (here he means 'European') regimes was the creation of a form of governance through the establishment of an 'economy'. European governments desired control of men and their relationships with 'things' like wealth and resources, and in the process, were 'as attentive as a father over his household'. See Michel Foucault, *Security, Territory, Population:*

Lectures at the College de France 1977–78, ed. M. Senellart, trans. Graham Burchell (London: Palgrave Macmillan, 2007), 133–34.

52. Copy of a Letter from the Officiating Deputy Commissioner, Delhi, to the Commissioner, Delhi Division, dated 21 August 1863, 12, No. 15–22A: No. 16, NAI Foreign Department, Genl., KW, January 1864.

53. Letter from T. Thornton Esquire, Officiating Deputy Commissioner, Delhi to Colonel G. W. Hamilton, Commissioner and Superintendent, Delhi Division, dated 21 August 1863, Box 5, 78/1863 CC, DSA RR.

54. Letter from the Commissioner of Delhi to the Deputy Commissioner, dated 18 February 1859, Box 5, 5/1859 CC, DSA RR.

55. Nawab Hamid Ali Khan's Clearances (henceforth HAC), List of Creditors of Nawab Hamid Ali Khan and Hajee Begum the Nawab's wife, n.d., Box 2, 5/1866, DSA RR.

56. Letter from the Deputy Commissioner, Delhi, to the Commissioner and Superintendent, Delhi, dated 11 December 1862, Box 2, 5/1866 HAC, DSA RR.

57. Letter from the Deputy Commissioner, Delhi, to the Commissioner and Superintendent, Delhi, dated 11 December 1862.

58. Letter from the Deputy Commissioner, Delhi, to the Commissioner and Superintendent, Delhi, dated 11 December 1862.

59. Letter to the Executive Engineer, PWD from the Deputy Commissioner, Delhi, dated 11 May 1859, Box 2, 10/1859 CC, DSA RR.

60. Letter from Lt. Col. Ommaney, Offg. Chief Engineer Punjab to Captain Hutchinson, Supt. Engineer 2 Circle Umballa, dated 15 February 1860, Box 5, 7/1860 ETC, DSA RR.

61. Letter from P. Egerton, Deputy Commissioner Delhi to the Commissioner and Superintendent, Delhi, dated 4 March 1860, Box 2, 19/1860 HAC, DSA RR.

62. Letter from P. Egerton, Deputy Commissioner Delhi to the Commissioner and Superintendent, Delhi, dated 4 March 1860.

63. Letter from Lt. Col. Ommaney, Offg. Chief Engineer Punjab to Captain Hutchinson, Supt. Engineer 2 Circle Umballa, dated 15 February 1860, Box 5, 7/1860 ETC, DSA RR.

64. Letter from P. Egerton, Deputy Commissioner Delhi to the Commissioner and Superintendent, Delhi, dated 4 March 1860, Box 2, 19/1860 HAC, DSA RR.

65. Letter from the Executive Engineer Delhi Division to the Commissioner of Delhi, dated 16 May 1859, Box 5, 12/1859 CC, DSA RR.

66. Letter from the Executive Engineer Delhi Division to the Commissioner of Delhi, dated 16 May 1859.

67. DSA RR Box 5, 39/1860 CC. Some of the names of these individuals include the wealthy merchants and bankers of Delhi like Lala Salig Ram and Mathura

Das, and leaders of minor territories with properties in Delhi, who ultimately supported the British during the rebellion, like the Raja of Jhind, Sardar Khan and Nawab Khan Jahan Khan.

68. Copy of a Letter from the Officiating Deputy Commissioner, Delhi, to the Commissioner, Delhi Division, dated 21 August 1863, 12, No. 15–22A: No. 16, NAI Foreign Department, Genl., KW, January 1864.

69. David Boyes Smith, *Report on Epidemic Cholera, as it Prevailed in the City of Delhi, at Goorgaon and the Surrounding Districts, During the Rainy Season of 1861* (Lahore: Government Press, 1861), 79.

70. Foucault suggests that in order to combat scarcity, European governments, from the eighteenth century onwards, developed economic models so that the seemingly 'natural' forces of demand and supply could operate and regulate the market. This 'naturalness' was allowed to develop through a process of non-interference based on the understanding that economic realities had self-curbing and self-regulatory qualities; Foucault, *Security, Territory, Population*, 64.

71. See Michel Foucault, *The Birth of Biopolitics: Lectures at the Collège de France, 1978–79*, ed. M. Senellart (New York: Palgrave Macmillan, 2008).

72. Copy of a Letter from the Officiating Deputy Commissioner, Delhi, to the Commissioner, Delhi Division, dated 21 August 1863, 12, No. 15–22A: No. 16, NAI Foreign Department, Genl., KW January 1864.

73. Copy of a Letter from the Officiating Deputy Commissioner, Delhi, to the Commissioner, Delhi Division, dated 21 August 1863.

74. Copy of a Letter from the Officiating Deputy Commissioner, Delhi, to the Commissioner, Delhi Division, dated 21 August 1863.

75. This was also a case of what Ritu Birla calls in her study of the Marwaris, 'folding into' new languages and practices of market governance and then using new subject positions to negotiate terms and conditions with colonial authorities; Ritu Birla, *Stages of Capital: Law, Culture and Market Governance in Late Colonial India* (Durham: Duke University Press, 2009), 6.

76. Copy of a Letter from the Officiating Deputy Commissioner, Delhi, to the Commissioner, Delhi Division, dated 21 August 1863, 12, No. 15–22A: No. 16, NAI Foreign Department, Genl., KW, January 1864.

77. Copy of a Letter from the Officiating Deputy Commissioner, Delhi, to the Commissioner, Delhi Division, dated 21 August 1863, 12.

78. Letter from Punjab Government, No. 165, dated 23 December 1863, 2, No. 15–22A, NAI Foreign Department, Genl., KW, January 1864.

79. In a subsequent declaration, Brandreth, too, issued instructions to suggest something similar:

Confiscated houses of equal value will be auctioned to provide compensation; you will buy at auctions, as you will not get the value of the demolished house in cash from Government: if the price of houses sold at the auction is more than the estimate, it will be rateably divided, and if less, then the loss will be distributed over those who wish for cash; those who buy confiscated houses being exempt from such a loss.

Copy of a Letter from the Officiating Deputy Commissioner, Delhi, to the Commissioner, Delhi Division, dated 21 August 1863, 13, No. 15–22A: No. 16, NAI Foreign Department, Genl., KW, January 1864.

80. Memorial of Thomas Cavendish Fenwick, Attorney for Messer's Healy, Rushton, Lalla Mull and other Dissident Ticket-holders of Delhi to His Excellency, Sir John Lawrence Bart, Viceroy and Governor General of India, dated 10 August 1864, No. 33–34 A: No. 33, NAI Foreign Department, Genl., September 1864.

81. Memorial of Thomas Cavendish Fenwick, Attorney for Messer's Healy, Rushton, Lalla Mull and other Dissident Ticket-holders of Delhi to His Excellency, Sir John Lawrence Bart, Viceroy and Governor General of India, dated 10 August 1864.

82. Jyoti Hosagrahar, *Indigenous Modernities: Negotiating Architecture and Urbanism* (London: Routledge, 2005).

83. Copy of a Letter from the Officiating Deputy Commissioner, Delhi, to the Commissioner, Delhi Division, dated 21 August 1863, 13, No. 15–22A: No. 16, NAI Foreign Department, Genl., KW January 1864.

84. Copy of a Letter from the Officiating Deputy Commissioner, Delhi, to the Commissioner, Delhi Division, dated 21 August 1863, 13.

85. Memorial of Thomas Cavendish Fenwick, Attorney for Messer's Healy, Rushton, Lalla Mull and other Dissident Ticket-holders of Delhi to His Excellency, Sir John Lawrence Bart, Viceroy and Governor General of India, dated 10 August 1864.

86. Memorial of Thomas Cavendish Fenwick, Attorney for Messer's Healy, Rushton, Lalla Mull and other Dissident Ticket-holders of Delhi to His Excellency, Sir John Lawrence Bart, Viceroy and Governor General of India.

87. Copy of a Report on Compensation for Demolitions at Delhi by the Punjab Government No. 165, dated 23 September 1863, Box 5, 92-B/1864 CC, DSA RR.

88. Letter from T. Thornton Esquire, Officiating Deputy Commissioner, Delhi to Colonel G. W. Hamilton, Commissioner and Superintendent, Delhi Division, dated 21August 1863, Box 5, 78/1863 CC, DSA RR.

89. Copy of a Letter from the Officiating Deputy Commissioner, Delhi, to the

Commissioner, Delhi Division, dated 21 August 1863, 13, No. 15–22A: No. 16, NAI Foreign Department, Genl., KW, January 1864.

90. Copy of a Letter from the Officiating Deputy Commissioner, Delhi, to the Commissioner, Delhi Division, dated 21 August 1863, 13.

91. Memorial of Thomas Cavendish Fenwick, Attorney for Messer's Healy, Rushton, Lalla Mull and other Dissident Ticket-holders of Delhi to His Excellency, Sir John Lawrence Bart, Viceroy and Governor General of India, dated 10 August 1864.

92. Copy of a Letter from the Commissioner, Delhi Division, to the Secretary to Government, Punjab, dated 27 April 1864, 3, No. 74–75A: No. 75, NAI Foreign Dept. Genl., June 1864. The overall number of tickets actually issued was 2,762, with a value of Rs 8,15,539, 6 Paisa and 4 Annas. During the whole process, only one individual refused to accept a ticket for his property, which was valued at Rs 6,612. This amount was thus deducted from the total value of compensation.

93. Letter from T. Thornton Esquire, Officiating Deputy Commissioner, Delhi to Colonel G. W. Hamilton, Commissioner and Superintendent, Delhi Division, dated 21 August 1863, Box 5, 17/1865 CC, DSA RR.

94. My argument for the colonial context develops upon political scientist Bernard Harcourt's argument that it is simplistic to call markets 'free' because they are always constrained by a variety of rules and political regulations. Tracing the historical antecedents of 'free markets' in America, Harcourt suggests that the notion of a 'natural order', that is, of an autonomous realm of economic exchange, is illusory and serves to hide the interventionist and regulatory capacities of modern states, their links with non-state organisations, as well as the legal frameworks in which such institutions are embedded. In contemporary America, Harcourt argues that the language of 'free markets' has obscured the real problems of distributional outcomes of wealth, and has left unchallenged the growing punitive interventionism of the state in the social sphere. See Bernard E. Harcourt, *The Illusion of Free Markets: Punishment and the Myth of the Natural Order* (Cambridge: Harvard University Press, 2011).

95. Copy of a Letter from the Officiating Deputy Commissioner, Delhi, to the Commissioner, Delhi Division, dated 21 August 1863, 13, No. 15–22A: No. 16, NAI Foreign Department, Genl., KW, January 1864.

96. Arjun Appadurai, *Modernity at Large: Cultural Dimensions of Globalisation* (Minnesota: University of Minnesota Press, 1996), 117.

97. Appadurai, *Modernity at Large*, 117.

98. Memorial of Thomas Cavendish Fenwick, Attorney for Messer's Healy, Rushton, Lalla Mull and Other Dissident Ticket-holders of Delhi to His

Excellency, Sir John Lawrence Bart, Viceroy and Governor General of India, dated 10 August 1864, No. 33–34 A: No. 33, NAI Foreign Department, Genl., September 1864.

99. For a background, see Veena Oldenburg, *The Making of Colonial Lucknow: 1856–77* (Princeton: Princeton University Press, 1984).

100. Oldenburg, *The Making of Colonial Lucknow*.

101. Anonymous Correspondent, *The Mofussilite*, 29 August 1862, 150.

102. Minute by The Hon. W. Ritchie to the Secretary to the Government of Punjab, dated 2 November 1861, Allahabad, No. 57–68A: No. 67, NAI Foreign Department, Pol., KW, November 1861. The problem for the authorities occurred over the legality of the sales and the question of whether the property formed a 'private' or 'public' part of the Nawab's household since the colonial state had annexed Awadh prior to the rebellion, and by virtue of that, had transformed all the rulers' property into government or state property. A confidant of the deposed Nawab called Anees ud Dowlah, along with the dependents of the ex-ruler, challenged the sales by claiming that the properties were not 'public' since they were not possessed in the name of the 'sovereign', but were under the Nawab's 'private' or individual capacity, and thus, redeemable by his heirs. Taking advantage of the government's policy for deciding cases under the 'Islamic personal law', the dependents claimed that the properties needed to be turned over to them, according to the legal provisions set by the state.

103. Copy of a Letter from the Officiating Deputy Commissioner, Delhi, to the Commissioner, Delhi Division, dated 21 August 1863, 14, No. 15–22 A: No. 16, NAI Foreign Department, Genl., KW, January 1864.

104. Memorial of Thomas Cavendish Fenwick, Attorney for Messer's Healy, Rushton, Lalla Mull and Other Dissident Ticket-holders of Delhi to His Excellency, Sir John Lawrence Bart, Viceroy and Governor General of India, dated 10 August 1864, No. 33–34 A: No. 33, NAI Foreign Department, Genl., September 1864.

105. Copy of a Letter from the Officiating Deputy Commissioner, Delhi, to the Commissioner, Delhi Division, dated 21 August 1863, 14, No. 15–22 A: No. 16, NAI Foreign Department, Genl., KW, January 1864.

106. Copy of a Letter from the Officiating Deputy Commissioner, Delhi, to the Commissioner, Delhi Division, dated 21 August 1863, 14.

107. Copy of a Letter from the Officiating Deputy Commissioner, Delhi, to the Commissioner, Delhi Division, dated 21 August 1863, 14. The profits from the auctions had originally been Rs 1,03,700, and this was raised to 19.77 per cent, that is, Rs 1,73,410-2, 2 Paisa and 7 Annas on all tickets with an original

value of 8,77,000. However, 19.77 per cent of Rs 8,77,000 actually totals Rs 1,73,382. There is thus just a slight difference between the two calculations, but the figures are broadly correct.

108. Copy of a Letter from the Officiating Deputy Commissioner, Delhi, to the Commissioner, Delhi Division.

109. Copy of a Letter from the Officiating Deputy Commissioner, Delhi, to the Commissioner, Delhi Division, dated 21 August 1863, 14.

110. Letter from Punjab Government, No. 165, dated 23 December 1863, 4–5, No. 15–22 A: No. 16, NAI Foreign Department, Genl., KW, January 1864.

111. Letter from Punjab Government, No. 165, dated 23 December 1863, 4–5, No. 15–22 A: No. 16, NAI Foreign Department, Genl., KW, January 1864, 5. Through this alteration of figures, the profits from the auctions, which had been Rs 1,03,700, were raised to Rs 1,73,410, 2 Paisa and 7 Annas (19.77 per cent) on all the tickets, which had an original value of Rs 8,77,000. Cooper further resolved to give 5 Annas and 4 Pies to settle the accounts so that no more claims would be put forward.

112. The battle was once again over the numbers that represented the figures of profit. Fenwick's assertion was that if Rs 2,17,000 worth of property that had been sold before the removal of certain property (Nawabi) led to a profit of Rs 92,000, then by this logic, the whole value of tickets, that is, Rs 8,08,000, would have yielded a profit of Rs 3,42,000. With interest, he further suggested, this was much more than what had been sanctioned by Mr Cooper; Memorial of Thomas Cavendish Fenwick, Attorney for Messer's Healy, Rushton, Lalla Mull and Other Dissident Ticket-holders of Delhi to His Excellency, Sir John Lawrence Bart, Viceroy and Governor General of India, dated 10 August 1864.

113. Memorial of Thomas Cavendish Fenwick, Attorney for Messer's Healy, Rushton, Lalla Mull and Other Dissident Ticket-holders of Delhi to His Excellency, Sir John Lawrence Bart, Viceroy and Governor General of India, dated 10 August 1864. The legal intervention not only opened the floodgates for disputes between Fenwick's ticket-holders and the government, but also left the question of Cooper's 5 Annas and 4 Pies assessment hanging. This meant that the case of profit for those who had bought houses (in accordance with Brandreth's compensation scheme) also remained unresolved.

114. Letter from J. Graham, Officiating Advocate General, to J. T. Wheeler, Assistant Secretary to Government of India, Foreign Department, dated 4 December 1863, No. 15-22A: No. 21, NAI Foreign Department, Genl., KW, January 1864.

115. For example, when it came to an examination of the rudiments of Brandreth's compensation plan, there was an unequivocal acceptance that this was simply the result of liberal impulses:

> [The decision] appears at first sight an arbitrary one, but on consideration it will be seen that it is nothing more than carrying out in a liberal manner the orders of the Supreme Government 'not to pay compensation in cash'. The supreme government said, 'give the ticket holders credit for the estimated value of their houses in the purchase of new houses'.

Copy of a Letter from the Officiating Deputy Commissioner, Delhi, to the Commissioner, Delhi Division, dated 21 August 1863, 25, No. 16, NAI Foreign Department, Genl., KW, January 1864.

116. Copy of a Letter from the Officiating Deputy Commissioner, Delhi, to the Commissioner, Delhi Division, dated 21 August 1863, 8.

117. Copy of a Letter from the Officiating Deputy Commissioner, Delhi, to the Commissioner, Delhi Division.

118. For example, the Advocate General declared the following:

> The majority of these tickets appear to be now in the possession of other persons than the owners of demolished houses. If the proposed offer (of compensation) be accepted, the signature of the original owner of the houses as well as the ticket holder should be required previously to payment being made so as to prevent any further claims by the former.

He further continued: 'The recognition of these ticket-holders as transferees of the original ticket-holders have hitherto been so fully recognised as standing in the position of the original owners, that the insisting on this condition will lead to further complaints, but I think it should nevertheless be adhered to'; Copy of a Letter from the Officiating Deputy Commissioner, Delhi, to the Commissioner, Delhi Division, dated 21 August 1863, 25, No. 16, NAI Foreign Department, Genl., KW, January 1864.

119. Letter from the Commissioner, Delhi Division to the Secretary to the Government of Punjab, dated 27 April 1864, Box 5, 90/1864CC, DSA RR.

120. Anonymous Correspondent, *The Mofussilite*, 1 October 1868, 6.

2

The Delhi Municipality and the Challenges of Urban Governance

INTRODUCTION

On 19 March 1863, J. H. Cooper, the Deputy Commissioner of Delhi, forwarded a printed list with 'subjects that demanded attention' to a select group of European and Indian elites who had formed a part of a new civic institution for the city, the Delhi municipality.[1] For their loyalty and support during the rebellion, rich bankers and merchants were offered roles as native members of the municipality, to help 'improve' the future state of Delhi. Under the Police Act of 1861, Cooper drafted a series of by-laws for the consideration of this coterie of municipal members, and listed core points around which the newly instituted municipality would conduct its future operations.[2] Drainage, encroachments on public streets, processions, conservancy, 'indecent or disgusting' mendicancy, and surveillance of 'sturdy beggars' were some core concerns listed for urgent consideration.[3]

As civic bodies instituted across India after 1858, municipalities carried a wide variety of powers to effect sanitation and conservancy, and to maintain order on public streets.[4] In Delhi, in addition to Cooper's memorandum, the Delhi municipality took it upon itself to keep a record of births and deaths, clear drains and sewers, ensure that streets were lit at night, and that octroi duties were collected to fund works of 'public utility'.[5] Plans were drafted for the creation of well-manicured gardens and a Town Hall.[6] The latter would soon stand on the site of the erstwhile

Mughal *Sarai* (a tavern or an inn; in the contemporary sense, a municipality, area or junction) and contain a library, reading rooms, museum and college, a school of design, and the space for a literary society (Figure 2.1).[7]

CLOCK TOWER CHANDNI CHOWK. DELHI.

Figure 2.1: Town Hall with Clock Tower, Delhi c. 1910

Source: This postcard was provided by the author.

Recent scholarship has added to our understanding of the operations of municipalities in colonial India and their enduring legacies. Arguments have been made to suggest that 'underdevelopment' in Indian cities is a legacy of the colonial era, arising as a result of the failure of the colonial regime to provide urban amenities, which understood the indigenous city through a politics of difference.[8] However, this suggests that municipal intentions were wholly consistent, that is, in terms of 'purposefully' neglecting urban spaces and spending finances on their promised schemes. The arguments in this chapter, however, build upon a body of work that questions a normative vision of colonial power and its intentions, revealing much more contradiction and ambiguity in the operations of its agencies.[9]

In examining Delhi municipality's attempts to reorganise public spaces in the city between 1863 and 1910, the chapter shows how the growth in, and the centralisation of, powers by the municipality to carry out its everyday operations created further challenges for the governance of its urban spaces. Colonial debates over the reorganisation of urban markets, the growing coercive power endowed through municipal acts, a hierarchical bureaucracy needed for surveillance, and the demand for technical expertise, all had the effect of increasing the scale, costs and complexity of municipal operations. This, in turn, carried the potential of igniting municipal conflicts with other departments as well as with the residents of the city. The larger point that this chapter makes is that while the growing complexity of municipal operations did indeed subvert its intentions, it also added to its bureaucratic strength and regulatory powers. In other words, as it 'failed' to do what it set out to, it was also 'fed' through an enlargement of its administrative capabilities.

MUNICIPAL RESPONSIBILITIES: STREETS AND THE REORGANISATION OF PUBLIC SPACES

As one-third of the city was being demolished, Cooper and other municipal members began laying out an agenda for the city. Only a few prominent merchants and bankers in Delhi were given a stake in the municipal enterprise in 1863, and they collaborated with the colonial government to undertake municipal operations. Together, they endorsed new spatial designs and practices that reflected the political project of improvement and the reordering of public spaces in the city.[10] A fundamental premise of municipal acts was to ensure that Indian streets remained free from obstructions, and from sanitary and building construction. This was based on European cultural norms that saw 'public' and 'private' as two distinct domains, the former being policed and maintained in the interests of the 'public'. Above all, public spaces such as streets were envisaged in metropolitan ideals as spaces of flows and movement, so that health and sanitation of the city could be improved. Thus municipal codes and plans espoused the circulation of 'free' and unencumbered bodies.[11]

In the colonial city, the reorganisation of public spaces was also based on the need to encourage the circulation of people and traffic. However, the rule of colonial difference meant that municipal governance in the colony was qualitatively different from that in the metropolis.[12] Indian cities were perceived as inherently dirty and disease-ridden, and as a result of this, a wide variety of native habits came under the surveillance of the municipality.[13] Surveillance and the force of the police was needed to discipline natives who conducted their sundry trades on streets, sold wares by blocking public pathways, and carried out insanitary activities that were injurious to the senses. One early description of Delhi from 1835 gives us an insight into how colonial perceptions about sensory deprivation in the city would later inform municipal policies and reinforce the need to police native habits. Describing a street scene, one guide recounted:

> The cries of the vendors of different articles of food, the discordant songs of itinerant musicians, screamed out to the accompaniment of the tom tom, with an occasional bass volunteered by the cheetah grumbling out in a sharp roar his annoyance at having being hawked about the streets for sale, with the shrill and distressful cry of the camel, the trumpeting of the elephants, the neighing of the horses and the grumbling of cart wheels are sounds which assail the ear from sunrise to sunset in the streets of Delhi.[14]

The assault on the ear, accompanied with the heat and dust somehow threatened or interfered with the experience of European travellers and prevented the 'legibility' of the street.[15] The public street therefore was seen to lack order and symmetry, and because of the confluence of activities, it carried the potential of sensory paralysis for European bodies. Descriptions like this differed from local perceptions and usages, which saw the street first and foremost as a social space.[16] For example, Nawab Quli Khan, a visitor to Delhi who stopped to see Chandni Chowk in the 1750s, described the hustle and bustle of street scenes in convivial terms and called it a haven for 'pleasure seekers'.[17] For him, the street did not have any rigid boundaries, and rather, it was a place where commerce, conviviality and recreation all unfolded at the same time. In describing the everyday happenings of Chandni Chowk, Khan reveals that there was no clear distinction between the 'public' space of the street and 'private' spaces of shops: 'The proprietors sit contentedly on one side of the passage while their subordinates carry out the daily trade .... Men can be found standing on the roads selling such a range of the choicest clothing that the wares of the shopkeepers are dull by comparison.'[18]

For Khan, this engagement with the social world of the street along with its commercial activities was a worthy pursuit, where commerce was inseparable from pleasure, and where the shop/street distinction did not exist. Moreover, unlike later colonial accounts, no concerns of filth, dirt or sensory assault were foregrounded, as they were not central to the understanding of street life.

With colonial attitudes towards Indians hardening after the rebellion of 1857, the need for policing Indian cities had become acute.[19] It was in this context that agencies like the Delhi municipality were formed in 1863. The lack of distinction between 'public' and 'private' spaces, degenerate habits and practices of most natives, and the insanitary nature of their surroundings led to the passage of the Police Act, under which municipal powers were first defined. If the municipality was to encourage circulation and movement in the Indian city, who could move where and when would remain firmly in its jurisdiction. It was for this reason that a large number of activities, ostensibly targetting the poor of the city (such as the 'sturdy beggars' in Cooper's note), came to be defined as 'nuisances', more so than in the metropole.[20] Indeed, the 'improvement' of cities and their populace was meant to be a political project in order to reshape the urban environment through new codes and regulations listed under municipal acts.

However, as we shall see, municipal reorganisation of 'public' spaces in Delhi was characterised by contradiction and inconsistency in its operations. The 'working' of municipal power in the city was effected through settling the boundaries between streets and markets, creating a hierarchical bureaucracy to affect policing, incorporating a wide range of municipal by-laws to check 'nuisances', and implementing technologies of improvement like sanitation and drainage facilities. The very complexity of the operations, the costs and the variegated opinions involved in such an enterprise could outstrip municipal intentions.

SETTLING BOUNDARIES: REBUILDING THE *SABZI MANDI*

One of the first drives towards the reorganisation of public space took shape with the reconstitution of the *Sabzi Mandi* of Delhi, or the main vegetable market of the city, between 1865 and 1874. The plot of the *Mandi* (market) formed a part of the extensive *nazul* properties of the Mughals that fell under the management of the municipality after 1857.[21] *Nazul,* in the words of the government, included 'innumerable patches and plots, cultivated and uncultivated, built upon and waste, lands and roads'.[22] Ground rents called *teh-bazari* were collected from such properties, and they became a source of income for the new municipality. *Nazul* plots, streets and squares were public spaces for the municipality, to be governed by rational principles, and divested of native nuisances and private encroachments.

The *Sabzi Mandi* was located a small distance away from the city and was a centre where all the fruit and vegetables from the suburbs of Delhi were brought for sale by gardeners and cultivators. It was well-placed since it was in the vicinity of gardens like the Roshanara and Sirhindi *Bagh,* which were parallel to the *Faiz Nahar* (the canal that brought water into the city).[23] Retailers and hawkers plying different markets within the city would purchase their goods from *dalals* (brokers) in the *Sabzi Mandi,* who were predominantly Punjabi Muslims. Goods brought to the *Sabzi Mandi* were sold by auction sales, and the *dalals* made a profit through commission.[24] Even products from outside the city, including Meerut and Saharanpur, made their way into the *Sabzi Mandi* auctions and were sold by the *dalals.*[25]

For the newly formed Delhi municipality, however, the market was a picture of chaos and confusion. One concern that was repeated in municipal accounts was the general over-crowdedness of the market when the auction sales of vegetables took place. Since the market plot belonging to the *Mandi* was listed as being only 20 feet square, the municipality argued that all transactions took place on what were 'public' roads.[26] Linked to this spillage of commercial activity onto public roads was the question of sanitation.[27] The *Mandi's* poor drainage facilities, insanitary habits of handling fruits and vegetables, and over-crowdedness aroused municipal fears of 'bad air' and vapours, along with 'unhealthy trades', which were defined by a succession of municipal acts passed after 1860, as responsible for the insanitary state of affairs in the country.[28] There was one more pressing reason for the municipality to spur itself into action. This was that the *Mandi* was near the Grand Trunk Road, the main communications route linking the eastern and western halves of the subcontinent, and it was argued that the transactions of the *Mandi* spilled over and obstructed traffic on the trunk road. The Deputy Commissioner and President of the municipality summed up all these reasons when recalling the state of the *Mandi* before municipal action:

> The crowd swelled out into all thoroughfares and interrupted traffic. The grand trunk road among others was often seriously interfered with. On this small spot and on the adjoining lanes and roads the fruit used to be in heaps on the ground. For an individual to pass from one end of the market to the other was a serious business, not only was he elbowed by the dense crowd but he had to make his way by a series of leaps over the heaps of fruit and vegetables, frequently causing no small damage.

He further stated:

> The want of space was not the only objection. The ground on that side of the subzee mandee is low and receives the drainage from the ground on the other side of the grand trunk road. There is no provision for allowing the water to pass off. Accordingly after a good shower or on a rainy day this market was fit for a duck pond and nothing else.[29]

Thus, the market was represented as being beset by a variety of impediments, including an overlap between over-crowdedness and a lack of drainage, improper trading activities, and even the encroachment of public roads. As Gyan Prakash has argued, colonial sanitary discourse produced a 'discriminatory sanitary order' in colonial India where the habits of Indians and their environment were seen as the source of diseases.[30] It was the fear of these 'insanitary' habits associated with Indian commercial activities, and the obstruction of goods and pedestrian traffic, which led the municipality to draft a serious 'improvement' initiative for the *Sabzi Mandi*.

In a carefully conceived plan of action, in 1865, the municipality applied to the government of India for the permanent transfer of a plot of land in Mauza Jahan Numa, a place near the site of the *Mandi* for an improved marketplace.[31] In the same year, the government acceded to the request and waived its proprietary rights to collect revenues in favour of the municipality.[32] In a burst of frenetic activity that followed, a market was created and fitted with new buildings and shops, along with storage areas for the products. The distance from the city to the new site was calculated, and the new area was kept within easy reaching distance from the same.[33] The municipality also took into account the catchment area, that is, the fruit and vegetable fields that were close to the older *Mandi*, and in accordance with it, chose an area that was about 400 yards away from the former. In the new market, it was decided that no levies were to be charged for storage of the items in the warehouses. It was claimed that all of this would induce the brokers and cultivators to shift to the new site and have the opportunity to conduct auctions as previously.[34] In total, the municipality spent Rs 12,000 to create an obstruction-free market with 'ample accommodation' for all parties by 1866.[35]

However, the neatness of municipal reorganisation was quickly thwarted by the refusal of the *dalals* and vegetable vendors to move their business.[36] At first, municipal officials decided to play the waiting game and had faith that the new market would indeed run smoothly. This wait was to last five years to no avail. In that time, the site was even converted into a makeshift police *thana* (police station) or office for a few months because of the heavy costs incurred in its construction.[37] By 1871, municipal patience had worn thin. After five years of waiting, Mr Knox, the Deputy Commissioner and President of the municipality, issued a verbal threat to the brokers and sellers that he would enforce a section of the Police Act of 1861 and eject them from the *Sabzi Mandi* altogether if they did not shift.[38] Following this threat, some brokers moved out of the premises, and into the new area, while others remained, leading to a situation where the disaffected individuals retaliated against the municipality violently, sparking a riot.[39]

What followed from this was a lengthy consultation and a series of debates over the reasons for the riot, whether the municipality needed to compensate the aggrieved parties for all their losses or if they should reconsider the site altogether. These debates, in turn, reveal how the diffuse nature of municipal power could create problems in its own operations. Knox's own verbal threat was an example of this. His actions were not condoned by other municipal members, and using the full force of the act, they were considered by some to be 'unfortunate to the administration' and 'very damaging to the case' because no written orders could be found, and the riot opened the way for legal cases.[40] Yet, if Knox's attitude was said to be impulsive, his orders were still within the bounds of municipal regulations. His lack of paperwork or official notice put the municipality in a bind because now an investigation was required to ascertain exactly what went wrong, so that claims of compensation could be assessed. At another level, his order served to project and reinforce a particular image, that of the capriciousness of the municipality and the brute force it was willing to use against the population.

The discussion over the reasons for the riot also revealed tensions between the municipality and other local authorities, who were at odds over what constituted the rights of the aggrieved *dalals* and sellers. For example, one of the most contentious issues was over the municipality's creation of new storage facilities. Municipal officials had created the new market based on the separation of commercial activities from dwelling houses, and these were in contradistinction to the old *Mandi* where the *dalals* stored fruits and vegetables in their own homes overnight.[41] Mr Benton, the new Deputy Commissioner and President of the municipality, was of the opinion that the *dalals* were making 'illegitimate' gains at the expense of the *maalis* (gardeners) and cultivators by appropriating their produce. Thus, he reinforced the perception that not only was the old market a 'disgusting scene', but the broker as a middleman was engaged in corrupt practices and exploitation.[42] This was to justify that the municipality had done nothing wrong and there was no need to discuss compensation claims since the 'legitimate gains' of the *dalals* did not suffer and the storage facilities were free of cost. The separation of functions between the household and market was therefore based on neat municipal distinctions between public and private spaces in order to remove the visual opacity (and hence, the charge of corruption) that the operations of the *dalals* were causing.

However, some officials were of a very different view. The Commissioner of the Delhi municipality, in responding to Benton's successor, for example, felt that 'old and intricate rights' had been interfered with.[43] He felt that Benton was trying to close the case of the *dalals* summarily, and this served to 'obliterate' their rights 'by an inference of fraudulent practices against the petitioners' of which there was no proof.[44] Thus, there were two competing positions based on two different ways of understanding the entitlements of the *dalals*.[45] One was that the *dalals* were making 'illegitimate' gains and were therefore corrupt—an undesired but necessary evil. This served to reinforce the stereotype of the corrupt middleman exploiting native cultivators, and thereby stifling market activity.[46] On the other side, there was the question of 'old and intricate rights' and whether municipal officials were interfering with these. The Commissioner, although not directly linked with the municipality, oversaw operations in the entire Delhi district and was wary about infringing upon indigenous rights and customs after the rebellion. For him, the *dalals*' entitlements were not 'illegitimate' gains, as Benton and others understood them, but instead they were 'old and intricate rights' of market practice, which were not clearly understood. He bemoaned the fact that municipal meddling had indirectly led to 'class favouritism' by privileging the rights of Hindu cultivators. By not having to pay a contribution to the Punjabi *dalals* who were predominantly Muslims, he felt that the cultivators gained at the new market, and this was against the government's policy of non-interference.[47] From the latter's standpoint, it was clear that the municipality had to arrive at some sort of a compensation by a sustained inquiry of exactly how the rights were injured and how much compensation could be paid in return. This again led to more municipal involvement through the re-assessment of claims.

Before his departure, Benton had come to the conclusion that the 'illegitimate' gains that the municipality took away from the *dalals* through its move led to the 'depreciation' in the price of the *dalals*' properties. This assessment was made when aggrieved parties were called to account for the losses that they had suffered.[48] However, defining such losses in monetary terms was more difficult than it seemed. While no rent was paid to the *dalals* for storage, it seems that they benefitted from the payment of a contribution by the fruit and vegetables salesmen. Benton's probe hinted at this when he suggested that the 'Punjabees allege they charge nothing for storage just as the municipality charge nothing.'[49] This could have also meant that their properties were sought after by other brokers and salesmen, and hence, there arose issue with the depreciation of property prices if the market was shifted.[50]

The assessment of 'depreciation' became more convoluted with further investigations. Another reason cited by the *dalals* was the availability of labour in their houses. It was argued that the presence of families, including wives and children, was beneficial as it meant that individuals were present to take care of the products and ward off the threat from white ants and other insects.[51] If the health of the city depended on the supply of unspoilt products from the *Mandi*, then, the *dalals* argued, this was only possible when household labour was available to inspect the fruits and vegetables.

So puzzling was the question of assessing the depreciated value of properties that the Commissioner of Delhi turned to the Punjab government for their counsel. Again, the Commissioner claimed that the rights of a 'laborious and enterprising section of the population' had been hurt, although no conclusion had been arrived at as to what these were. In the interim, the Commissioner even called for investigations to see if operations in the old *Mandi* could be restored with new drainage facilities for 'space and convenience', all in the hope that this would balance municipal needs as well as show that the administration was acting in a 'conciliatory spirit'.[52] Thus, it was not as if the Commissioner was opposed to any interference. Rather, his alternative vision was also based on the same need to uphold the tenets of the civilising mission. He, too, was committed to an orderly marketplace with a rational distribution of space, but one that balanced the 'old and intricate rights', a way of understanding native *difference*, within it.

When the Punjab government came back with an answer, the investigations and proposals that the Commissioner had voiced were stalled. The government disagreed with the Commissioner, called the *dalals* 'monopolists', and dismissed the vested rights that they claimed were lost.[53] The new Secretary of the municipality saw this as an opportunity to avoid further municipal losses and expenditure, and quickly took advantage of the Punjab government's proclamation. In a municipal proclamation, he declared:

> Never did the municipal committee perform a more disinterested act than this one, and they confess to surprise at being called upon to pay for imaginary losses, and of kind the commissioner himself declares it impossible to define. The complainants are dallals and in no sense were they the proprietors of the market, inasmuch as it was held on the public road and was a daily nuisance. These dallals get the same percentage on sales as they did in the old market hence the loss on their part is simply impossible.[54]

These pitched battles over 'imaginary' losses revealed internal tensions within the municipality, and between it and other local authorities.

Questions over the use of municipal coercion or competing ideologies of colonial difference, that is, over whether ancient rights were disturbed or whether the case was a simple matter of 'illegitimate' accumulation, confounded operations and stalled the functioning of the new market. However, this did not mean that the lack of order or systematicity had no real effects. If we recall Knox's order again, we know that it indirectly reinforced the capriciousness of the municipality and its will to use force despite the originally intended efforts at inducing a shift to the new *Mandi*. Moreover, the Commissioner's orders to assess 'old and intricate' rights led to an intensive drive to clarify who was injured by the relocation, and how. The need to prove that his view was wrong gave a sense of purpose to municipal authorities, and it also justified more intrusive and exhaustive fact-checking. In effect, confusion and disagreements extended the bureaucratic responsibilities of the municipality.

When the Punjab government sided with the municipality, there was an opportunity to jettison the investigation of compensation claims and liabilities, as this was now a matter for the civil courts to resolve.[55] This promised a clean slate for the municipality to continue its policy of restructuring and policing urban markets. Yet, as we have seen, the archival trail left by the *Sabzi Mandi* case reveals how internal tensions and competing claims of the government departments over rights and usages created chaos and confusion for municipal operations. This was, in a way, a productive break, which led to an increase in investigations and expanded the work of the municipal enterprise through investigations and surveys.

In the next section, I consider the increasing regulatory powers of the municipality that were endowed through municipal acts. Successive municipal acts gave municipalities the ability to create by-laws to tackle what were perceived as building or sanitary 'encroachments' in the city. However, as I show, an expansion in the coercive powers of the municipality created severe challenges for municipal operations. Examining the case of the *chabutra* (a masonry or wooden platform), which is used for various purposes in Delhi's shops and houses, I show how the expansion of municipal powers to curtail encroachments increased conflicts between the municipality and the residents of the city, and also in a similar manner as the *Sabzi Mandi*, within the colonial government itself.

MUNICIPAL ACTS AND COERCIVE POWERS: PLATFORMS AS 'ENCROACHMENTS'

As we have seen in the case of the *Sabzi Mandi*, the *dalal*s and vendors of the market were blamed for insanitary transactions on public roads by municipal authorities. By the using of the broad definition of 'public nuisance', the municipality sought to discipline such activities and refashion urban spaces.[56] It was in light of this that a new market with clear boundaries between public and private spaces was desired. In conjunction with the drive to re-settle markets and police commercial activities, a target of municipal regulation and by-laws were the dimensions of buildings and their use. Building additions such as plinths, balconies and over-hangings were particularly threatening to the rational and systematic ordering of spaces since they 'encroached' upon public land. In addition, as objects on streets and in *bazaar*s, they had the potential to block the circulation of goods traffic, prevent drainage or sanitation works, and thus, create a haven for disease.[57]

As an example of how the municipality policed encroachments in Delhi, I discuss how the construction of *chabutra*s intersected with municipal designs to reorganise the city into neat divisions between 'public' and 'private' spaces and check the spread of insanitary obstructions. As in the case of the *Sabzi Mandi*, this was a contradictory process that increased conflicts not only between the municipality and different sections of the population, but also within the colonial government itself.

In Delhi, platforms such as *chabutra*s were placed in front of shops in order to meet people or conduct business and financial transactions (see Figure 2.2).[58] They formed a liminal space between the shop and the street, and blended into the street-shop spaces. Emily Metcalfe, the daughter of Thomas Metcalfe, the British resident and agent of Delhi in the years leading up to the rebellion of 1857, gave an account of the shops at Chandni Chowk:

> The front room (*of the shop*) being open to the street, without doors, carpeted with a white cloth on which one or two men would be sitting …. If a European stopped at a shop he generally sat on the edge of the floor of the shop, which was always raised a few feet above the road, and bargained for any new articles he wanted.[59]

Figure 2.2: Dye-Maker on Pukka Chabutra, Delhi c. 1920s

Source: This postcard was provided by the author.

While the terminology of the *chabutra* was not explicitly mentioned in Metcalfe's narrative, her account pointed to the elevated space of the shop floor that extended to the road, and which in this case was used to host European customers. Instead of shutting off the front of the shop by way of a door, the street traffic was invited in during business hours. At times, the doors of the shops were themselves portable and could be folded to create a platform or plank that doubled up as a *chabutra*.[60] In fact, the term 'chabutra' could be applied to multiple objects that projected onto the streets.[61] It is probable that the owners of the *chabutra*s paid rent in the form of duties to the *bazaar* headmen or to the *kotwal* (magistrate), the collection rights of which in the early-nineteenth century were rented out or sold off to local notables.[62] Further, *chabutra*s could be rented out to individuals to sell their wares and formed a means for shopkeepers to enhance their income.[63]

Prior to 1857, there was no coherent policy prohibiting *chabutra*s in Delhi. In fact, the opposite seems to be the case for some of the largest

THE (UN)GOVERNABLE CITY

markets and thoroughfares like Chandni Chowk. For example, Sir Syed Ahmad Khan, a resident of Delhi prior to the rebellion, wrote in his account of the city that *chabutra*s in official marketplaces were repaired under government initiative.[64] Along with the repair of several main drains of the city in 1853, the *chabutra*s in front of all the prominent *bazaar*s were redesigned in red sandstone as part of government policy.[65]

With colonial attitudes towards Indians hardening after the rebellion of 1857 and disease being seen as closely linked to the Indian environment, what puzzled European visitors was how shopkeepers could sit on their *chabutra*s, oblivious to the filth of their surroundings. *The Mofussilite*, an English-language newspaper commenting upon the putrid nature of the streets of Delhi, in 1868, reported that there was a 'peculiar sort of delight experienced from sitting on a wooden or masonry platform in front of a shop, raised about a foot or so above the black slush, and watching the "mud larks" toiling and staggering through it'.[66] The evocation of 'black slush' and the presence of scavenging natives in the form of 'mud larks' conveyed a sense of the filth and degeneracy of the Indian street, neighbourhood and the shopkeeper, from the perspective of a spectator enjoying daily life unfold on the streets. However, critical as the report was of Indian *bazaar* life, it hinted that beyond the purely economic or commercial reasons, sitting on a *chabutra* was also a form of leisure, where the platforms were important for viewing the spectacle of the streets.[67]

With the Delhi municipality's establishment in 1863, the regulation of *chabutra*s became a particular concern of the colonial government. As large and obtrusive features protruding out of shops, *chabutra*s were seen as encroachments upon public land. In addition, they fuelled anxieties about reduced visibility and traffic congestion on the streets. This point is evident from the reports of municipal officials documenting the process of *chabutra* creation in Delhi. A municipal official reporting on the *chabutra* issue in the city wrote:

> Evidence [of such encroachments] is forthcoming in almost all the bazars of the city to a careful or to an old observant and to the most idle eye in suburban wards of our own town and almost all the towns of the Delhi Division. The usual way of additions and encroachments is by allowing a little malba outside the shop, then to add a few stones to it, evidently as a foot-step for going and coming out of the shop …

The description further continued thus:

> ... then on some rainy day to make it into the form of a chabutra as wide as the breadth of the lane would permit; then by permission or otherwise on the pretext of repairing turn the existing chabutra into a pakka one; then to protect the chabutra by a thatch or wooden saeban, and then to make a pakka slanting cover or to enclose the chabutra into the shop itself, and finally to add a new chabutra in the same way as before till they render large and wide streets narrow enough for cart traffic.[68]

The burgeoning practice of the street *chabutras* was thus seen as obscuring the visibility of street and preventing the smooth circulation of carts and people.

Municipal acts allowed for a wide range of activities to be checked. The Police Act of 1861, under which *chabutras* were first identified, allowed municipalities to demolish any kind of building extensions that they felt were a nuisance. By-laws could be created and fines could be levied as a deterrent in accordance with Section 5 under the said act.[69] In March 1864, almost at the same time as the shift of the *Sabzi Mandi*, the Delhi municipality passed an unequivocal order for the demolition of all *chabutras* on the streets.[70] The *chabutras* were now seen as blocking 'public' spaces. The age of the *chabutras* was a point of contention since the municipality was confronted with a situation where *chabutras* of different ages stood in the marketplaces, and were a feature of the city prior to British rule. The sweeping order given was that irrespective of their age, *chabutras* in all 'public thoroughfares' in the city were to be demolished.[71] In the following year, the municipality extended its orders further to include the protocol that the shops of the city, particularly those of the *halwaies* or confectioners, were to be of a uniform width and that they would be inspected by the civil surgeon to ensure that this rule was adhered to.[72]

However, an examination of the municipal records reveals that the order passed in 1864 to demolish the *chabutras* was rescinded in 1866, when the municipality decided that the construction of *chabutras* was allowed, but the consent of the municipality was necessary in every case.[73] The issue of age had been dropped, and now the permission of the municipality was to be attained when *chabutras* were sought to be 'erected, altered or repaired'.[74] In 1869, the decision was reiterated in a general meeting of the municipality:

> It is the opinion of the commissioners that all chabootras erected in shop fronts by the sides of the streets in the city are built on land belonging to the public and that the occupiers have no right to them: Having however had the possession of such chabootras for many years occupiers of the shops may be permitted to use them but that they have no right whatever to sell either chabootras or the land on which they stand.[75]

Because of the fragmentary nature of the municipal records of the period, it is difficult to conclude exactly why the decision was overturned; but it can be suggested that the municipality faced considerable opposition from shopkeepers over the ban of *chabutras*. In other colonial cities of the British Empire, municipal control of the physical fabric of the city created considerable trouble for the local administration in the form of not only violent opposition such as riots, but also everyday acts of subversion.[76] In a similar manner, the reversal of the decision in a short span of five years could have been a product of the underlying tensions between the users of the *chabutras* and municipal officials. As the age of the *chabutra* was dropped and the municipality suggested that those who were in possession of *chabutras* for many years were to continue using them, the 'antiquity' of the *chabutra* as a claim could have also been raised by shopkeepers. Moreover, the sale of the *chabutras* to others also indicates the complex web of relationships that were associated with their use. This was perhaps a stumbling block when ascertaining the rights of individuals. The legitimation of the *chabutra* as a part of the municipal regulations should also be seen in light of the fact that there was often a slippage between intention and effect in the implementation of municipal plans to remove 'encroachments'. While the municipality was adventurous enough to formulate grand schemes, its fiscal conservatism did not match up to its aptitude for planning.[77] It was perhaps easier to regulate the spread and construction of *chabutras*, issuing punishments where necessary, instead of having to spend funds on litigation and assessing questions of proprietorship of land, which may have ensued as a result of the order for outright demolition.

As local municipalities like Delhi moved from 'demolition' to 'regulation', they found more support in municipal acts that allowed revisions to by-laws, and this invested them with increasingly sophisticated powers for the 'punishment of all offences partaking of the character of public nuisances which were not otherwise provided for by law'.[78] The Municipal Act of 1884, or Act XIII of Punjab, for example, allowed municipalities to frame laws to ensure that ventilation, drainage, the free passage of air and movement were prioritised in the city, and that building projects that went beyond the 'regular line of a public street' could be penalised.[79] Accordingly, the Delhi municipality framed rules, and the permission to rebuild encroachments like *chabutra*s upon public land was forbidden. If applications were made to rebuild *chabutra*s on private land, the owner would have to prove that the ground was his own property. Even in case of the latter, the municipality would have the final say regarding whether permission was to be granted or refused. Along with these rules, the question of repairs to existing *chabutra*s, an issue which had caused problems in the past, was taken up, and it was decided that ward members could give permission, but with instructions that neither was the *chabutra* to be raised, nor was the style of its erection to be altered.[80]

However, while these new guidelines and ordinances were designed to ensure that urban spaces were regulated and natives understood boundaries between private buildings and the 'public', they ultimately landed the Delhi municipality in a bigger predicament and subverted their designs for the city. The powers granted by municipal acts and by-laws were accompanied by ambiguous legal terminology, the interpretation of which was often puzzling, and had the potential to increase municipal liabilities. For example, municipal acts such as the Punjab Act VII of 1884 sanctioned set amounts of compensation for acts such as the removal of *chabutra*s. This was payable to the party under a sub-section of the act, which guaranteed that if the *chabutra* was 'lawfully in existence at the time of the passing of the municipal act', a reasonable compensation by the municipal authorities would be paid.[81] However, the term 'lawfully in existence' was ambiguous, and this ambiguity raised the possibility of paying large amounts in compensation, and frustration with civil courts and their judgements. In 1892, Girdhari Lal, a member of the Delhi municipality, expressed his dismay at the misunderstandings that he felt occurred when *chabutra* cases were settled in court. In a report to the Deputy Commissioner of the city on a *chabutra* encroachment case that had taken a substantial investment of his time and energy, he wrote:

> Now surely the word lawfully in existence means in my opinion not the [above] described existence of a chabutra, unless it has been in existence for the last 60 years, so as to bar the claim of the government. But some lawfully existing ones are such as by license, purchase, & c. The interpretation put on them by our civil court is, I am sorry, against its apparent meaning, and in many cases the Committee has lost the point if the plaintiff proved the existence of chabutra for the last 12 years.[82]

The helplessness of the situation was also echoed by other members of the municipality at that time, like Robert Clarke, the Deputy Commissioner who was Girdhari Lal's superior. Clarke claimed that the Delhi municipality had been 'most unfortunate' in cases of this kind where they had appeared before the civil courts either as plaintiffs or defendants. He felt that it was 'useless' for the municipality to try and prevent encroachments 'when the question of lawful existence is certain to be decided against them, and when fabulous sums are awarded against them when reasonable compensation has got to be settled by the courts.'[83]

The removal of *chabutras* proved costly for the municipality when the civil courts ruled against them over the meaning of the term 'lawfully in existence'. Even when the municipal authorities had earmarked *chabutras* for demolition, the ambiguous nature of legal terms could be used by enterprising individuals to claim a substantial amount of compensation in court. The astuteness by which the Evidence Act was used to bring to light transactions of purchase or transfers of licenses reveals the ways in which colonial bureaucratic codes were used by people. Legal decisions, if they went up to the courts, were injurious to the finances of the municipality. Moreover, the expenses of having cases appealed to the Chief Court in Lahore often tempted municipal officials to settle payments then and there to avoid further losses.[84] As much as municipal acts provided greater powers of coercion to municipalities over cases like the *chabutra*, they also increased the possibilities of legal entanglements, conflict, and internal disagreements over the ambiguity of municipal ordinances.

SANITARY SURVEILLANCE OF PUBLIC SPACES: ADMINISTRATION AND THE PROBLEMS OF VISIBILITY

A constant concern raised in municipal acts and local ordinances was to ensure that public spaces were free from encroachments and building constructions. Whether this created tensions between shopkeepers or *chabutra*-users, on the one hand, or led to municipal complaints about the inherent ambiguity of government proclamations, on the other, there was little doubt on the part of government officials that the increased visibility and policing of public spaces such as streets would discipline native habits. Censuses, registration practices, maps and surveys were essential tools in this civilising mission, and they were meant to isolate, classify, discipline, and ultimately, awaken the natives to the dirt and degeneracy of their environment. In 1868, A. C. C. De Renzy, the Sanitary Commissioner of Punjab, proudly proclaimed the superiority of registration practices and how they had the potential to reform the evils in Indian society. In his yearly report on the progress of municipalities, he wrote about the veil of ignorance that prevented India from understanding her diseased state, and on how registration would be the first step in inspiring Indians to take stock of their own society:

> When the natives see their sanitary evils accurately reflected in the Registration returns, and the full import of the facts represented has had time to sink into their minds, they cannot fail to be inspired with a desire to cooperate in the prevention of diseases which cause so much misery and poverty. They have hitherto regarded sanitary improvement with repugnance, owing to their unconsciousness of unhealthiness, and their failure from ignorance to trace the connection between sickness and the causes which produce it; but registration will lift the veil which has concealed from them the knowledge of their condition.[85]

Yet, in order to police public spaces, the municipality had to walk the streets. Put another way, surveillance, and the generation of facts, figures and reports was an expensive and labour-intensive process, which required manpower to patrol the spaces of the city regularly. The municipality needed a large and hierarchical framework of municipal administration, with a chain of command extending from senior-level

English administrators to local Indian staff, if municipal designs for the city were to be effective. As Prakash has pointed out, the need for enumerating and surveying the native population's demographic, economic and epidemiological properties 'set into motion a powerful process of bureaucratic expansion' in an effort to centralise power.[86] However, as we shall see, it was this very administrative reorganisation and enlargement that created more challenges for the municipality over its effectiveness to govern urban spaces.

In 1871, the Delhi municipal authorities proposed to divide the city and suburbs into wards or *ilakas*, each one under a sub-committee of members of the municipality, whose responsibility was to undertake 'all investigations, inspections or questions of law' in their *ilaka*.[87] Madho Pershad, a municipal representative speaking of the *ilaka* system in 1921, wrote that the express purpose of the system was to make sure that 'every evil was brought to light'.[88] Instituted in its final version in 1875, the *ilaka* system required one municipal member and his five assistants to visit each ward under their assignment at least once a week and report on any transgressions on the streets and *kuchas* (areas or corners leading to a cluster of houses and shops), so that this could be taken up at municipal meetings.[89]

This expansion in the municipal administration was based on the notion that constant surveillance of the streets would reduce the tyranny of encroachment and nuisances. The new arrangements of the *ilaka* were superimposed over the existing measures, which included the recruitment of *mohalla* sweepers for sanitary purposes and policing by the municipality. Sweepers or *jamaadars* were used by the municipality to collect registration statistics, that is, an account of births and deaths, along with performing their usual conservancy duties such as the collection and disposal of refuse from external privies.[90] Hosagrahar writes that sweepers 'achieved police status as well as visibility and legitimacy in official eyes' because of their admission into households and their familiarity with the neighbourhoods.[91] Since a direct intrusion by municipal officials into households was perceived as distasteful, sweepers were appointed to overcome such obstacles. In time, sweepers also reported information on neighbourhood building constructions or sanitary 'nuisances'. Thus, *ilaka* members and their army of local staff and sweepers became a hierarchical structure of municipal administration, created with the intention of regulating the urban domain, reporting sanitary and other building encroachments, so that in all cases, the city could be made 'visible' to official eyes.

However, extending bureaucratic involvement did not end the problem of policing sanitary or other encroachments for the municipality. Rather, the addition of a new bureaucracy meant that the wards became the sole domain of the *ilaka* members, and the policing of encroachments rested upon, in the words of one official, 'the honesty of the ward jamadar, and the loyalty to the committee's policy which the ward member is prepared to exhibit'.[92] If the residents of the city could cultivate ties with the *ilaka* representatives and staff, there was a chance that sanitary violations could be overlooked and building applications pushed forward for approval. Although instituted with great fanfare, *ilaka* arrangements raised tensions within the municipality because of a flood of applications that were recommended for building additions. In time, the municipality had to issue hasty notices to ward members, stating that they were to pay 'due attention' to the by-laws and 'recommend applications as are absolutely necessary and cause no obstructions'.[93]

However, many of these problems of surveillance were not because of the inherent corruptibility of Indian officials, but they were rather the product of municipal policies and the inequities of colonial rule. Sweepers or *jamaadars*, although employed by the municipality, were regularly penalised for any municipal shortcomings. Financial conservatism meant that municipalities like Delhi relied heavily on the labour of sweepers, exploiting their services while apportioning blame to them for any lapses.[94] In this way, colonial rule and its municipal bureaucracy was equal to, and sometimes, even more repressive in its policies towards sweepers than earlier.[95] In Delhi, for example, if there were arrears in the payment of rent for the use of any municipal land or services by individuals, the *jamaadars* of the ward were forced to pay from their own pockets instead of those who had violated the by-laws paying the amount.[96] Added to this was the fact that the *jamaadars* were paid extremely poorly. As one municipal official would later admit, a sweeper in Delhi could get 'better pay as a coolie'. The threat of instant dismissal, along with limited opportunities for promotion, made it impossible to retain *jamaadars* for a substantial period of time.[97] Till the 1880s, the sweepers of the city tried to resist being formally employed as municipal servants, and in rare instances, they even filed suits against municipal authorities when they felt their rights to sell night soil were being taken away.[98] In light of the harsh working conditions and outright exploitation, the sweepers were willing to receive money from other sources or turn a blind eye when it came to reporting sanitary or building encroachments.

While sweepers were at the bottom of the municipal hierarchy, those at the other end of the spectrum, that is, the *ilaka* members, and after the local self-government scheme of 1882, the 'elected representatives', were also willing to overlook encroachments and other transgressions. For the elected representatives, forging friendships with wealthy merchants and shopkeepers was a way of securing votes at the municipal elections. Lord Ripon's local self-government reform of 1882 had extended the municipal franchise and promised Indian elites greater political participation.[99] This opened the way for wealthy and propertied sections or rate payers of Indian society to vie for political influence with those who were deemed to be the 'natural' leaders of their communities and religious groupings.[100] During times of election, as Douglas Haynes writes, the backing of local magnates such as bankers and shopkeepers was required by councillors to secure votes because of the former's influence over the urban householders.[101] Moreover, ties of reciprocity were also influenced and shaped through this new language of 'elections' and 'voting'. To be elected as a ward member meant that one had to grant concessions from time to time and elide any 'encroachments'. Thus, the extension of municipal power had the potential effect of subverting its operations and plans for the reordering of urban spaces. Clarke, the Deputy Commissioner of Delhi in 1892, revealed both a sense of anger as well as helplessness about the inconvenience to the public that municipal arrangements were causing. In a distraught letter to the government of Punjab, he wrote:

> There is no doubt that as the ward member's position upon the votes of the residents in his ward, he has a distinct incentive to wink at conveniences to themselves secured by his constituents at the expense of the public; at the same time I am not prepared to even insinuate that the ward members, as a rule, neglect their duties in this respect in Delhi.[102]

Girdhari Lal, the official encountered earlier, also lamented that an increase in bureaucracy was actually inefficient and caused greater problems in checking municipal offences. In a report to Clarke in 1892, he wrote that it was 'very easy to win the low paid Jamadar to his side for a wealthy shopkeeper'; and on the other hand, the ward member himself, 'whose very existence' depended on the votes of these individuals, did sometimes 'connive in the matter'.[103]

Yet, a mere acknowledgement of the situation did not mean that the faith in the municipal enterprise or its structural limitations was challenged. Rather, as elsewhere in the colonial world, the cure for an inefficient bureaucracy came in the form of more bureaucracy.[104] Stronger laws and regulations were perceived to be a remedy for ineffectual local procedures.[105] In the case of encroachments, for example, Girdhari Lal proposed that a new map of the town was needed to record the dimensions of buildings and streets as they then stood, so that the municipality would have a better chance of challenging insanitary encroachments in the future. This, he felt, needed a 'responsible' official who would go around getting signatures of the owners of houses or shops, recording the state of their buildings in the presence of two other witnesses.[106] This recommendation was again premised on a reorganisation of current administrative methods and more direct bureaucratic involvement. In the case of the sweepers, if the municipality acknowledged that their remuneration was inadequate, its fiscal conservatism led it to act otherwise.[107] On the other hand, as Clarke's statement reveals, it was difficult to suggest the complicity of ward members in allowing 'public nuisances' without undermining the municipal administration itself. To do this as a senior colonial administrator was unthinkable.

It was felt that detailed surveys and maps were the solution towards a more effective administration and an end to sanitary and building encroachments. Contradictions lay at the core of municipal bureaucratic expansion, and it was believed that only through constant reorganisation and restructuring could effective measures be implemented and problems resolved. Indeed, these recommendations were part of a cyclical process that enlarged the powers of the bureaucracy further, and simultaneously stifled its prospects of sanitary surveillance.

In the next section, we will see how technical expertise and its influence on the creation of infrastructure affected municipal operations in Delhi. Since the establishment of the municipality in 1863, sanitary officials and commissioners recommended the creation of water supply and drainage facilities in light of their superiority over prevailing Indian practices. An ambitious municipality was also keen to harness technologies that were necessary for the 'improvement' of the population. As the narrative reveals, however, the growing complexity of expertise and colonial sanitary knowledge carried with it the potential to subvert municipal procedures through the sheer scale and cost of interventions that they suggested. These caused huge delays in municipal operations, restricted the municipality from carrying out its daily duties, and ultimately, made it a target of local criticism.

GRAND INTENTIONS: TECHNICAL EXPERTISE, DRAINAGE, AND THE PROBLEMS OF MUNICIPAL GOVERNANCE

For the municipal authorities, along with the removal of obstructions, the streets and *bazaars* of the city had to be freed from the tyranny of waste and refuse if they were to be truly 'improved'. Water and drainage infrastructure promised a technological means of encouraging this process.[108] Influenced by the growing body of colonial knowledge and research, sanitary inspectors and commissioners were resolute in their opinion that municipalities were to turn to technology to resolve the problems of sanitation and disease in India. As experts in their field, these officials acted in a supervisory capacity to municipalities, and possessed vast executive powers and responsibilities unlike in Britain.[109]

In 1869, under the influence of 'scientific' expertise, the Delhi municipality classified the water in the wells of the city as 'bad on sanitary grounds'.[110] The poor health of the colonial troops was a significant matter in the move towards this classification, as it was felt that the 'emanations from the city filth' had infiltrated the water and were causing bodily infections, made visible by the presence of boils.[111] Sanitary officers working with the municipality felt that a system of water-works, bringing fresh piped water from the Yamuna River outside the city was needed as an antidote to the impure water within the wells. As Awadhendra Sharan has argued, the debates over piped water in Delhi, which was imagined through a grid-work of bricks, stone and iron, were rooted in the politics of difference. Narratives of pollution guided the preference for a new scheme of water supply rather than the use of traditional sources of water, which were ignored by the colonial government.[112] Since the municipality's inception, however, financial considerations shaped the implementation of plans, as the water-works scheme was deemed too costly to be a means of investment by the colonial government.[113]

At the same time, as the debates over a system of water-works started, the question of drainage was brought to the fore by various government authorities. Delhi had a network of underground drains that ran across the city in a crisscross manner, which had been made in the days of emperor Shah Jahan. As the road-level of the city rose, the drains became quite a long way below the surface.[114] From the earliest days of the British Residency in Delhi, these had been cleaned irregularly.[115] The Delhi municipality, since its inception, followed a similar policy as its predecessor. The drains were largely neglected, and because of the piecemeal nature of the operations, the municipality became a target of criticism in the local newspapers.[116]

To understand the municipality's early operations and its neglect of the Shahjahani drains, we need to consider the influence of colonial expertise and the often inconsistent and contradictory nature of 'improvement' policies. If the repair of the Shahjahani drains was patchy, the municipality enthusiastically began constructing a network of underground drains between 1871 and 1873, with the intent of giving the streets of the city a 'cleanly appearance'.[117] However, just as these drains were completed, municipal efforts were criticised by senior government authorities as improper on the basis of the fact that the drains that had been constructed were akin to cesspools. The then Sanitary Commissioner for Punjab, A. C. C. De Renzy wrote in his report in 1873 that the sewers in Delhi had been constructed 'in an aimless, haphazard way, on no definite principle'. Rather than a boon, he felt that this was a 'curse to the city' and a warning 'to other towns not to set about the construction of under-ground sewers without competent advice'.[118] This criticism sheds light on the ambiguity surrounding notions of 'correct' procedures, and at times, competing sanitary models or recommendations clashed in local contexts. The PWD engineers hired by the municipality were often at the centre of these controversies and were often stopped from conducting their responsibilities by sanitary officials in light of new research or professional opinions. Indeed, there was often confusion in terms of what was to be implemented, how this was to take place, and in many cases, the construction of technology was a process of moving one step forward and two steps backwards.

Sanitary Commissioners, experts in their field, believed that surface or gutter drains were better than any underground drainage system. In 1878, Dr Bellow, the Sanitary Commissioner for Punjab, advocated a complete abolition of underground drainage systems and recommended that surface drains, a European import, be created since they rested on a sound 'scientific basis'.[119] Bellow recommended this vision of urban drainage for 'all streets as distinguished from narrow lanes' because of the inherent 'superiority' of the plan over the 'native method'.[120] Intimately connected with these proclamations of European 'scientific' superiority was the question of the cost-effectiveness of drain-clearing and repair work in Indian cities. In other words, the reason sanitary experts also began advocating surface drainage systems in places like Delhi was because it provided a cheap alternative to the continuous cleaning, repair or reconstruction of older underground drains.[121] What this meant was that municipalities like Delhi had to freeze not only the construction of their novel underground drains, but also the repairs of the old Shahjahani drains, until the government sanctioned a comprehensive drainage plan, with details on how surface drainage in the city was to be conducted. In other words, local engineers and the municipality often awaited instructions from experts on new plans in light of their criticism of prevailing practices. For example, in 1880, the local engineer of the PWD in Delhi recommended that the repair and maintenance of drains should be halted, fearing that any expenditure and effort would be defeated by a drainage scheme, which, he felt, was in the offing. A note written by the municipality captured this predicament vividly when it declared that it was 'impossible to proceed with the service drainage of lanes and kuchas' since the work was complicated, and its engineer pointed out that 'the whole work would have to be done over again when the drainage scheme came out'. Had this not been the case, the municipality suggested, then it 'would have proceeded to level, pave and drain all minor streets'.[122]

While the municipality waited for updates about a new drainage scheme, higher authorities at the level of the government of Punjab began considering whether both the drainage and water supply of the city could be initiated together, in a comprehensive plan for water and drainage in the city.[123] The creation of a comprehensive plan as a total solution resulted not from arbitrary whims, but from the increased complexity of colonial sanitary discourses and expertise. Just as underground drains were abandoned in favour of surface drainage, which, in turn caused engineers to await a new scheme with bated breath, technical expertise again had a role to play in complicating the way in which local drainage schemes were implemented. Sanitary experts and government officials were constantly developing and perfecting a range of 'scientific' techniques and knowledge to reform Indian society, and this was a key premise of the civilising mission. However, a growing body of knowledge had the potential to increase the scale of pending projects, as well as their complexity, costs and government involvement. In the case of a comprehensive water supply and drainage scheme, as we shall see below, this led to a process where projects were constantly altered, there were delays over the question of financial assistance, and this ultimately created more problems for municipal operations in the city.

Piped water, as outlined above, was seen as a remedy to the polluted water supply of the city, and above all, it was meant for the use of the troops. Yet, in the 1860s, this scheme was held back on account of the lack of finances and until estimates met the approval of the Punjab government.[124] Now it was the influence of new theories on malarial fevers that suggested that water supply and drainage schemes had to be combined together to alleviate sanitation problems in cities. While the demand for pure river water loomed large in the minds of sanitary officials and municipalities, in the 1870s, colonial sanitary discourse began to associate *excess* water in native environments with debilitating health problems and disease. The experience of sanitary officers working in the villages irrigated by the Ganga Jumna Canal in the Delhi district had led them to make a connection between well-irrigated tracts and spleen disease.[125] Excess salinity, 'oversaturation' of the soil, and seepages from colonial water supplies were beginning to be suspected of 'malariousness'.[126] Interestingly, the ground for this had partly been prepared from colonial research conducted in the area since the 1840s.[127] In Bombay, the influence of this research had begun to be felt as early as 1852, when sanitary officials were discussing the need for water-works projects to be conducted in conjunction with new drainage and sewerage facilities.[128] By 1879, the Sanitary Commissioner of the Army formally declared that excess water would lead to an increase in the mortality rates, and that the drainage of the cities like Delhi and its suburbs had to proceed 'pari-passu with the water supply'. In a damning indictment, he suggested that if this condition was overlooked, more water would lead to more epidemic mortality.[129]

As the fortunes of both water supply and drainage were being tied together, the whole process entailed a rethinking of project costs. The Delhi municipality was not only alive to the need of creating a comprehensive project, but was also wary that the proposed expenditures had to be scaled down if the government of Punjab was to sanction both the schemes simultaneously. In an address to municipal members in 1882, the Vice President of the municipality reflected upon how professional opinions had influenced the decision to create an integrated plan and the need to ensure that the drainage scheme would not cost too much on its own:

> A project for the drainage of the city bears so close a relation to that for the water supply, that we have professional opinions in carrying both projects out together. Under these circumstances, the financial aspect of the drainage scheme and its main features must be borne in mind in considering the present scheme. The revised drainage project is approaching completion under the able hands of Mr Morley, and will be brought up for consideration in a few days from the present time.[130]

Predictably, however, when revised plans and estimates were sent to the provincial authorities, the outlay involved was considered too much. In 1882, for example, the municipality proposed to borrow an amount of Rs 12,50,000 in the open market and requested a contribution of Rs 2,50,000 from the imperial government, but this was refused.[131] This was the second time that a scheme was refused on account of a lack of funds by the imperial government.[132]

This meant that plans had to be redrafted again and again, and the municipality had to prepare a scheme that was affordable and acceptable. Again, in 1886, when funds were asked for by the municipality and even agreed upon by the provincial government of Punjab, the government of India refused to sanction the amount.[133] Meanwhile, the threat of sicknesses and disease meant that the municipality began carrying out selective cleaning of older drains from time to time.[134] In contravention to government directives, some drains were also constructed; but even this policy was scaled back, and the municipality considered it unwise except in 'special cases', to go on making drains, 'which might not fit in with the general project'.[135] Thus, the hope remained that the government would soon sanction money, and both water supply and drainage works would be underway in the city.

The tardiness and the piecemeal manner of the municipality's operations received heavy criticism from local newspapers. The *Safir-i-Hind*, for example, derided the municipality for proposed increases in octroi taxation on account of the water supply scheme, which the authorities were beginning to prioritise ahead of drainage facilities.[136] The municipality, it suggested, should have 'taken steps to introduce an improved system of drainage before it thought of constructing the water works'.[137] With drains clogged and the municipality unwilling to take further action, residents of the *mohallas* and *kuchas* took it upon themselves to find solutions in order to discard dirty water from their houses. In 1883, for example, a Delhi correspondent of a Lahore newspaper, the *Anjuman-i-Panjab*, reported that while the municipality had washed its hands of building or cleaning drains till the water-works project was underway, in certain quarters of the city, people started sinking earthen vessels into the ground in order to collect dirty drain water, which was then thrown in the lanes.[138] This was deeply ironic, inasmuch as the municipality had been trying for some time to check 'public nuisances' on the streets; but now residents were taking matters into their own hands.

Finding funds for both the schemes, which were tied together by the growing complexity of sanitary discourses, thus led to a situation where the municipality's own intentions to check 'public nuisances' were subverted. In other words, discourses of disease led to the creation of a large and complicated plan of municipal management, which, because of insufficient funding was frozen in its tracks. This led to a vicious cycle, where a desperate municipality had to revise plans over and over, waiting and hoping that the imperial government would come around and sanction the funds for the water-works and drainage schemes. The municipality of the city, in anticipation of the constantly deferred schemes, stopped even the little that it was prepared to do to resolve drainage issues. Individuals faced with an overrun of dirty water had to invent solutions and ultimately threw the water into the lanes in a desperate effort to keep their *mohallas* and *kuchas* clean. Thus, what the municipality labelled as insanitary 'nuisances', actually increased.

When the Delhi municipality had finally prepared cost-effective plans for the water-works and drainage schemes that were approved by the government in the 1890s, more problems surfaced. For example, technical issues with the water-works scheme meant that more money was required over the original outlay.[139] By 1897, an amount of Rs 10,40,000 had been spent on the water-works scheme, and another Rs 2,00,000 was required over and above the former amount.[140] Money that was made available for the drainage scheme came in a piecemeal manner, and by 1899, the municipality still needed a sum of Rs 6,00,000 just to complete the drainage of the area within the city walls.[141] There was no mention of the condition of extra-mural drainage, which was subordinated to the plans for the city.[142] When the sporadic construction of drains did start to occur in the city, there was an even bigger irony. The creation of drains on a 'scientific' basis resulted in more friction with the residents of the city since the building extensions like *chabutras* had to be demolished in certain areas. As we have seen, the dimensions of these 'obstructions' were regulated through by-laws, and the municipality had avoided outright demolitions after 1866. However, by 1897, the municipality once again found itself demolishing street obstructions that were in the way of the newly assigned works and had to pay compensation to the owners.[143]

Colonial sanitary expertise had inadvertently trapped the municipality between huge borrowing costs and paying out substantial amounts as compensation to owners of buildings that were to be demolished. The municipality increased its fines and taxes to offset the costs. The *modus operandi* of the municipality at the end of the 1890s was to compound petty offences and charge a hefty sum of Rs 50 for technical breaches, including building regulations. This was significantly in excess of the limit of Rs 5 sanctioned in the by-laws, and had the potential to ignite more lawsuits.[144] In effect, these measures brought the municipality into conflict with local residents who were disgruntled at the lacklustre sanitary arrangements and the arbitrary method of taxation and fines that it had devised.[145]

Colonial sanitary expertise was, then, a double-edged sword. In the name of 'progress' and 'improvement', professionals and sanitary commissioners enthusiastically recommended the creation of water-works and drainage technologies for municipalities in the belief that infrastructure needed to rest not on an indigenous, but a 'scientific' basis. However, the growing complexity of technical expertise and colonial sanitary discourses created more problems for municipalities, as they increased the scale and expense of projects, and often led to a long wait in the hope that funds would be sanctioned by higher authorities. Proposals had to be redrafted constantly, and went back and forth between higher authorities who were unwilling to sanction funds, and desperate municipal officials keen to have 'superior' technology. At the local level, the anticipation of forthcoming projects led to smaller operations being irregular or being stopped entirely, increased what were considered to be 'public nuisances', and further embroiled the municipality in legal disputes with the residents of *mohalla*s and *kucha*s.

CONCLUSION

By 1910, the Delhi municipality had a large and hierarchical administration, and it also possessed considerable powers of coercion endowed through municipal ordinances. It could boast that extensive maps of the city were being designed, sanitary surveys and registration records had been kept, and effective regulations were in place to check the creation of sanitary and building 'encroachments'. In other words, the Delhi municipality's expansion of its own bureaucratic powers after 1863 had been tremendous. Yet, the growth of municipal powers to check and reorganise 'public' spaces in the city was a deeply chaotic, inconsistent and irregular process. As this chapter has suggested, the growing complexity of municipal operations, their costs, and the professional opinions of experts created conditions in which 'intentions' were constantly being subverted.

Indeed, the desire to 'improve' native habits was ever-present in the attitude of the municipality. Although, when intent was put into practice, it revealed contradictions that set the municipality on a very different course than it had planned. The settling of 'public' roads and the *Sabzi Mandi*, for example, revealed that there were internal disagreements over how rights and customs were to be understood and assessed. The municipality waited for almost six years before issuing a threat of eviction, and when the latter was passed, senior officials talked of backtracking plans and pressurised the municipality to assess whether the old market could be restored. There were talks of 'conciliating' the *dalals* and paying them compensation for the injury to their 'old and intricate rights'. Between 1871 and 1874, endless internal investigations caused long delays and threatened to derail municipal plans for neat 'public' roads and a new marketplace. Similarly, sanitary surveillance required a large set of staff and officials to police the streets, and this created more problems than it resolved for the municipality. Sweepers who were exploited for their services took their chances and were often willing to turn a blind eye when it came to recording and reporting sanitary or building violations.

Voting, a new but intentionally limited means of representation, created to secure the support of intermediaries, also created contradictions. The need for votes during times of election meant that the ward members were also willing to overlook 'encroachments'. When technological solutions were foregrounded to 'improve' the city, the precarious situation that the municipality found itself in grew more acute. In light of growing research and theories about native environments, colonial sanitary discourses advocated grand 'scientific' plans, which entailed huge costs. Municipal operations were deferred in the hope that it would be provided with imperial funds and patchy construction, and incomplete operations marked the implementation of works of 'public utility'. With few funds available, the municipality considered only 'special' cases for the repair and cleaning of drains, and privileged certain areas in the city over others. Thus, urban sanitation problems increased as a result of the contradictions within the colonial government itself. It was no surprise, then, that the municipality became a target of local criticism and annoyance. Its incomplete and unfinished projects, the seemingly arbitrary method of its operations, and heavy fines resulted in lawsuits and compensation claims where possible.

By paying close attention to the working of municipal power in the reorganisation of public spaces in Delhi, the chapter has highlighted the paradoxical nature of municipal governance. On the one hand, there were contradictions within the colonial government that created challenges for municipal operations in the city. On the other, these contradictions and subsequent difficulties went hand in hand with strengthening the municipality's bureaucratic and regulatory powers.

NOTES

1. Proceedings of General Meetings from 1 June 1863 to 5 April 1869, Memorandum from Mr Cooper, dated 19 March 1863, DMC, Town Hall, Delhi.

2. Preliminary Correspondence, Memorandum from Mr Cooper, dated 12 March 1863, DMC, Town Hall, Delhi.

3. Proceedings of General Meetings from 1 June 1863 to 5 April 1869, Memorandum from Mr Cooper, dated 19 March 1863.

4. See Hugh Tinker, *Foundations of Local Self-government in India, Pakistan and Burma* (London: Athlone Press, 1954), 29–30; and Kenneth L. Gillion, *Ahmedabad: A Study in Urban History* (Berkeley: University of California Press, 1968), 105–52.

5. Rai Sahib Madho Pershad, *The History of the Delhi Municipality: 1863–1921* (Allahabad: Pioneer Press, 1921), 8–10.

6. Anonymous, *Friend of India*, 17 December 1863, No. 1511, 1431.

7. Letter from Lt. Colonel McNeile, Offg. Commissioner, Delhi to Mr Fitzpatrick, Deputy Commissioner, Delhi, dated 2 December 1867, DSA Deputy Commissioner Office (henceforth DCO) 4/1863.

8. See Michael Mann, 'Delhi's Belly: On the Management of Water, Sewage and Excreta in a Changing Urban Environment during the Nineteenth Century', *Studies in History* 23, no. 1, 2007, 1–31.

9. See, for example, Prashant Kidambi's book on the work of the Bombay Improvement Trust. Prashant Kidambi, *The Making of an Indian Metropolis: Colonial Governance and Public Culture in Bombay, 1890–1920* (Aldershot: Ashgate, 2007), 71–114. See also Cunningham Bissell's study of urban planning in colonial Zanzibar. W. C. Bissell, *Urban Design, Chaos and Colonial Power in Zanzibar* (Indiana: Indiana University Press, 2011).

10. See William J. Glover, *Making Lahore Modern: Constructing and Imagining a Colonial City* (Minneapolis: University of Minnesota Press, 2007), 59–98.

11. Patrick Joyce, *The Rule of Freedom: Liberalism and the Modern City* (London: Verso, 2003), 86–89.

12. See Partha Chatterjee, *The Nation and its Fragments: Colonial and Postcolonial Histories* (Princeton: Princeton University Press, 1993).

13. Gyan Prakash, *Another Reason: Science and the Imagination of Modern India* (Princeton: Princeton University Press, 1999), 131.

14. Anonymous, *The Tourists' Guide from Delhi to Kurrachee: Describing the Various Towns: Commerce: Railways: River Communications: & C: & C: With a Map* (London: British Library, 2011), 8.

15. Swati Chattopadhyay has argued that early European artists and painters in colonial Calcutta foregrounded concerns like filth, heat and dust of the city in their paintings since they faced difficulty in mastering and representing the landscape visually. See Swati Chattopadhyay, *Representing Calcutta: Modernity Nationalism and the Colonial Uncanny* (London: Routledge, 2005), 21–75.

16. Nikhil Rao, *House but No Garden: Apartment Living in Bombay, 1898–1948*, PhD Thesis, University of Chicago, 2007, 21.

17. Chander Shekhar and Shama Mitra Chenoy, *Dargah Quli Khan, Muraqqa-e-Dehli: The Mughal Capital in Muhammad Shah's Time* (Delhi: Deputy Publication, 1989), 24.

18. Shekhar and Mitra Chenoy, *Dargah Quli Khan*, 24–25.

19. Veena Oldenburg, *The Making of Colonial Lucknow: 1856–77* (Princeton: Princeton University Press, 1984).

20. See Awadhendra Sharan, 'In the City, Out of Place: Environment and Modernity, Delhi 1860s to 1960s', *Economic and Political Weekly* 41, no. 47, 2006, 4905–11.

21. Jyoti Hosagrahar, *Indigenous Modernities: Negotiating Architecture and Urbanism* (London: Routledge, 2005), 133.

22. Report on the Administration of the Delhi Crown Lands, 1910, 13-II Box 64, DSA CCO.

23. Mirza Sangin Beg, *Sair ul Manazil* (New Delhi: Ghalib Institute, 1982), 193.

24. Letter from A. Benton Esquire, Officiating Deputy Commissioner to Lt. Colonel Cracroft, Commissioner and Superintendent, Delhi, dated 26 March 1872, File 3-198, 1876, Box 22, DSA CCO.

25. Letter from the Commissioner and Superintendent, Delhi to the Deputy Commissioner, dated 30 March 1872, File 3-198, 1876, Box 22, DSA CCO.

26. Letter from A. Benton Esquire, Officiating Deputy Commissioner to Lt. Colonel Cracroft, Commissioner and Superintendent, Delhi, dated 26 March 1872.

27. Letter from A. Benton Esquire, Officiating Deputy Commissioner to Lt. Colonel Cracroft, Commissioner and Superintendent, Delhi, dated 26 March 1872.

28. See Sharan, 'In the City, Out of Place', 4906.

29. Letter from A. Benton Esquire, Officiating Deputy Commissioner to Lt. Colonel Cracroft, Commissioner and Superintendent, Delhi, dated 26 March 1872.

30. Prakash, *Another Reason,* 132.

31. Letter from the Commissioner of Delhi to the Deputy Commissioner and Superintendent, Delhi Division, dated 19 August 1865, File 3-198, 1876, Box 22, DSA CCO.

32. Copy of a Letter from the Secretary to the Government of Punjab to the Lieutenant Governor, Punjab, dated 9 August 1865, File 3-198, 1876, Box 22, DSA CCO.

33. Letter from A. Benton Esquire, Officiating Deputy Commissioner to Lt. Colonel Cracroft, Commissioner and Superintendent, Delhi, dated 26 March 1872.

34. Letter from A. Benton Esquire, Officiating Deputy Commissioner to Lt. Colonel Cracroft, Commissioner and Superintendent, Delhi, dated 26 March 1872.

35. Copy of a Docket, from the Secretary of the Municipal Committee to the Deputy Commissioner, Delhi, dated 2 June 1874, File 3-198, 1876, Box 22, DSA CCO.

36. Letter from the Commissioner and Superintendent, Delhi to the Deputy Commissioner, dated 30 March 1872.

37. Letter from Lt. Colonel Cracroft, Commissioner and Superintendent, Delhi to T. Thornton Esquire, Secretary to the Government, Punjab, dated 27 April 1874, File 3-198, 1876, Box 22, DSA CCO.

38. Letter from Lt. Colonel Cracroft, Commissioner and Superintendent, Delhi to T. Thornton Esquire, Secretary to the Government, Punjab, dated 27 April 1874.

39. Letter from Lt. Colonel Cracroft, Commissioner and Superintendent, Delhi to T. Thornton Esquire, Secretary to the Government, Punjab, dated 27 April 1874.

40. Letter from Lt. Colonel Cracroft, Commissioner and Superintendent, Delhi to T. Thornton Esquire, Secretary to the Government, Punjab, dated 27 April 1874.

41. Letter from A. Benton Esquire, Officiating Deputy Commissioner to Lt. Colonel Cracroft, Commissioner and Superintendent, Delhi, dated 26 March 1872.

42. Letter from A. Benton Esquire, Officiating Deputy Commissioner to Lt. Colonel Cracroft, Commissioner and Superintendent, Delhi, dated 26 March

1872.

43. Letter from the Commissioner and Superintendent, Delhi to the Deputy Commissioner, dated 30 March 1872.

44. Letter from the Commissioner and Superintendent, Delhi to the Deputy Commissioner, dated 30 March 1872.

45. For another study that highlights how different perspectives on conceiving and governing the population could lead to a failure of the stated aims of government agencies, see Stephen Legg, 'Governmentality, Congestion and Calculation in Colonial Delhi', *Social Geography* 7, no. 5, 2006, 709–29.

46. Thus, this one prevailing view was based on an understanding that the parasitic intermediary corrupts the natural laws of the market. However, as Denis Vidal's contemporary work points out through an examination of the role of intermediaries in Delhi's grain *bazaar* (the *Naya Bazaar*), intermediaries in India actually facilitate market practice and business links rather than distorting them and should be understood as essential to the development of a market economy. Denis Vidal, 'Markets and Intermediaries: An Enquiry about the Principles of Market Economy in the Grain Market of Delhi', in *Delhi: Urban Space and Human Destinies*, ed. Veronique Dupont, Emma Tarlo and Denis Vidal (Delhi: Manohar, 2000), 125–39.

47. Letter from the Commissioner and Superintendent, Delhi to the Deputy Commissioner, dated 30 March 1872.

48. Letter from the Commissioner and Superintendent, Delhi to the Secretary to the Government, Punjab, dated 7 April 1874, File 3-198, 1876, Box 22, DSA CCO.

49. Letter from A. Benton Esquire, Officiating Deputy Commissioner to Lt. Colonel Cracroft, Commissioner and Superintendent, Delhi, dated 26 March 1872.

50. Letter from A. Benton Esquire, Officiating Deputy Commissioner to Lt. Colonel Cracroft, Commissioner and Superintendent, Delhi, dated 26 March 1872.

51. Letter from the Commissioner and Superintendent, Delhi to the Secretary to the Government, Punjab, dated 7 April 1874.

52. Letter from the Commissioner and Superintendent, Delhi to the Deputy Commissioner, dated 30 March 1872.

53. Letter from A. Thornton, Secretary to the Government, Punjab to Colonel Cracroft, Commissioner and Superintendent Delhi, dated 20 April 1874, File 3-198, 1876, Box 22, DSA CCO.

54. Letter from A. Thornton, Secretary to the Government, Punjab to Colonel Cracroft, Commissioner and Superintendent Delhi, dated 2 May 1874, File 3-198, 1876, Box 22, DSA CCO.

55. Letter from A. Thornton, Secretary to the Government, Punjab to Colonel Cracroft, Commissioner and Superintendent Delhi, dated 20 April 1874, File 3-198, 1876, Box 22, DSA CCO.

56. Sharan, 'In the City, Out of Place', 4906.

57. Hosagrahar, *Indigenous Modernities*, 66.

58. Email correspondence with Shamsur Rahman Faruqi, dated 13 April 2010.

59. M. M. Kaye (ed.), *The Golden Calm: An English Lady's Life in Moghul Delhi: Reminisces by Emily, Lady Clive Bayly, and her Father, Sir Thomas Metcalf* (Exeter: Webb and Bower, 1980), 210–11.

60. Email correspondence with Shamsur Rahman Faruqi, dated 13 April 2010.

61. Evidence of this is present from the latter half of the nineteenth century, when the municipal authorities of the city classified *chabutras* as 'encroachments' upon public spaces. In correspondence with senior figures of the government, the Deputy Commissioner of Delhi wrote that encroachments upon the city took the form of *chabutras*. See Proceedings: March 1893, Letter from R. Clarke B. A., C.s. Deputy Commissioner, Delhi, to the Commissioner and Superintendent, Delhi Division, dated 2 June 1892, No. 48-57 A: No. 55, OIOC P/4320, Punjab Board and Committees.

62. C. A. Bayly writes that colonial interference in the *bazaars*, that is, through the official abolition of towns duties in the early-nineteenth century, did not mean an end to the collection of duties since those rights were rented or sold by the 'ancestral owners' of *bazaars* to local strongmen; C. A. Bayly, *Rulers, Townsmen and Bazaars: North Indian Society in the Age of British Expansion 1770–1870* (Cambridge: Cambridge University Press, 1983), 316.

63. Proceedings: March 1893, Letter from R. Clarke B. A., C.s. Deputy Commissioner, Delhi, to the Commissioner and Superintendent, Delhi division, dated 2 June 1892.

64. Syed Ahmad Khan, *Aasaar us Sanaadeed* (Delhi: Urdu Academy, 2006), 135.

65. ' … *bare bazaron mein donon taraf dukanon ke niche pukhta badarooen bana kar shahr ke bahar pani nikal diya aur dukanon kea aage sang sarkh ke khoobsurat chabootre bana gae …* ' (' … On both sides of the big bazaars, solid drains were made to let the water out of the city and beautiful red sandstone chabutras were made in front of the shops … '); Khan, *Aasaar us Sanaadeed*, 135.

66. Anonymous, *The Mofussilite*, 6 October 1868, 6.

67. The category of the *chabutra* could itself be used to designate seating plinths like *takht*s (seating plinths) which were found in shops and houses.

68. Proceedings: March 1893, Copy of a Letter from Lala Girdhari Lal, Member, Municipal Committee, Delhi to the Deputy Commissioner, Delhi, dated 28 April 1892, No. 48-57: No. 55, Board and Committees.

69. Proceedings of a Special Meeting, dated 14 December 1863, No. 48-57: No. 55, Punjab Board and Committees.

70. Proceedings of General Meetings from 1 June 1863 to 5 April 1869: Works Sanctioned and Ordered to be Commenced, dated 9 March 1864, DMC.

71. Proceedings of General Meetings from 1 June 1863 to 5 April 1869: Works Sanctioned and Ordered to be Commenced, dated 9 March 1864, DMC.

72. *Koh-i-noor*, Native Newspaper Reports (henceforth NNR), Punjab, 23 September 1865, 445.

73. Proceedings of General Meetings from 1 June 1863 to 5 April 1869: Proceedings of a General Meeting, dated 19 March 1866, DMC.

74. Proceedings of General Meetings from 1 June 1863 to 5 April 1869: Proceedings of a General Meeting, dated 19 March 1866.

75. Colonel McNeile in Chair, Resolution 15, Proceedings of General Meetings from 5 April 1869 to 18 December 1871: Monthly General Meeting held on 6 December 1869, DMC.

76. Brenda Yeoh, *Contesting Space: Power Relations and the Urban Built Environment in Colonial Singapore* (Kuala Lampur; Oxford: Oxford University Press, 1996), 269-70.

77. Vijay Prashad, 'The Technology of Sanitation in Colonial Delhi', *Modern Asian Studies* 35, no. 1, 2001, 113-55.

78. Copy of a Letter from the Governor General of India to the Right Hon. Secretary of State India, dated 27 October 1884, File 2296, 27 October 1884: No. 3, OIOC L/PJ/6139.

79. Copy of a Letter from the Governor General of India to the Right Hon. Secretary of State India, dated 27 October 1884.

80. Proceedings of the Municipal Committee: Rules Framed under Section 24 (1) Act XIII of 1884 (The Punjab Municipal Act) for Regulating the Building of Balconies & C., Overhanging Public Streets and Land within the Municipality of Delhi, and Passed at a Special Meeting, Held in the Town Hall on 3 June 1889, S. no. 73, 49-B (3), Box No. 53, 1895-96, Vol. IV, DSA Commissioner's Office Files (henceforth CO).

81. Proceedings: March 1893, Copy of a Letter from Lala Girdhari Lal, Member, Municipal Committee, Delhi to the Deputy Commissioner, Delhi, dated 28 April 1892.

82. Proceedings: March 1893, Copy of a Letter from Lala Girdhari Lal, Member, Municipal Committee, Delhi to the Deputy Commissioner, Delhi, dated 28 April 1892.

83. Proceedings: March 1893, Letter from R. Clarke B. A., C.s. Deputy Commissioner, Delhi, to the Commissioner and Superintendent, Delhi division, dated 2 June 1892.

84. Proceedings: March 1893, Letter from R. Clarke B. A., C.s. Deputy Commissioner, Delhi, to the Commissioner and Superintendent, Delhi division, dated 2 June 1892.

85. Copy of a Letter from A. C. C. De Renzy, Sanitary Commissioner Punjab to T. Thornton Esquire, Secretary, to the Government, Punjab, dated 24 July 1868, No. 5-6 A: No. 5, 7 November 1968, NAI Home Sanitary.

86. Prakash, *Another Reason*, 126.

87. Proceedings of Ordinary Meetings (Executive Committee) from 14 June 1869 to November 1871: Ordinary meeting dated 29 May 1871, DMC.

88. Pershad, *The History of the Delhi Municipality*, 34.

89. Proceedings of Municipal Meetings 4 January 1875 to 4 November 1878: Ordinary Meeting, dated 26 July 1875, DMC.

90. Hosagrahar, *Indigenous Modernities*, 107–08.

91. Hosagrahar, *Indigenous Modernities*, 109.

92. Proceedings: March 1893, No. 48-57 A: No. 55, Letter from R. Clarke B. A., C.s. Deputy Commissioner, Delhi, to the Commissioner and Superintendent, Delhi Division, dated 2 June 1892.

93. Proceedings of Municipal Meetings 4 January 1875 to 4 November 1878: Ordinary Meeting, dated 5 July 1875, DMC.

94. Prashad, 'The Technology of Sanitation', 127.

95. See Jim Masselos, 'Jobs and Jobbery: The Sweeper in Bombay under the Raj', *Indian Economic and Social History Review* XIX, no. 2, 1982, 101–39.

96. Delhi Municipal Proceedings, Proceedings of an Ordinary Meeting, dated 20 May 1895, S. No. 73, Box 53, 1895–96, Vol. VI, DSA CCO.

97. Delhi Municipal Proceedings 1907–08: Proceedings of a Special Meeting, dated 23 December 1907, S. No. 171, 1907, Box 62, DSA CCO.

98. Pershad, *The History of the Delhi Municipality*, 47–48.

99. John G. Leonard, 'Urban Government under the Raj: A Case Study of Municipal Administration in South India', *Modern South Asian Studies* 7, no. 2, 1973, 227–51.

100. Douglas Haynes, *Rhetoric and Ritual in Colonial India: The Shaping of a Public Culture in Surat City, 1852–1920* (Berkeley: University of California Press, 1991).

101. Haynes, *Rhetoric and Ritual in Colonial India*, 146–47.

102. Proceedings: March 1893, Letter from R. Clarke B. A., C.s. Deputy Commissioner, Delhi, to the Commissioner and Superintendent, Delhi division, dated 2 June 1892.

103. Proceedings: March 1893, Copy of Letter from Lala Girdhari Lal, Member, Municipal Committee, Delhi to the Deputy Commissioner, Delhi, dated 28 April 1892.

104. Bissell, *Urban Design, Chaos and Colonial Power*, 269.

105. In Bombay, for example, the perceived difficulty of policing neighbourhoods through 'indirect' influence in the 1890s led to the consolidation of police powers under the Police Act of 1902. Rather than being a panacea for colonial policing, the legislation caused the police to be more directly involved in the affairs of the neighbourhoods, raising the potential for more friction between the police and plebeian sections. See Kidambi, *The Making of an Indian Metropolis*, 115–56.

106. Proceedings: March 1893, Copy of a Letter from Lala Girdhari Lal, Member, Municipal Committee, Delhi to the Deputy Commissioner, Delhi, dated 28 April 1892.

107. Proceedings of a Special Meeting of the Delhi Municipality, dated 4 November 1895, S. No. 73, 1895–96, Vol. VI, Box 53, DSA CCO, DMC. The fragmentary evidence from the municipal files reveals that even when some ward members recommended that the pay of the sweepers should be increased, the municipality as a whole was against it.

108. For a study of the role of technology as a tool of colonial dominance, see Michael Adas, *Machines as the Measure of Man* (Cornell: Cornell University Press, 1990).

109. See Prakash, *Another Reason*, 131.

110. Pershad, *The History of the Delhi Municipality*, 15.

111. Letter from A. Taylor, Civil Surgeon Delhi to Lt. Colonel McMahon, Commissioner and Superintendent, dated 2 April 1874, No. 11-15 A: No. 14, July 1874, NAI Home Sanitary. The 'Delhi boil', as it was labelled, generated a huge debate within the colonial administration. Moreover, while parallels for the infection that led to the boils were found with Europe, the boils were thought to emanate from purely local circumstances, namely the presence of organic impurities and salts in water.

112. Awadhendra Sharan, 'From Source to Sink, "Official" and "Improved" Water in Delhi, 1868–1956', *Indian Economic and Social History Review* 48, no. 3, 2011, 425–62.

113. From planning to early construction, it took 20 years for the scheme to start. See Mann, 'Delhi's Belly', 18.

114. Wilberforce H. Greathed, *Report on the Drainage of the City of Delhi and on the Means of Improving It* (Agra: Secundra Orphan Press, 1852).

115. Greathed, *Report on the City of Delhi*.

116. *Urdu Akhbar*, NNR Punjab, 16 April 1871, 181.

117. Letter from A. C. C. De Renzy, Esq., Sanitary Commissioner, Punjab to the Secretary to the Government, Punjab, dated 4 December 1873, No. 2 A, Vol. 5, December 1873, CSA Punjab Home Proceedings.

118. Letter from A. C. C. De Renzy, Esq., Sanitary Commissioner, Punjab to the Secretary to the Government, Punjab, dated 4 December 1873.

119. Letter from Surgeon Major J. Fairweather, Sanitary Commissioner, Punjab to the Secretary to the Government, Punjab, dated 14 February 1880, No. 12 A, Vol. 12, February 1880, CSA Punjab Home Proceedings.

120. Letter from Surgeon Major J. Fairweather, Sanitary Commissioner, Punjab to the Secretary to the Government Punjab, dated 14 February 1880.

121. Margrit Pernau, *Ashraf into Middle Class: Muslims in Nineteenth-Century Delhi* (New Delhi: Oxford University Press, 2013), 347–48.

122. Pershad, *The History of the Delhi Municipality*, 48.

123. No. 11-16 A: No. 98, dated 24 March 1882, NAI Home Municipal, Government of Punjab, KW, June 1882.

124. Pershad, *The History of the Delhi Municipality*, 15.

125. Government of Punjab, *Gazetteer of the Delhi District: 1883–84* (Gurgaon: Vintage Books, 1988), 15.

126. Elizabeth Whitcombe, 'The Environmental Costs of Irrigation in British India, Waterlogging, Salinity, Malaria', in *Nature Culture and Imperialism: Essays on the Environmental History of South Asia*, ed. David Arnold and Ramachandra Guha (New Delhi: Oxford University Press, 1996), 251–52.

127. Government of Punjab, *Gazetteer of the Delhi District*, 15.

128. Mariam Dossal, *Imperial Designs and Indian Realities: The Planning of Bombay City, 1845–1875* (New Delhi: Oxford University Press, 1991), 98–99.

129. No. 11-16A: No. 98, dated 24 March 1882.

130. No. 11-16A: No. 98, dated 24 March 1882.

131. Letter from A. Mackenzie, Esq. Secretary to the Government of India, to the Secretary to the Government, Punjab, dated 2 June 1882, No. 15, NAI Home Municipal, Government of Punjab Government of Punjab, KW, June 1882.

132. Copy of a Letter from the Commissioner and Superintendent, Delhi to the Secretary to the Government, Punjab, dated 14 September 1877, No. 12-14 B, July 1879, NAI Home Municipal. The first time, the imperial government was asked to sanction a total amount of Rs 10,00,000.

133. Pershad, *The History of the Delhi Municipality*, 74.

134. Pershad, *The History of the Delhi Municipality*, 56.

135. Pershad, *The History of the Delhi Municipality*, 83.

136. *Safir-i-hind*, NNR North-west Provinces, 31 August 1887, 551.

137. *Safir-i-hind*, 31 August 1887, 551.

138. *Anjuman-i-Panjab*, NNR Punjab, 24 March 1883, 273.

139. Proceedings of a Special Meeting of the Delhi Municipal Committee Held at

the Town Hall, Delhi, on Monday, 10 May 1897, S. No. 84, Box 54, Vol. VIII, 1897–98, DSA CCO.

140. Proceedings of a Special Meeting of the Delhi Municipal Committee Held at the Town Hall, Delhi, on Monday, 10 May 1897.

141. Pershad, *The History of the Delhi Municipality*, 126. The drainage scheme was further divided into two parts: while the money that was raised for the first part was utilised by the municipality by 1897, the drainage plans for the second part had to wait until more funds were released by the government.

142. Pershad, *The History of the Delhi Municipality*, 141. Till 1902, only surveys had been undertaken for the suburbs.

143. Proceedings of a Special Meeting, dated 8 November 1897, S. no. 84, Box 54, Vol. VIII, 1897–98, DSA CCO.

144. Letter from the Secretary to the Government, Punjab to the Commissioner and Superintendent Delhi, dated 10 August 1897, S. no. 82, B-2, Box 53, 1897, DSA CCO.

145. *The Aftab*, NNR Punjab, 8 December 1907, 14.

3

The Outskirts

Natural Landscapes and the Ordeal of 'Improvement'

INTRODUCTION

The previous chapter suggested that municipalities set agendas to 'improve' the city through the reordering of its 'public' spaces, so that streets remained free from 'private' encroachments. 'Improvement' was, of course, a powerful tenet of the civilising mission, underpinned by the belief that colonial rule existed for the moral and material betterment of India.[1] This chapter further extends the discussion on improvement by highlighting the importance of nature and natural landscape improvement policies followed by the colonial government in Delhi after 1857.

The historian David Arnold has analysed how colonial observers and naturalists used the doctrine of 'improvement' to understand and evaluate the material environment of India in the early-nineteenth century. Arnold argues that beyond a strictly economic agenda, discernible in the early drives for 'improvement' were aesthetic motives, botanical enthusiasm, and moral judgements about India's poverty, and its deficient or harsh environment.[2] The 'tropical' landscape of India, simultaneously an object of 'fear and desire, utility and aesthetics' provided legitimacy to ideas of 'improvement'; and Arnold argues that this was a prelude and precondition for the physical transformation of the Indian countryside.[3] Although focusing on the early-nineteenth century, his arguments provide us with a comprehensive framework for understanding the linkages between 'improvement' impulses, the natural landscape, and the multiple and sometimes contradictory imperatives that they contained.[4]

Yet, the colonial 'improvement' of nature, conceived and implemented through the creation of botanical gardens and arboriculture practices, was not simply restricted to the Indian countryside, but it extended to the city and its suburbs. It is argued in this chapter that in the second half of the nineteenth century, the 'improvement' of nature and the natural landscape became a central feature of colonial governance in the city and the suburbs of Delhi. Building upon Arnold's insights, this chapter suggests that policies and practices of 'improvement' such as the need to ensure that garden cultivation and forest plantations remained financially productive, worked together with aesthetic considerations and broader political aims, such as the moral upliftment of the natives and the alleviation of insanitary conditions in the tropics. As is revealed, the fear of decaying 'tropical' vegetation and its effects on the health of the European troops stationed in the cantonment and in elite areas like the Civil Lines went hand in hand with motives such as moral and material 'improvement'. This chapter suggests that the 'improvement' of nature, and the multiple, and sometimes contradictory objectives embedded within it, also provide us the ability to examine the city and its suburbs within a single analytical frame.[5]

Finally, this chapter highlights the network of people and agencies that were involved in projects to 'improve' the natural landscape. The complexity of improvement schemes required an assembly of professionals and agencies, whose consultation, advice and recommendations the colonial government could not do without. This chapter shows that the numerous and often conflicting claims made in the name of 'improvement' entangled local administrations in disputes with sanitary professionals, forest departments, military officials, and other state agencies. If these struggles within the colonial government exacerbated tensions, they were also productive, as they provided legitimacy and justification to 'improvement' plans and served to extend local administrative control over the natural landscape.

'NATURAL' LANDSCAPES AND DELHI'S *NAZUL* LANDS: THE 'IMPROVEMENT' OF THE CITY AND ITS SUBURBS, 1863–75

Seen as inherently filthy and insanitary, Indian cities were perceived as 'diseased organisms' to be 'improved' under colonial public health reforms after 1857.[6] The concern over the health of the European troops stationed in north Indian cities after the rebellion, the threat of mysterious tropical illnesses, and the political agenda of 'civilising' the natives, all coalesced into improvement policies pursued by agencies like the municipality.[7] As has been suggested, the 'improvement' of the natural surroundings of the city also fulfilled multiple agendas for colonial administrations of cities like Delhi. From political concerns of civilising the natives, anxieties over the health of the troops, to the encouragement of economic productivity and aesthetic refinement, the natural landscape of the city formed an important field of intervention for agencies like the municipality and for 'scientific' personnel. As Richard H. Drayton has argued, nature was at the heart of an 'imperialism of improvement' in which natural sciences and colonialism were inextricably linked.[8]

In colonial cities like Delhi, newly established municipalities, sanitary officials and foresters worked to further this vision of 'improvement' of nature. For example, right from the clearance of the city after the demolitions, trees were planted in the open area cleared between the fort and Indian quarters of Delhi, to aid the 'purification of the atmosphere', providing much needed circulation of air to the troops located in the fort. It also served as a remedy to the crowded spaces of the city.[9] Almost concurrently, sanitary experts recommended that the decaying deciduous vegetation, such as the wild cactus of the Kudsia gardens, should be cleared because they were growing on low-lying alluvial soils and had the potential to cause epidemic diseases in the elite area of the Civil Lines.[10] As revealed in Chapter 2, troop mortality, in particular, was a source of distress for the colonial government. The notion that European 'constitutions' were biologically unsuited to 'tropical' climates like India had gained currency ever since the 1820s under the aegis of East India Company medical surgeons.[11] The racialisation of the tropics, an emphasis on the distinctiveness of its disease environment and the degenerate habits of the natives, played into the fears that the climatic conditions of India were debilitating to European bodies.[12] In order to alleviate these health anxieties, medical officers recommended tree-planting (or arboriculture) and flora transfers from different destinations in accordance with local climatic conditions.[13]

In a similar manner, manuals on arboriculture, with 'scientific' expertise proclaiming the economic, aesthetic and sanitary benefits of trees, were made available for the benefit of district officials and foresters in cities like Delhi. Official guides were replete with recommendations for the plantation of 'exceedingly ornamental' rose shrubberies and tree clumps at road corners and town crossings.[14] In Delhi, the municipality was lavished with praise for its tree-planting drives along the roadsides of the city. Colonial visitors admired the special attention given to trees, and also the fact that they were enclosed within brick-worked walls to prevent cattle from trespassing them.[15]

Gardens, too, were objects of 'improvement', and in conjunction with profit motives, their maintenance was deemed necessary by colonial sanitary experts for the moral upliftment of the natives, providing them recourse from their squalid surroundings and unhealthy living conditions.[16] For example, De Renzy, the Sanitary Commissioner in 1873, wrote that gardens were an 'indispensable means of cultivating and refining the taste of the people, not to speak of the advantages to health to be derived from having a place where people can escape from the squalor and closeness of their houses and streets to enjoy the open and fragrant air'.[17] In Delhi, municipal officials took charge of former Mughal gardens within the city, such as the Begam Ka *Bagh* near Chandni Chowk, right after the rebellion. The former garden, re-named and anglicised as 'Queens Gardens', was an 'improved' botanical expanse, the largest 'public' garden in the city.[18] Full of different varieties of fruits, trees and plants, the Queens Gardens was meant to convey a vision of colonial order, salubrity and aesthetic superiority, in contrast to the lacklustre spaces of the city. Travel guides like Fredrick C. Cooper's *Handbook for Delhi* lionised the Queens Gardens as a perfect specimen of colonial 'improvement':

> Here it will be observed a well-kept cricket ground, tropes of mangoes, pomegranates and plantains, vineries and strawberry beds, and well-arranged flower pots. A canal flows through the garden, along the banks of which a foot passenger may enjoy a shady and picturesque promenade. In the centre of the garden is a band-stand around which flowers and shrubs display a luxuriance and beauty not often found in upper India.[19]

While the gardens within the city had been showered with great attention, municipal management and care of the gardens, orchards and trees outside the city remained patchy till the beginning of the 1870s as a result of overlapping jurisdictions and the claims of the provincial government to outlying *nazul* properties. As described in Chapter 2, *nazul* properties formerly belonged to the Mughals and fell into the hands of the colonial government after the rebellion. These were scattered plots and roads, both within and outside the city, and the municipality had begun to manage them as 'public' properties and spaces after 1863. Till 1874, however, municipal limits and boundaries were ill-defined, and the outlying *nazul* lands and gardens were either contracted out by the government of Punjab or appointed to the care of committees under the district administration of Delhi.[20] Between 1871 and 1874, Lieutenant Colonel Cracroft, a government official and the Commissioner of Delhi, zealously undertook the task of establishing municipal control over all *nazul* lands outside the city, and with it, the task of 'improvement' of the suburbs.

Cracroft argued that the extension of municipal limits and centralisation of authority through the municipality needed to be pushed forward urgently to check the neglect of outlying *nazul* properties and prevent them from 'encroachments', which the multifarious district committees had been incapable of checking. Echoing a familiar concern in government circles, he felt that scattered *nazul* properties around Delhi were becoming 'more or less the food of a hungry population eager for spoliation'.[21] In a typical paternalistic tone, he called for executive action to 'protect the rights of the government and the public'.[22] Anxieties about native encroachment over government properties, and the belief that direct municipal control would lead to effective management and 'good governance', impelled Cracroft to suggest that it was best if all *nazul* properties in the suburbs came under municipal control. Cracroft was convinced that if this could be done, it would lead to financial profitability of the municipality, add to the health and comfort of both the city and its neighbourhood, and enable the display of 'immensely prized' properties as trophies of the empire.[23]

In this schema of 'improvement', of particular importance to Cracroft was nature itself. *Nazul* lands to the north and north-west of Delhi included a varied green expanse containing garden plots, orchards and extensive shrub and tree-cover around suburbs like *Sabzi Mandi* and Kishenganj.[24] At the height of Mughal power, this cover engulfed the rocky outcrop known as the 'ridge' and extended for two miles outside the city.[25] While forested areas like the Ridge had experienced gradual deforestation since the eighteenth century, after the rebellion of 1857, colonial authorities had also encouraged tree-felling in gardens like the Kudsia and Tis Hazari *Bagh*.[26] Cracroft argued that this expanse, particularly large Mughal gardens like the Roshanara and Kudsia *Bagh*, needed to be gradually improved by stocking them with trees of 'superior descriptions' where canal water was available, or otherwise, by planting timber trees so that the land could be 'turned to best account.'[27] For Cracroft, it was incumbent for imperial science and botanical expertise to bring order to the unruly natural landscape with 'superior' descriptions of trees while maintaining the productivity of land.

Aesthetically, there were further advantages of 'improving' the natural landscape of the suburbs. Just as Cracroft was concerned that prized *nazul* properties needed to be displayed as trophies of the empire, he argued that Delhi's vast gardens, too, needed to be lifted out of their neglected state and converted into ornaments of distinction. He wrote to the Punjab government that as relics of a Mughal past, gardens like the Roshanara *Bagh*, in particular, were of aesthetic significance. He also said that they were more than worthy of being presented to select dignitaries and visitors. Cracroft explained:

> Dehlie [*sic.*] is a place visited by many foreigners and persons of distinction who cannot fail to draw inference unfavourable to our administration when they see the state of the surroundings of Dehlie [*sic.*] and the neglected state of the gardens which would be an ornament in any capital in Europe if properly managed and kept up.[28]

However, rather than simply 'restoring' the gardens to their former state, Cracroft's impulse was an expression of colonial political power, and one rooted in the spirit of 'improvement'. While the local officials found much to appreciate in the former gardens, especially the varieties of fruits and flowers that they contained, English landscape gardening practices and colonial visions of ordered beauty provided the framework with which to transform them. This was a process of eclectic borrowing, where some features of the older Mughal gardens were preserved, but only because they were in line with colonial ideological imperatives and 'improvements'. In other words, the restructuring of the gardens had parallels with colonial architectural projects of the time, inasmuch as they were like 'objects' whose forms could be 'selected, rejected or altered'.[29]

In connection with the above-stated aims, the last pressing reason discernible in the move towards the improvement of the natural landscape outside the city was that of sanitation. As mentioned earlier, trees had been planted in the city with the intention of improving the health of the troops, and gardens were characterised as islands of salubrity, in contrast to the diseased city. Vegetation and greenery was repeatedly touted in English-language newspapers for its health-giving potential and its ability to 'gladden the senses' of the 'smoke dried denizens' of the city.[30] Outside the city, the 'improvement' of the health of the agricultural population of the *Sabzi Mandi* found expression in Cracroft's proposals for the control of the vast gardens and natural landscape surrounding Delhi.[31] Since the 1860s, sanitary experts had castigated the dwellings in the *Sabzi Mandi* for being too crowded, and thus, providing a fertile environment for the spread of epidemics.[32] If we recollect, as early as 1865, the municipality had set out to create a new market, citing congestion and the insanitary state of the area.[33]

In 1873, Dr Taylor, the Civil Surgeon of Delhi classified the area around the Roshanara gardens, to the north-west of Delhi, as waterlogged and responsible for the spread of spleen disease and malarious fevers in the neighbouring population of the *Sabzi Mandi*.[34] The watercourses of the Roshanara gardens were connected to a branch of the Western Yamuna canal for irrigation purposes; but the surface drainage systems were found to be too shallow to prevent the water from standing. During the rainy season, these plots of garden land transformed into 'ponds' and the vegetation became, in the words of Dr Taylor, 'drying and dead, the undergrowth jungly and rank or rotting'.[35] Stagnant pools of water, and rank vegetation acted upon by sunlight and excess humidity, reinforced the exceptional nature of 'tropical' climates and the deleterious effects of disease in Indian environments. An orderly and regulated green expanse was salubrious, and economically and politically beneficial. However, its obverse in the form of unruly and waterlogged 'jungles' were not only reminders of diseases lurking at the city's doorsteps, but also an affront to the 'civilising mission' of colonial authorities and their plans for 'improvement'.

Cracroft would later write to the provincial government of Punjab that the drainage of the western gardens in the western suburbs was conceived hand in hand with ensuring that the 'productive capacity' of the gardens was maintained. In doing so, the health of the neighbouring agricultural population would 'improve', and this was an 'incalculable boon' to the city and suburbs at large.[36] From his perspective, economic motives, the strategic display of garden properties, and health prerogatives were interconnected, and necessitated control through a single agency like the Delhi municipality instead of disparate government bodies. In asking the provincial government of Punjab for an opportunity to re-negotiate municipal boundaries, Cracroft urged the transfer of all *nazul* properties and lands under direct municipal management. He made this with the recommendations that the municipality would employ and oversee the services of forest officers and other experts, as deemed necessary.[37]

However, if Cracroft's energetic call for the 'improvement' of the outlying lands of the city was accepted by the provincial government, this was a long and arduous process because of the multiple jurisdictions that existed over *nazul* properties outside the city. Moreover, Cracroft's 'improvements' and the multiple objectives within it needed an assemblage of sanitary experts, foresters, engineers and local officials to see them through. As we will see in the next section, the multiple objectives envisaged in 'improvement', the professional views of authorities needed to carry them forward, and the existing arrangements of control over the *nazul* lands created its own set of contradictions and complexities. There were tensions between state bodies and officials over the nature, scope and cost of 'improvements'. However, these disputes also served to drive state intervention and legitimise its plans regarding the 'improvement' of the natural landscape. The latter was evident in the 'improvement' of the Roshanara *Bagh*, one of the largest *nazul* reclamation projects undertaken between 1871 and 1874.

GARDEN DESIGNS: THE CASE OF THE ROSHANARA *BAGH*

One of the largest *nazul* properties that Cracroft wished to bring under his 'improvement' plans and the eventual control of the municipality was the

Roshanara *Bagh*. Under Mughal patronage, tracts to the north and north-west of Shahjahanabad were converted into extensive pleasure gardens.[38] Their vastness and luxuriance had fascinated European travellers like Bernier, who visited the city in the seventeenth century.[39] The Roshanara *Bagh* was created in 1650 by its namesake and Shah Jahan's daughter, Roshanara *Begum* (princess). Upon the patron's death, she was entombed within the garden in the Mughal *chahar bagh* (quadrilateral garden) style.[40] Surrounded by water channels, trees and orchards of various descriptions, the Roshanara *Bagh* was redolent in its display of paradisiacal imagery. For the elite, the use of such gardens was multifold; they were not only spaces of formal intercourse and pageantry, but also spaces of conviviality and leisure.[41] At another level, and beyond the sphere of elite consumption, gardens like the Roshanara *Bagh* were important for the sustenance of the local area. It was essential for the legacy and prestige of the patron to live on long after his or her death, and this was done by providing for the wider neighbourhood.

The Roshanara *Bagh* sat between other garden tracts, it was not enclosed, and inhabitants of nearby areas like the *Sabzi Mandi* and Mughalpura were permitted to access the site and its facilities.[42] Moreover, gardens like the Roshanara gave various entitlements to land and trees such as the *Sardarakhti*, which allowed cultivators to take their produce to wholesale markets like the *Sabzi Mandi* without harassment.[43] The latter meant that a cultivator or *Sardarakhtidar* was responsible for the maintenance of trees in a garden and could not be ejected from the land until the trees stood there. A small amount in rent was payable to the proprietor if fruit trees were involved.[44] All in all, the Roshanara *Bagh* was an example of how Mughal gardens could support a range of occupations and activities as well as be metaphors of Mughal power.

After 1857, and under the tenure of Colonel Cracroft, the prized Roshanara garden would eventually acquire new meanings and functions through 'improvement' plans. Envisaged as government property and a 'public' garden, with implications for the city and suburbs alike, Cracroft was determined to carry out two measures at the very outset: determine and remove 'encroachments' from the land, and expand and consolidate the Roshanara by incorporating the smaller *nazul* gardens that lay adjacent to it. Several garden plots, namely the Sirhindi, Bahadur Khan, Saadat

Khan, Lal Khan, Mokurrus Khan and Mohsum Khan *Baghs*, which lay near the Roshanara, were considered to be an 'integral part' of the garden that was believed to have fragmented over time. Cracroft felt that it was better to have 'compact property in a ring, rather than manage a multitude of small parcels' in different areas.[45] The right to amalgamate the gardens into one was based on the belief that by virtue of their superior knowledge and expertise, Cracroft and the local administration were best equipped to discharge matters over the design, dimensions, usage and functions of the natural landscape around the city.

The fact that the efficient management and best use of the natural landscape was the prerogative of an enlightened government had been used to justify imperial control over forests and natural resources in many colonies.[46] As the complete transfer of *nazul* lands into municipal hands was as yet incomplete, local arbitrators, namely Munshi Amir Ali, *Raises* Sahib Singh and Mahesh Das, all of whom were Indian members of the municipality, were assigned to assist district committees, like the Local Committee and the Local Cess Committee, in discharging their duties, consolidating government land, and settling 'encroachment' disputes as the first steps towards 'improvement'.[47]

However, exhaustive enquiries over *nazul* lands immediately revealed difficulties and yielded results quite different from what Cracroft and others had expected. In the case of the Roshanara Bagh, Cracroft was forced to admit that 'encroachments' had indeed taken place; but this was only one side of the story. The *nazul* garden plots, Cracroft concluded, had been 'much interfered with, partly by grants, partly by sale and partly by encroachments'.[48] This admission was laced with irony since the government had itself alienated its *nazul* land in the preceding years. Before the East India Company seized the city in 1803, a combination of sectarian plunder and internal conflict within Delhi meant that income from the lands around Shahjahanabad dwindled and the hold over the area outside the city became tenuous for Mughal elites.[49]

As early as 1826, the local colonial administration had begun selling off several garden plots in the vicinity of the *Sabzi Mandi*. Deemed 'escheated' property, the lands were considered transferrable by sale or grants.[50] Discernible in these early attempts to transfer *nazul* gardens was a different vision of 'improvement' from Cracroft's centralised control and consolidation of garden lands. Prior to the rebellion, local officials felt that garden lands along the *Sabzi Mandi* were much more 'profitable' under individual owners than under government proprietorship.[51] This line of thinking stemmed from a notion that the administration's actions were in accordance with Mughal policies, under which garden lands were the 'sole and undisputed property' of individuals who purchased the ground, planted trees, and ultimately 'enjoyed the produce of fruits and vegetables, raised through the medium of labouring gardeners'.[52] Under Cracroft's administration, however, the pervasive notion that the colonial government was itself an ideal landlord, best suited to 'improving' and managing its valuable garden lands, took root. Now, in addition to establishing what 'encroachments' had taken place, the administration began buying back or reclaiming those *nazul* gardens that were to be ring-fenced, thus effectively undoing the 'improvements' by previous British administrations.

The process of undoing the work of the previous administration was accompanied by disputes among several departments that were involved in the 'improvement' scheme. For the first two years of the Roshanara project, the municipality worked jointly with provincial authorities like the Local Cess Committee and the Local Committee of the Delhi district.[53] As mentioned above, Indian members of the municipality were appointed as arbitrators to settle disputes and to grant compensation for land or trees that were included in the ring-fenced garden. Indian arbitrators were particularly useful when it came to assessing entitlements like the *Sardarakhti*, whose holders were compensated by a like-for-like exchange of *nazul* land and trees outside the Roshanara.[54] This was a cost-effective way of consolidating the government holdings and ensuring that loyal native elites settled delicate questions of rights and customs. As the exchanges began, Captain Bartholomew, a local official, triumphantly proclaimed in his report:

> Outlying plots, which in our hands were of little value, have been exchanged for valuable garden lands adjacent to the Roshanara Gardens, of which they form an integral part. Troublesome rights to the shares of produce have been transferred from the government in exchange for valuable land. Injury to fruit trees has been assessed at a much lower rate, than that which was obtained

from the authorities of the Rajputana State Railway, and yet the claimants are not dissatisfied. Only the small sum of Rs. 350 remains to be paid in cash.[55]

Bartholomew's optimism, however, was short-lived when more exchanges in lieu of interior plots were proposed. During this time, the municipality threatened to stop the contribution of funds and resources towards the Roshanara project, citing the fact that it was not under their exclusive management.[56] The overlapping jurisdictions, the delayed transfer of *nazul* properties, and claims of various authorities over their use caused a considerable amount of friction among different colonial departments; and this would be a recurring theme of urban governance in Delhi.[57] In the context of the Roshanara project, government disputes caused the dissolution of the local arbitration committee of Indian municipal members in 1874, and the task of settling compensation claims fell upon the shoulders of the Local Committee.[58] Without experienced native hands to arbitrate, settling the intricate claims became complicated and caused inordinate delays. Local cultivators and *Sardarakhtidars* took advantage of this confusion to demand cash payments, citing that the plots that the government planned to exchange were barren and inferior in comparison to the properties that had been exchanged earlier. Faced with settling complex claims, bitter internal disputes and long delays, officials like Bartholomew suggested that it was better to compensate the remaining claimants in cash, an exercise that could now 'hardly be avoided'.[59]

A government that was financially conservative, of course, never overtly desired cash payments. However, clashes between different branches, delays and complexities of compensation procedures, and resistance offered by the cultivators made it easier to simply pay cash and carry on with the project. No department was willing to abandon the 'improvement' of the garden halfway, for, as Cracroft had stated earlier, imperial prestige was at stake. For officials like Bartholomew who seconded this, cash compensation became, by default, a way out of the messy situation and a means to get on with the 'improvement' plans.[60]

Fulfilling multiple aims within the 'improvement' plans also added to the complexity of the Roshanara project. Professional views on what kind of 'improvement' was to be prioritised extended the scale and costs involved, and created friction between departments and officials. This became glaringly apparent when officials spent more money on a particular aspect of 'improvement' such as aesthetic alterations over other priorities. As mentioned earlier, Cracroft's administration felt that the Mughal gardens could be kept up for display and made accessible to foreign visitors. In order to 'improve' the Roshanara gardens' aesthetic potential, great strides were made by Major Tighe, the Deputy Commissioner of Delhi. As a municipal member and District Officer, Tighe was considered by Cracroft and the provincial authorities to be the best candidate to take charge of the scheme, coordinate the various operations of departments, and oversee the progress of the Roshanara project.

Tighe, however, had even larger and extensive plans for the aesthetic renewal of the Roshanara project, which surpassed the plans laid down by Cracroft. Within the first two years, Tighe carried out the 'ornamentation' of the gardens. Along with essential drainage and ventilation improvements, he supervised the creation of a network of roads with side drains, culverts and bridges to great 'aesthetic effect'.[61] The highlight of Tighe's efforts was the creation of an ornamental road leading from the direction of the elite enclave of the Civil Lines, providing an 'improved' approach by avoiding the *Sabzi Mandi* and the Grand Trunk Road altogether. When called to account for the huge expenses that were involved in the creation of the road, Tighe defended it as 'essentially a part of the scheme', one that could not be excluded.[62] Further investigations revealed that Tighe had, in fact, spent the bulk of the funds reserved for the 'project' for ornamentation purposes and had failed to keep accounts over what was spent where. Pinned down, Tighe in turn attacked Cracroft for his ill-conceived project of improvement and the inadequate finances that were budgeted for it:

> I could not help perceiving that you were hardly aware of the cost of these improvements and my opinion being that they were too costly to be borne out by the limited funds at the disposal of the committee .... this led to my not co-operating with you in these schemes in the manner you felt you had a right to expect from me as district officer, but in so acting I have only done what I considered my duty as the executive officer through whom these funds are collected and disbursed.[63]

In his own way, Tighe was acting in what he thought were the best interests of the colonial government. Indeed, in the case of the road, private access had been given to the European and Indian elites of the Civil Lines, avoiding the insanitary huts and dwellings in the *Sabzi Mandi* and the traffic of the Grand Trunk Road. In the interests of colonial power, racial and class considerations always mattered when it came to 'improvements'. It made sense to prioritise elite interests, especially since there were limited funds available for the scheme. However, the fallout of this was that Tighe's aesthetic ventures exhausted the funds that were available for the project. By the end of 1873, the Roshanara project had cost a total of Rs 60,000 and left Cracroft needing Rs 15,000 more to finish the 'improvements'.[64] As a consequence, the provincial government of Punjab came down heavily upon Cracroft, castigating him over the lack of accountability and inappropriate use of funds. From time to time, the works undertaken were condemned by higher authorities and sanitary experts for being deficient on economic and sanitary grounds, the other principles embodied in 'improvement', and local officials were accused of treating the whole project with 'a spirit of dilettantism'.[65]

Yet, rather than seeing these criticisms as wholly dismissive of Cracroft's efforts to 'improve' the gardens, it should be noted that they also provided legitimacy to future 'improvement' plans. Put in another way, the contradictions of the scheme, failures of implementation, and endless criticisms of deficiency laid the groundwork for the future 'improvement' of the natural landscape. The best example of this was represented by the criticism of De Renzy, the Sanitary Commissioner, who we have come across earlier. De Renzy started by asking Cracroft why expansive garden tracts *outside* the city needed to be maintained by the civil authorities in the first place, when the Queens Gardens *inside* the city were perfectly suited to the needs of the people.[66] For De Renzy, this was first and foremost a problem of respecting boundaries and jurisdictions. In other words, he hinted that the maintenance of gardens and their improvement under the provincial authorities would have been just as beneficial without Cracroft's ambitious plans and their huge expenses.

However, as the gardens were now under civil control, De Renzy lambasted Cracroft by suggesting that his style of 'improvements' were too aesthetic, and that the costs incurred entirely outstripped the fee simple of the gardens. Too much effort had been focused on aesthetics and too little on ensuring that the gardens remained remunerative. To him, the ornamental roads were of little 'industrial value', and while 'improvements' had indeed been made, the works were too ostentatious even for sanitation and drainage purposes. He wrote in a report:

> ... [T]he condition of the gardens has been vastly improved by the measures carried out by Colonel Cracroft, but I regret that I am compelled to say that in my opinion a very large portion of expenditure incurred was unnecessary on sanitary grounds, and that there are no valid reasons for charging any portion of the expense to municipal funds .... nothing more was required than to open up the old drainage channels which had become obstructed. Instead of this a net-work of roads greatly in excess of the requirements has been constructed, provided with side drains, culverts and bridges.[67]

If De Renzy was dismissive about the sanitary works undertaken under Cracroft, it was because he felt that gardens required simple measures such as regular cleaning of drains and thinning of fruit trees from time to time.[68] Simplicity in this case was 'scientific', and the reason De Renzy felt so was because of his belief—that suburbs of cities were generally much healthier than the city itself. Colonial scientific knowledge had constantly posited the Indian city as a site of disease. In Delhi, since the 1860s, sanitary specialists had criticised the 'impure atmosphere' and lack of ventilation inside the city.[69] As we have seen, in comparison to the city, the green tracts of the suburbs and the smell of fresh vegetation was considered infinitely healthier. If rotting tropical vegetation could be threatening, lush gardens and verdure were, simultaneously, objects of desire. This contradiction, as Arnold has shown, was central to the way in which the Indian landscape was understood.

De Renzy was firm in his belief that the claims of sickness in the suburbs of Delhi were greatly exaggerated, and he challenged Dr Taylor, the civil surgeon who advised Cracroft on the sanitary side of 'improvements'. He stated that Taylor's calculations to assess spleen disease in the neighbourhood of Roshanara were erroneous because his averages were based on too small a number of instances. Averages based on 40–50 instances were, in his opinion, 'obviously fallacious'.[70] He went to great lengths to prove that although malarial illnesses existed in the neighbourhood, the 'improvements' were conceived on miscalculations, and all that was required to keep the Roshanara in shape were simple measures taken from time to time.

In foregrounding Cracroft's inability to carry out 'improvements' in the manner he deemed necessary, De Renzy reinforced the primacy of colonial scientific knowledge. Science dictated that 'improvements' in the suburbs, by virtue of their healthiness, needed to be minimal. In future, De Renzy hoped that simple aesthetic and sanitary measures would be taken and that the economic productivity of *nazul* gardens would be kept in mind first. This was, as we have seen, practised under the provincial authorities before the *nazul* transfer, when the gardens were contracted out to other agencies. Indeed, the logic of improvement itself was never questioned by officials, for the discourse of improvement was linked to colonial claims to authority and power. The question was simply about how it could be made more effective. The discussions, debates and criticisms were therefore also productive, inasmuch as they provided legitimacy to future paradigms of 'improvement' and proclaimed the superiority of colonial 'scientific' claims.

It is also pertinent to reiterate that the 'improvement' of the Roshanara did indeed have tangible effects, and it impacted the relationship between the city and suburbs. As an 'ornament' of Mughal times, the 'improvement' of the Roshanara transformed the garden in its form and meaning. The ringed fence around the property, a physical distinction between garden plots outside the premises and the *Sabzi Mandi* served to mark 'public' property with its protocols of use and conduct, which were governed by agencies like the municipality. Racial and class distinctions shaped the design of the Roshanara, which had an ornamental road called the Roshanara Boulevard, an exclusive entrance for the Civil Lines.[71] Renaming the road as a 'boulevard' was in itself a political statement to distinguish it from the native entrances of the *Sabzi Mandi*. Moreover, the creation of the boulevard led to the displacement of a locality of lime burners and masons who had, in Cracroft's mind, rendered the place 'formerly incapable of being visited'.[72]

Within the gardens, aesthetic changes like those made by Tighe had greater resonance, and for all the contradictions and complexities of the scheme, helped situate colonial claims in Delhi's Mughal heritage. Several Mughal buildings in the newly fenced area were removed, except the tomb of Roshanara Begum along with a portion of the canal, thus ridding it, as one colonial official called, of its 'peculiar oriental features'.[73] In effect, upon entering the Roshanara, the viewer was meant to gaze upon the solitary tomb in a garden fashioned in the form of an 'English landscape'.[74] New roads cut up the garden with broad gravel sweeps to create an aesthetic effect that helped the eye focus on nothing but a tomb in the distance.[75] The terrain was also shaped in such a way that the vestiges of the rebellion, like the 'General's Mound', were visible above the trees on the slope of the Ridge that was behind the garden.[76] 'Improvement' was thus carried out in terms of an English landscaped garden where reminders of the rebellion were visible. All of these features helped to situate the colonisers' own claim to Delhi's Mughal heritage.

PLANTATIONS AND SUBURBAN LANDS: THE *BELA* LANDS OF DELHI, 1863–1900

Reclaiming and maintaining garden properties was one way of ensuring that the natural landscape was 'improved', while transforming fertile alluvial tracts into forest plantations was another. One of the longest examples of colonial 'improvement' in the suburbs of Delhi was the transformation of the *bela* lands immediately outside the city walls. The *bela* was a local term used for the riverine land running on both sides of the Yamuna River. Distinct for its soil and vegetation, *bela* tracts stretched from the base of the *Lal Qila* (Red Fort) to the village of Chandrawal that lay to the north of the city. As a component of *nazul* property, the colonial government confiscated vast tracts or *bighas* (a unit of measurement) of *bela* lands after the rebellion.[77] A total area of 650 *bighas* of land on the right bank of the Yamuna and 607 *bighas* of land on its left came to be classified as 'government property' by the local authorities in the 1860s.[78] The 'improvement' of the *bela*, like the initiatives undertaken by Cracroft to transform the gardens, was driven by multiple, and sometimes, contradictory motives. Various government agencies like the Delhi municipality, the forest department and military authorities had a stake and participated in plans to fashion the landscape of the *bela*. Yet, fulfilling a mix of sanitary, aesthetic and political objectives through the *bela* and the claims raised by different departments in the name of 'improvement', created severe challenges for the colonial government.

Prior to colonial rule, the fertile land of the *bela* served the inhabitants of the city and suburbs in multiple ways. At one level, the *bela* formed a means of approach to the city before the railways, when a bridge of boats traversed to enter through the gates of Delhi. Circuits of movement over the *bela* lands also linked villagers of Chandrawal to the city, as they crossed over the *bela* to enter and collect night soil and take it to their fields.[79] The *bela* lands also provided for the city since agricultural activities like manure-intensive melon cultivation were carried out on its banks.[80] Last, in ritualistic and symbolic terms, the *bela* lands occupied an important place for different sections of Delhi's residents. For Hindu devotees, the banks of the Yamuna were a sacral space, littered with bathing and burning *ghats* (river banks usually accompanied by a flight of steps), to carry out ritual ablutions or cremate the dead. In popular sentiment, the city's fortunes were linked to the changing course of the river; the 'displeasure' of the river was even a theme captured by chroniclers of the city after the rebellion.[81] For the Mughals, the *bela* was a carefully configured space for the performance and display of imperial power. The *bela* was where people assembled to catch a glimpse of the emperor through the *Jharokha Darshan* (the trellis window) in the *Lal Qila*.[82] Thus, the Yamuna and its *bela* lands were important as a space of myth, as well as a symbol of ritual performance, economic sustenance and communication.

As the lands fell into the hands of the colonial government after the rebellion, debates ensued over what 'improvements' could be made to the *bela*, its economic and aesthetic potentialities, and the sanitary measures that were needed to keep it in check. One powerful economic argument came from the forest department of Punjab, which was to convert the fertile alluvial land into a commercial *Sisu* (Dalbergia Sissoo) 'plantation' on the banks of the Yamuna.[83] India's integration into a colonial economy and the beginnings of a railway network from the mid-1860s was carried out with a rationale of providing railway companies with timber.[84] The heavy costs of importing coal from England and the limited availability of coal in India made timber, a cheap source of fuel, incredibly attractive for railway purposes.[85] For a ready supply of wood, the government of India promoted the growth of timber plantations across Punjab, which continued till 1880.[86] The alluvial soil of the Yamuna, a representative of the forest department argued, was 'naturally adapted for the purpose' of a plantation.[87] Seen as economically useful, and with a possibility of the whole area behind the city becoming an 'extensive shady grove' in future, the plantation proposal immediately struck a chord with the provincial government of Punjab.[88]

Yet, this enthusiasm was not readily matched by the municipal authorities, who again rued the fear of rotting plants and rising miasmas in such close proximity to the city. The municipality had, of course, begun the reclamation of *nazul* properties by the early-1870s, and the purported transfer of the *bela* lands to the forest department meant losing control over valuable *nazul* lands that were in the vicinity of the city. While careful to not dismiss the plantation entirely, it argued that whatever course was followed, the *bela* required careful and regular maintenance, which was a necessity to prevent the creation of a dense and rank jungle.[89] Cracroft, who was at the helm of the district administration, also suggested that instead of a plantation, it was better to leave an open grazing ground on the banks of the Yamuna, so that the civil authorities could transform it into a sheep farm in future.[90] Thus, like the gardens of the Roshanara, a variety of motives were recognisable in the 'improvement' plans voiced by different authorities. Arnold's argument about the natural landscape being understood as an object of 'fear, desire, utility and aesthetics' again rings true in this case. Economic priorities were echoed through the suggestion of creating a plantation along with concerns for aesthetic renewal, that is, the creation of a shady grove behind the city. However, fears of rank and rotting vegetation and the threat of tropical diseases simultaneously fuelled anxieties and prompted debates over whether plantations near the city were ideal. This was again reflected in the tension between authorities like the municipality and forest department, the latter ostensibly answering to the government of India.

Eventually, colonial ideological interests in maintaining a barrier between the Civil Lines and the burning *ghats* triumphed over the tensions between the forest department and the municipality. The latter accepted a plantation on the premise that trees would not only form a barrier, but on the advice of the civil surgeon, they also believed that this would benefit the dwelling houses to the south of the Civil Court.[91] In the interests of health, fortifying areas near to the Civil Lines from contamination by native dead bodies was paramount for the civil authorities, and could not be neglected in any scheme to 'improve' the natural landscape of the city. While the forest department had succeeded in convincing the provincial government of the benefits of establishing a plantation, the civil authorities and agencies like the municipality constantly voiced the fear that an unruly jungle expanse could engulf the river banks. As we will see, tensions among the municipality, forest department, and later, the military authorities would shape the course and direction of 'improvements' in the *bela*.

COMPETING COLONIALISMS: 'IMPROVEMENTS' AND THE STRUGGLE FOR CONTROL OF THE *BELA* LANDS

As an outcome of final deliberations, a *Kikar* (Prosopis Juliflora) plantation was created on the *bela* tracts as a fuel reserve in the vicinity of the city.[92] A sketch created by the local authorities (see Figure 3.2) shows us the extent and location of the *bela* area that was eventually demarcated and handed over to the forest authorities. Immediately after the transfer, however, the civil authorities received a flurry of petitions complaining about the conduct of the forest department. Archival information records these cases under the category of the question of 'rights', which were compromised by the demarcation of the area by the forest authorities. As suggested in Chapter 2, different government authorities were confused over what constituted 'ancient rights and customs' of the natives; and yet, such internal disputes fuelled the expansion of the bureaucratic apparatus of the colonial government. In the case of the *bela* lands, similar fears about encroaching upon the rights of the people and a desire to ensure that a space of free movement prevailed across the expanse exacerbated tensions between the civil authorities and the forest department.[93] This would fuel the demands for civil control of the *bela* and its incorporation into municipal designs for 'improvement'.

As mentioned earlier, the *bela* lands had been used by the villagers of Chandrawal to cart night soil away from the city towards their fields.[94] The permission to use this manure was originally given to the *zamindars* (landlords) of the area by the municipality after 1863, and the soil was carried away towards Chandrawal over the *bela* through two places, the Nigambodh and Kela *ghat* gates running alongside the city walls.[95] The creation of a plantation now meant that a circuitous route had to

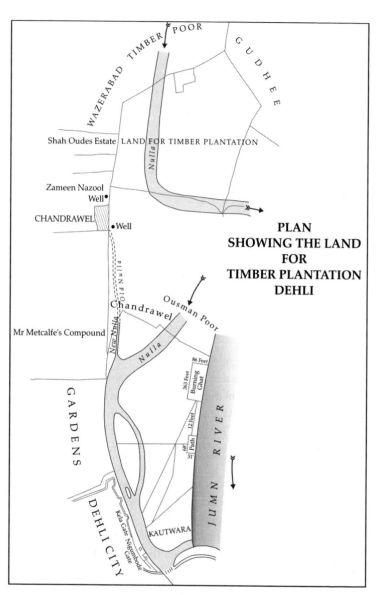

Figure 3.1: *Bela* Lands Entrusted to the Forest Department in 1869

Note: The image has been modified by the author.
Source: F.No. 3/1882, DCO, Delhi Archives, Government of NCT of Delhi, India.

be taken to carry away the manure since the forest department claimed that any trespassers would damage tree saplings.[96] The municipality was particularly alarmed at this development as, first, the sale of manure was first and foremost a very lucrative trade. Second, the municipality had stopped the ingress and egress of manure traffic from other routes of the city a few years earlier to keep the Civil Lines free from disease. Anxiety regarding preserving the health of the Civil Lines, and the profits from the manure trade made the municipality launch a spirited attack on the forest department. It was absolutely necessary, a Deputy Commissioner argued, to enable bullock carts to carry manure over the *bela*. This was because the plantation had resulted in the carts crossing three branches of the river before reaching their destination, much to the anger of the *zamindars*.[97]

Yet, more arguments were made by the civil authorities and the municipality to criticise the forest department for encroaching upon the 'religious rights' of the people. The Brahmins of the city had sent petitions claiming that the creation of a plantation absorbed some land at a point between the Kudsia *bagh* and the riverfront, which was previously used for ritual ablutions.[98] Clearly, the municipality argued, this was a blatant case of suppression in which the religious rights of an influential section of the population had been harmed. They lobbied for the creation of a separate area by the forest department for the aggrieved parties so that the latter could perform their bathing rites and rituals.[99] A combination of colonial paternalism and a fear of government intrusion in religious customs led to repeated calls for the abandonment of the plantation by the forest authorities and its takeover by the municipality instead. As one Deputy Commissioner wrote to his superior:

> You are aware that the lands alluded to are close to the city and on the banks of the Jamuna .... Daily numbers of people go from the city to bathe, burn their dead, and wash clothes & c. and it appears to me the advantages of having a kikar plantation on the ground are not be compared with the great inconvenience it is to the people to be at all restricted in their movements. I would recommend that the forest department remove their establishment from the grounds in the neighbourhood of the city altogether.[100]

In return, the forest department, which was in no hurry to transfer control over the plantation, blamed native ignorance and habits for trespassing. It also reassured the civil agencies that the plantation would itself prove to be a civilising force in due course. The latter was best expressed by Baden Powell, the Conservator of Forests, in a letter to the civil authorities at Delhi. He noted:

> My experience of several visits is that people insist on trespassing off the road, trying to cut off corners and wander about over the whole place. This of course leads to necessary protective action for which the people have only to thank for themselves. This difficulty, however, is purely temporary, as the young seedlings will soon attain a height sufficient to mark out definitely where the thoroughfares are, and being thorny, will down a natural barrier to trespassers.[101]

The fact that the forest department stood its ground increased squabbles between the department and the civil authorities. The latter lobbied stridently for the creation of well-defined spaces for bathing and burning *ghat*s for the city-dwellers, and eventually forced the forest department to create a plot measuring 50 feet long and 30 feet wide along the river.[102] In due course, more concessions were granted and clear pathways to the *ghat*s were created and kept in repair by the forest department.[103] The mobility of the *zamindar*s of Chandrawal, along with recommendations that a passage along the Kudsia gardens should remain open for manure traffic, was reconsidered.[104] These attempts by civil authorities to uphold the demands of the population of the city and suburbs are significant for several reasons. On the one hand, this showed the operation of a distinct political rationality in the post-rebellion scenario—to uphold what were deemed to be the 'natural rights and customs' of the natives. We have seen this previously in the case of the relocation of the *Sabzi Mandi*, for example. At another level, concerns to preserve the health of the Civil Lines made it imperative to examine the ways in which night soil was carted out of the city. As mentioned above, the municipality forbade manure carts to enter or exit through the city gates in the direction of the Civil Lines, and in lieu, it gave permission to use the *bela* lands. This was also advantageous, inasmuch as it supplied municipal funds with a constant source of revenue. Thus, we see how a variety of economic and political reasons impelled civil authorities and the municipality to assert their right to manage the plantation.

However, as suggested in this chapter, civil authorities and agencies like the municipality had their own designs for the 'improvement' of the natural landscape. Officials like Colonel Cracroft once again voiced their disapproval over the fact that the most 'valuable' *nazul* properties had been taken by forest authorities and were included within the plantation, and that thousands of rupees were being made through the sale of grass and tree produce in the area.[105] This, in their opinion was a rightful part of local revenues, unjustifiably seized by the forest department.[106] In conjunction, Cracroft argued that it was perhaps best to abandon ideas of keeping a plantation near the city walls for sanitary reasons. He pointed out that Delhi was 'hemmed in' by a high Ridge overgrown with trees, and the only open space was the river, which had been receding to the east. In his opinion, this was not a 'good thing either for salubrity or with respect to the railway bridge and other considerations'.[107] He spoke of the 'overgrowth' of unruly vegetation near the city and the poor soil of the riverbed that had been jeopardised by planting trees. If economic and sanitary reasons were foregrounded in the removal of the plantation and its subsequent 'improvement', Cracroft also hinted at aesthetic motives. He felt that it was best to keep some trees above the line of the city wall, near the Kashmiri gate, all with the intention that the *bela* would not degenerate 'into a jungle interspersed with high grass and become a refuge of wild beasts'.[108]

The fear of dense and rank vegetation rotting in the *bela* and the need for conservancy measures gave the municipality its chance for 'improvement' in 1878.[109] The sanitary condition of the *bela* lands had been found to be so poor that the provincial authorities accepted its transfer from the forest department. Attributing the impeding of the drainage of the city to the 'inferior' size of osiers and trees, the municipality took charge of the plantation with the forest department, now acting in an advisory capacity along with sanitary officers.[110] The victory of the civil authorities, however, brought with it a new series of complications. The land transferred to the municipality had suffered from a cycle of repeated inundations and droughts.[111] In the late-1870s, the *bela* had also been plagued by an infestation of rats, which had destroyed the plants that were grown by the forest authorities.[112] In addition, sewage from the Shahjahani drains of the city passed through the *bela* lands at a time when the river had changed its course further eastwards.[113] These examples of the uncontrollable and erratic effects of the river upon the *bela* lands reveal, as Christopher Otter suggests, that the matter had 'multiple and unpredictable effects'.[114] This unpredictability of the river, and the resultant combination of sewerage and soil infertility alarmed Delhi's colonial military establishment and cantonment authorities, as the *bela* plantation lay in close proximity to the fort where British troops were garrisoned.[115] The military authorities voiced a palpable fear of malarial miasmas resulting from a dense jungle in the *bela* and urged the municipality to take action.[116]

Thus, although the municipality fought to bring the *bela* under its own brand of 'improvement', new obligations to preserve the health of the troops after 1878 created a contradiction. While civil authorities like the municipality had earlier upheld the customary rights of people in response to the forest department, it now itself began charging the natives with polluting the *bela* lands. The fear of filth and unhygienic habits corrupting the water of the *bela* and spoiling its soil, particularly near the fort, heightened colonial anxieties. If any 'improvement' of the *bela* was to take place, officials argued, the first requirement was to ensure that no native waste flowed into the *bela* channel leading towards the cantonment.[117]

As a consequence, municipal efforts were directed towards keeping the military establishment at the Salimgarh fort free from disease. Salimgarh, a sixteenth-century fort on the banks of the Yamuna, was connected to Shah Jahan's palace or the *Lal Qila* by the means of a bridge (see Figure 3.3). If we recall, after the rebellion, the military authorities had stationed British troops within the *Qila*, as a means of security. Although Salimgarh and the Red Fort ostensibly fell under the aegis of military authorities, the cooperation of the civil administration and municipality was required from time to time, particularly in matters of sanitation.[118] Moreover, the *bela* lands and the river extended from the areas under the care of the municipality in Chandrawal, close to the walls of the *Qila* and Salimgarh, which came under military jurisdiction. Thus, to protect the European troops, the cooperation of both agencies was needed.

Since the *bela* lands were close to the fort, civil authorities took measures to divert drain water from indigenous quarters away from falling within the *bela* area. To 'improve' the *bela*, it was ensured that the Salimgarh channel did not receive drain water from other areas except from the Civil Lines; and a proposal was made that all sewers could be realigned in such

Figure 3.2: Photograph of Bridge Connecting the Fort (Left) and
Salimgarh (Right) c. 1890s

Note: A section of the *bela* on either side of the Yamuna River near the fort.
Source: Provided by the author.

a way that the city's waste only exited through the Delhi gate.[119] Finally,
the then Conservator of Forests argued that it was incumbent upon civil
authorities to prevent the *bela* grounds from being used as a public latrine,
as people flocked to it due to the denseness of its undergrowth.[120] Echoing
the oft-repeated trope that the Indian habits and the distinctiveness of
its environment were responsible for the unhealthy state of the *bela*, the
conservator stated in a letter to provincial authorities:

> I can testify from personal experience that the air in it is in a dreadful state,
> especially near the city wall. In going away from the latter the air improves
> considerably which seems to me to show that the unhealthiness is in reality
> not so much produced in the bela as carried in to it from the city, partly by the
> people, and partly by the drains, which empty themselves into it.[121]

Yet, if there was so much trouble in policing native habits, the question
then is, why was the *bela* not cleared completely? Part of the answer
lies in the multiple objectives envisaged in 'improvement'. To clear the
bela of all vegetation was to end the revenue that was generated from
grazing rights and the sale of grass.[122] Cracroft, if we recall, was keen on

bringing into local accounts the 'thousands of rupees' collected from the sale of grass. Conversely, the huge expenditure involved in clearing the plantation, from the overgrowth to its roots, made the government shy away from any sizeable investment towards its clearance.[123] There were, however, other reasons that prevented any systematic denudation of the *bela*. While on the one hand, some civil officials mulled over its clearance, professional opinions of the forest authorities were different. In the 1880s, the foresters did not perceive that the trees in themselves harmed the sanitation of the area; rather, they argued that the regular removal of the undergrowth would alleviate any sickness or malarial fevers.[124] The fact that a plantation was an effective means of balancing the water table had been suggested repeatedly in different imperial contexts.[125] The lineage of this conservationist argument was based on the notion that land could not be left waste, for that was an anathema to 'improvement'.[126] Moreover, as the statement of the Conservator of Forests reveals, the 'problem' was not the *bela* in itself, but the fact that the natives polluted it, which in turn gave rise to malarial miasmas. After all, trees and natural vegetation were salubrious, and the suburbs, particularly as one went away from the city, were much healthier. This was something that De Renzy had argued several years earlier. Thus, a contradiction that arose from competing understandings of the natural landscape, which was at once a source of fear and desire, also prevented the clearance of the *bela*.

If contradictory opinions allowed 'improvements' to carry on, so did confusing notions of what was required to keep the soil of the *bela* in order. Controlling the cultivation of melons in the alluvial tracts of the *bela* was an example of this. In 1880, officials like the Sanitary Commissioner of Punjab were in favour of removing the cultivation of melons from near the fort on account of the heavy use of manure, which was presumed to be detrimental to the health of soldiers. The officers of the forest department, on the other hand, had claimed just a couple of years earlier that melon grounds were, in fact, beneficial for the area.[127] Their argument was that the cultivation of melons was a local practice that was meant to improve the fertility of the soil.[128] It appears that as a compromise between these two contrasting positions, melon grounds were permitted to stand, but it was urged that the manure be mixed with the soil or be used with an equal portion of earth if used as a top dressing.[129]

Clearly, in the light of conflicting opinions and contradictory advice, local officials found that it was better to modify regional practices rather than risk further soil degradation by removing them altogether.[130] Conflicting opinions and ambiguity over whether the *bela* needed to be cleared or not created a stalemate, and in the end, 'improvement' continued under municipal authorities. Attention was given when questions of sanitation became unavoidable and the municipality carried on the periodic practice of removing the undergrowth.[131] The consequences of such measures for the health of the people living in the city were disastrous. As Delhi resident and scholar Munshi Zakaullah recalled much later, malarial sickness became a debilitating problem in Delhi, ravaging its citizens time and again.[132] Even in the 1890s, when the government of India was asked for financial help for clearing the *bela*, the request was denied because of the huge costs involved and the investment needed to lengthen the bridges that had been created over the river.[133]

By the beginning of the twentieth century, debates over the 'improvement' of the *bela* and the gardens of the city took a different turn. As discussed in the next section, a renewed colonial aestheticism, with its focus on creating park-like landscapes, characterised 'improvement' impulses. This emphatic turn towards the aesthetic, however, did not mean that 'improvement' policies were implemented in a uniform or consistent manner. Rather, the aesthetic agenda itself brought agencies like the municipality into conflict with other authorities like the military department and their designs for the improvement of the *bela* lands.

'PARK-LIKE' VISIONS: AESTHETIC RENEWAL AND 'IMPROVEMENT'

In 1903, Delhi witnessed the grand spectacle and pageantry of the Delhi *Durbar* (ceremonial court), held at the behest of Lord Curzon, the Viceroy of India. The Curzon era was marked by the deployment of an aesthetic impulse, particularly in the domain of archaeological practice, where buildings were abstracted from their contemporary contexts and put within 'picturesque' garden surroundings.[134] If in the 1870s Colonel Cracroft had not found favour within the provincial government because of his excessive aestheticism and 'ornamentation' of gardens, now there was a growing consensus among the upper echelons of the imperial establishment that green surroundings could be used to 'improve' Mughal tombs and buildings as relics of the past. Increasingly, there came to be a pervasive view that Indian gardens were 'interwoven' with buildings, and studies of either its architecture or gardens could not be separated from one another.[135]

These discussions were pivotal in increasing the garden establishment in Delhi, and they led to the recruitment of European gardeners to care for *nazul* gardens like the Roshanara and Kudsia *Baghs*, and other scattered properties around the city. As W. C. Rennouf, the Director of Agriculture, remarked in 1909:

> In the importance, beauty and number of its ancient monuments and in historical interest, Delhi, the old imperial capital of India, stands absolutely pre-eminent among Indian cities. We know how the charm of Agra monuments has been enhanced by the work of the European gardener in charge. We have absolutely neglected Delhi in the past. I consider that Delhi has a claim to similar treatment to Agra, and the expenditure which ensures that its beautiful historical buildings are suitably set off is amply justified.[136]

Beyond the focus on creating monuments with a picturesque backdrop, discussions over colonial aesthetics also revolved around whether 'landscape and flower effects' were to be toned down in a country where conceptions of gardens revolved around shade and their productiveness as fruit orchards.[137] At the same time, some advocates took an extreme view: to purge the influence of English gardening practices from the landscape and show the raw essence of an essentially 'Indian' garden craft.[138] This also reveals a subtle difference from the aestheticism that was pervasive during Cracroft's time. These discussions sought to create an authentically 'Indian' landscape, removing gardening practices that were 'imported'. As we recall, Cracroft, on the other hand, saw the Roshanara as part of an English garden landscape.

By the early decades of the twentieth century, this colonial aestheticism also extended to discussions over the *bela* plantation. Indeed, Lord Curzon himself had wanted the *bela* lands to be used to commemorate the *Durbar* of 1903, and had desired the conversion of the riverfront into an area from where an elaborate imperial memorial would be visible.[139] This renewed aestheticism, however, did not mean that sanitary or economic agendas in 'improving' the plantation were eliminated. Rather, these aims worked in tension with the aesthetic designs put forward by agencies like the municipality.

The municipality had not wished to incur any significant expenditure by itself over the removal of the *bela*, and the sporadic sanitary efforts that were made put the needs of the cantonment and the Civil Lines before those of the rest of the city. In 1904, the case of the *bela* was re-opened by civil authorities in trying to assess the situation of the 'jungle' that was visible from the walls of the fort.[140] In the interim, the *Kikar* trees of the *bela* had grown tall enough to form a backdrop to the city wall, particularly where the post and telegraph offices, kutchery and the Church were located.[141] The undergrowth of tamarisk shrub provided a source of revenue for the municipality, and much to the relief of the officials, the *bela* was less dense in the run-up to the fort, as special care was given to remove vegetation between trees.[142]

While the original use of the *bela* as a fuel plantation no longer appealed to the authorities, the Commissioner was unwilling to consider a move that would sweep away 'a plantation deliberately made by responsible authorities'. This was because it would reveal inconsistency in the administrative procedure, and not to mention, the cost it would require in the removal of the *bela*.[143] Moreover, significantly, the Commissioner argued, the plantation over time had become 'a pleasing feature of the river bed which would be missed if removed'.[144] Clearly, the Commissioner's desire was for the *bela* to form a pleasing backdrop to the city, a landscape aesthetic in which the Mughal city was entwined with its green surroundings. This view heralded a new beginning in the life of the *bela*.

Now, under the trappings of a cost-effective solution, which could potentially rid the banks of the Yamuna of its poor soil, the aesthetic clearance of certain portions of the *bela* was deliberated. It was argued that the cost of meeting such a clearance could be taken care of from the sale of grass and of some wood from trees that were felled.[145] In fact, from both economic and sanitary points of view, this aesthetic clearance was deemed beneficial by the civil authorities in Delhi. The Chief Engineer, for example, claimed that the cleared land could be let out to *zamindars* for the cultivation of 3–4 crops a year, and this would also remedy the longstanding sanitary problems of the city.[146] This kind of a clearance of the *bela* had been recommended in 1881, when the forest authorities suggested that the *bela* lands could be let out for cultivation in a way that reflected the cultivation patterns of Punjabi fields. However, this was ignored at the time.[147] The reappearance of these recommendations at this juncture reinforces the powerful influence of colonial aesthetics on 'improvement' designs.

Like the experience of previous interventions, however, the aesthetic improvement of the *bela* was anything but straightforward. If the municipality had started drafting plans to remodel the *bela*, by this time, military authorities had begun to formulate their own designs for its improvement. In 1905, military authorities requested the government of India for direct control over sections of the *bela* so that cavalry regiments could be supplied with grass.[148] Unlike the aestheticism that the municipality espoused, the *bela* was seen by military authorities primarily in economic terms, as the best measure to offset the exhaustion of grazing lands in the old cantonments.[149] Within a year, the government of India granted a total of 341 acres of the *bela*, running from the fort northwards, to the military authorities, to create a grass farm.[150] The government of India, if we recollect, had the power to alienate *nazul* lands, although the municipality was responsible for its care and management. Significantly, in a complex series of arrangements, the lease of the *bela* was drafted between the municipality and military authorities, and through this, the municipality preserved entitlements such as the right to sell forest produce.[151] Unsurprisingly, immediately after the transfer, the military began accusing the municipality of making a profit through the sale of sewage, which was still allowed to enter the grass farm, thus shirking away from its obligations to ensure the safety of the troops.[152]

Colonial sanitary expertise was also responsible for subverting municipal plans by increasing the scale and costs of improvements. By the 1900s, new medical developments established that parasites and its malarial vector, the *anopheles* mosquito, were responsible for the prevalence of malarial disease.[153] By this logic, disease could be found anywhere with stagnant water and was not simply reserved to lands like the *bela*. Initially, the military department still claimed that since disease persisted after 'every effort had been made by medical officers to reduce the unhealthiness of the fort', the main factor in the causation of sickness had to be the bad condition of the *bela* lands rather than that of the fort itself.[154] By 1910, however, the Commissioner of Delhi was suggesting differently, that the condition of the *bela* was 'not entirely' linked to the health of the troops. In the light of new research and recent surveys, he argued that it was, in fact, the fort's drainage that was found to be defective and therefore responsible for the ill-health of the troops.[155] However, this was a pyrrhic victory. As it had now been established, both the *bela* and the fort needed sanitary maintenance, the municipality became involved in plans to remedy both.[156] As argued in Chapter 2, sanitary expertise was a double-edged sword. Medical theories were constantly being modified in the light of new developments and research. Yet, through their recommendations, medical theorists and sanitary experts increased the costs and scale of colonial interventions. In the process, local administrations found it difficult to carry out their schemes.

In cognisance of the large expenditure that was now required, the aesthetic improvements were scaled back further. Initially, there were suggestions within the colonial establishment that the park-like model could be extended to bring the river back to its original course under the city walls, which had changed course after the construction of the railway bridge built in the 1860s.[157] It was considered that the suggestion would be popular with the inhabitants of the city, bringing back these people to use old *ghats* and bathing places from which they had been displaced. Now, the costs involved in the operation, and the fact that sewage from the city would have to be purified before entering the river made the authorities scale back their ambitions and abandon any such benevolent ideas.[158]

By 1911, the hackneyed 'park-like' design of the *bela* was scrapped altogether, but by a larger aesthetic intervention. Selected for the display of imperial power, the *bela* became one of the sites to host the Delhi *Durbar* celebrations of 1911. Finally drained, the *bela* lands were cleared for the *Durbar* so that the King and Queen could address their audience from the Mughal *Jharokha* of the Fort.[159] This again attests to one of the main arguments made in this chapter. The 'improvement' of the natural landscape was an internally contested process, and reflected the designs and priorities of different agencies and departments. This final aesthetic clearance revealed the intervention of a different scale of government and its 'improvement' of the natural landscape.

CONCLUSION

We have seen that the 'improvement' of nature was a central feature of colonial governance after the rebellion of 1857, and it encompassed both the city and its suburbs. The improvement of gardens and plantations fulfilled multiple, and sometimes, contradictory aims such as ensuring the productivity of land in strictly economic terms, improving the health of suburban 'agricultural' populations, and imparting aesthetic effects. Political aims such as the moral upliftment of the natives and the colonial preservation of native 'rights and customs' were also espoused through the improvement and control of the natural landscape.

Yet, 'improvement' was a contested discourse within the state, with several authorities laying claims to the natural landscape simultaneously. In the light of these tensions, the outcomes of colonial interventions were often unpredictable. In certain cases, internal conflicts mounted severe challenges for colonial authorities. Disputes over jurisdictions and territory were a case in point. While civil agencies like the municipality and other district authorities sought to extend improvements of *nazul* lands outside the city, at different times, the overtures of the provincial authorities, and forest and military departments resisted their advances. Disputes over who would 'improve' the natural verdure, gardens and plantations reveal that the city was witness to multiple interventions that were bitterly contested among different colonial departments.

The point that has to be made, however, is that these clashes and challenges could also be productive. In Cracroft's case, De Renzy's critique established the primacy of a *particular* brand of colonial knowledge and expertise. Similarly, productivity can also be understood through the extension of civil designs for the control of the natural landscape. Rivalries between the civil agencies, such as that between the municipality and the forest department, for example, fuelled the former to extend control over the *bela* plantation and champion the 'rights and customs' of the natives. Last, another productive outcome was the continuation of improvement policies in the light of the sometimes conflicting colonial practices and knowledges. For example, it was always simpler for the municipality to continue conducting the 'improvement' of the *bela* by modifying its practices slightly than choose between the recommendations of either the sanitary officials or the forest department. Whether the melon grounds were to be removed or kept for soil fertility was unclear, given the claims of the two different authorities; and in recognition of this, the municipality chose to modify regional practices and carry out its improvements.

In the middle of these competing claims and tensions, it became acute for the colonial government to address questions of 'difference'. Major Tighe's aesthetic ornamentation of the Roshanara was a case in point. If we recall, Tighe privileged the interests of the colonial and native elite by designing a separate entrance to the Roshanara for the Civil Lines area. This, in his opinion, deserved priority, given the insignificant funds that were allocated by Cracroft towards the project. Indeed, for local officials like Tighe, it was sensible to privilege the rights of select groups on political considerations when the budget for improvements was so tight. Similarly, although the municipality championed indigenous rights to challenge the forest department, over the course of time, this stance shifted as it came to control the *bela* lands. The same native rights then seemed questionable, particularly in the context of the health of the troops and their sanitary welfare. The 'improvement' of nature was thus configured in the midst of the overlapping, and at times, contradictory colonial impulses.

NOTES

1. For a brief discussion on how the civilising programme changed over the course of colonial rule, see Michael Mann, 'Torchbearers Upon the Path of Progress: Britain's Ideology of Moral and Material Progress in India. An Introductory Essay', in *Colonialism as Civilising Mission: Cultural Ideology in British India*, ed. Harald Fischer-Tiné and Michael Mann (London: Anthem Press, 2004), 1–28.

2. David Arnold, 'Agriculture and Improvement in Early Colonial India: A Pre-History of Development', *Journal of Agrarian Change* 5, no. 4, 2005, 505–25. See also David Arnold, *The Tropics and the Traveling Gaze: India, Landscape and Science*, 1800–56 (New Delhi: Permanent Black, 2005).

3. Arnold, 'Agriculture and Improvement'; see also Arnold, 'The Tropics and the Travelling Gaze'.

4. In fact, Arnold argues that the groundwork for 'tropicalisation' had been laid even before the rebellion of 1857. Although he shows that there were tensions within this process, for example, a romantic fascination with India coexisted with harsher appraisals for the 'improvement' of its landscape, by the mid-century, the natural sciences had indeed served to appropriate the land for colonial transformation. Arnold allies himself with the historiography of tropical medicine and the work of historians like Mark Harrison, who suggest that by the 1820s, radical shifts in perceptions about the harshness of the Indian 'climate' contributed towards the idea of alterity of the tropics and its diseased environment. For the latter, see Mark Harrison, *Climates and Constitutions: Health, Race, Environment and British Imperialism in India, 1600–1850* (New Delhi: Oxford University Press, 1999).

5. Only recently has there been a move to reconsider the relationship between the city and its suburbs. For a brief discussion of this problematic, see Swati Chattopadhyay, 'Introduction: The Historical Legacy of the Suburbs in South Asia', *Urban History* 39, no. 1, 2012, 51–55. For studies that examine the fluidity and interconnections between the city and its provincial units, and the process of suburbanisation and identity in the colonial period, see Tania Sengupta, 'Between City and Country: Fluid Spaces of City and Provincial Administrative Towns in Nineteenth-century Bengal', *Urban History* 39, no. 1, 2012, 56–82; Preeti Chopra, 'Free to Move, Forced to Flee: The Formation and Dissolution of Suburbs in Colonial Bombay, 1750–1918', *Urban History* 39, no. 1, 2012, 83–107; and Nikhil Rao, *House but No Garden: Apartment Living in Bombay, 1898–1948*, PhD Thesis, University of Chicago, 2007.

6. Jyoti Hosagrahar, *Indigenous Modernities: Negotiating Architecture and Urbanism* (London: Routledge, 2005), 85.

7. Hosagrahar, *Indigenous Modernities*, 85.

8. Richard H. Drayton, *Nature's Government: Science, Imperial Britain and the Improvement of the World* (Yale: Yale University Press, 2000), xv.

9. Letter from A. Taylor, Civil Surgeon Delhi to Lt. Colonel McMahon, Commissioner and Superintendent, dated 2 April 1874, No. 11-15 A: No. 14, July 1874, NAI Home Sanitary.

10. Letter from D. B. Smith, Assistant Civil Surgeon, Delhi to Colonel Hamilton, Commissioner and Superintendent, Delhi, dated 26 October 1863, S. No. 163, 1863, Box 10, DSA CCO.

11. Harrison, *Climates and Constitutions*.

12. Harrison, *Climates and Constitutions*.

13. James Beattie, 'Imperial Landscapes of Health: Place, Plants, and People between India and Australia, 1800s–1900s', *Health and History* 14, no. 1, 2012, 100–20.

14. 'Aboriculture in India', *The Times of India*, 15 March 1872, 4 (Reproduced from *The Pioneer*, 13 March 1872).

15. Fredrick F. Wyman, *From Calcutta to the Snowy Range: Being the Narrative of a Trip through the Upper Provinces of India to the Himalayas Containing an Account of Monghyr, Benares, Allahabad, Cawnpore, Lucknow, Agra, Delhi and Simla* (London: Tinsley Brothers, 1866), 256.

16. Unlike the growing corpus of literature that examines the relationship between architecture and colonialism, gardens in colonial India have largely remained a neglected aspect of study. One notable exception that examines the linkages between gardening practices and colonial dominance is Eugenia. See W. Herbert, *Flora's Empire: British Gardens in India* (Pennsylvania: University of Pennsylvania Press, 2011).

17. Letter from A. C. C. De Renzy, Sanitary Commissioner, Punjab to the Secretary to Government, Punjab, dated 4 December 1873, No. 2 A, December 1873, Vol. 5, CSA Punjab Home Proceedings.

18. Anonymous, *The Mofussilite*, 10 May 1863, 302.

19. Fredrick C. Cooper, *The Handbook for Delhi: With Index and Two Maps, Illustrating the Historic Remains of Old Delhi and the Position of the British Army Before the Assault in 1857 &c. &c.* (Lahore: T. C. McCarthy, Lahore Chronicle Press, 1865), 125.

20. Letter from Lt. Col. Cracroft, Commissioner and Superintendent, Delhi to I. Frizelle, Officiating Deputy Commissioner, Delhi, dated 16 April 1874, 17/1874, DSA DCO.

21. Letter from Lt. Col. Cracroft, Commissioner and Superintendent, Delhi to the Deputy Commissioner, Delhi, dated 12 February 1874, 17/1874, DSA DCO.

22. Letter from Lt. Col. Cracroft, Commissioner and Superintendent, Delhi to the Deputy Commissioner, Delhi, dated 12 February 1874.

23. Letter from Lt. Col. Cracroft, Commissioner and Superintendent, Delhi to I. Frizelle, Officiating Deputy Commissioner, Delhi, dated 16 April 1874, 17/1874, DSA DCO.

24. Michael Mann and Samiksha Sehrawat, 'A City with a View: The Afforestation of the Delhi Ridge, 1883–1913', *Modern Asian Studies* 2, no. 43, 2009, 547.

25. Narayani Gupta, 'Delhi and its Hinterland: The Nineteenth and Early Twentieth Centuries', in *Delhi Through the Ages: Selected Essays in Urban History, Culture and Society*, ed. R. E. Frykenberg (New Delhi: Oxford University Press, 1994), 142.

26. Mann and Sehrawat, 'A City with a View', 549–50.

27. Letter from Lt. Col. Cracroft, Commissioner and Superintendent, Delhi to

I. Frizelle, Officiating Deputy Commissioner, Delhi, dated 16 April 1874, 17/1874, DSA DCO.

28. Letter from Lt. Col. Cracroft, Commissioner and Superintendent, Delhi to Col. R. Maclagan, Sec. to the Government, Punjab, dated 24 October 1872, 15/1872 No. 167, Box 70, Vol. 1, DSA DCO.

29. T. R. Metcalf, *Ideologies of the Raj* (Cambridge: Cambridge University Press, 1994), 159.

30. *The Mofussilite*, 21 May 1868, 7.

31. Letter from Lt. Col. Cracroft, Commissioner and Superintendent, Delhi, to the Secretary to the Government, Punjab, dated 24 Februry 1874, 15/1872 No. 167, Box 70, Vol. 2, DSA DCO.

32. D. Boyes Smith, *Report on Epidemic Cholera, as it Prevailed in the City of Delhi, at Goorgaon and the Surrounding Districts, During the Rainy Season of 1861* (Lahore: Government Press, 1861), 28.

33. See Chapter 2, this book.

34. Report on the Sanitary Survey of the North Western Suburbs of Delhi, dated 28 October 1873, Misc. 27/1873 Box 70, DSA DCO.

35. Report on the Sanitary Survey of the North Western Suburbs of Delhi, dated 28 October 1873.

36. Letter from Lt. Col. Cracroft, Commissioner and Superintendent, Delhi, to the Secretary to the Government, Punjab, dated 24 February 1874, 15/1872 No. 167, Box 70, Vol. 2, DSA DCO.

37. Letter from I. Frizelle, Offg. Deputy Commissioner, Delhi to Lt. Col. Cracroft, Commissioner and Superintendent, Delhi, dated 12 May 1874, 17/1874, DSA DCO.

38. Shama Mitra Chenoy, *Shahjahanabad: A City of Delhi 1638–1857* (New Delhi: Munshiram Manoharlal Publishers, 1998), 108–09. Gardens were, of course, part of a wider urban complex, comprising tombs, settlements, *bazaars* and *mohallas*, which linked the city to the suburbs. For a description, see Stephen Blake, *Shahjahanabad: The Sovereign City in Mughal India, 1639–1739* (Cambridge: Cambridge University Press, 1991), 57.

39. F. Bernier, *Travels in the Mogul Empire: AD 1656–1668* (Delhi: Low Price Publications, 2005), 242.

40. There is extensive literature on the form, functions and meanings of Mughal gardens. See, for example, Sheila Haywood and Susan Jellicoe, *The Gardens of Mughal India* (London: Thames and Hudson, 1972); J. L. Wescoat Jr. and J. W. Bulmahn (eds), *Mughal Gardens: Sources, Places and Representations* (Harvard: Harvard University Press, 1996); Ebba Koch, 'The Mughal Waterfront Garden' in *Gardens in the Time of the Great Muslim Empires*, ed.

Attilio Petruccioli (Leiden: Brill Publishers, 1997), 140–60; and Ebba Koch, *The Complete Taj Mahal and Riverfront Gardens of Agra*, (London: Thames and Hudson Ltd, 2006).

41. See J. F. Richards, 'The Historiography of Mughal Gardens', in *Mughal Gardens*, ed. Wescoat Jr. and Bulmahn, 259–66.

42. On the topic of access to gardens under Mughal rule, Irfan Habib suggests that instead of there being one policy for all imperial gardens, access was 'varied' in nature. So while the Taj Mahal, for example, may have been open to visitors and the poor who received alms there, the inner chamber containing the grave was closed off to everyone except a select audience. See I. Habib, 'Notes on the Economic and Social Aspects of Mughal Gardens', in *Mughal Gardens*, ed. Wescoat Jr. and Bulmahn, 127–38.

43. See Chapter 2, this book.

44. Report on the Administration of the Delhi Crown Lands, 1910, 10–11, 13-II Box 64, 1910, DSA CCO, Lahore.

45. Letter from Lt. Col. Cracroft, Commissioner and Superintendent, Delhi, to the Secretary to the Government, Punjab, dated 24 February 1874, 15/1872 No. 167, Box 70, Vol. 2, DSA DCO.

46. See Drayton, *Nature's Government*, 221–68.

47. Letter from Captain Bartholomew, Sec. Local Committee, Delhi to I. Frizelle, Offg. Deputy Commissioner and President, Local Committee, Delhi, dated 5 November 1874, 15/1872 No. 167, Box 70, Vol. 2, DSA DCO.

48. Letter from Lt. Col. Cracroft, Commissioner and Superintendent, Delhi, to the Secretary to the Government, Punjab, dated 24 February 1874, 15/1872 No. 167, Box 70, Vol. 2, DSA DCO.

49. C. A. Bayly, *Empire and Information: Intelligence Gathering and Social Communication in India, 1780–1870* (Cambridge: Cambridge University Press, 1996), 84.

50. Extract of Political Letter from Bengal, dated 17 November 1826, F/4/1028 No. 28168, OIOC.

51. Copy of a Letter from H. Middleton, Assistant in Charge of the Centre Division, to W. Fraser Esq. Deputy Superintendent of Delhi Territory, dated 16 February 1821, F/4/813 No. 21730, OIOC.

52. Extract of Political Letter from Bengal, dated 17 November 1826, F/4/1028 No. 28168, OIOC.

53. Letter from A. Benton Esq. Assistant Commissioner and Secretary, Local Fund Committee, to Lieutenant Colonel Cracroft, Commissioner and Superintendent, Delhi, dated 5 July 1873, 15/1872 No. 167, Box 70, Vol. 2, DSA DCO.

54. Letter from Captain Bartholomew, Sec. Local Committee, Delhi to I. Frizelle, Offg. Deputy Commissioner and President, Local Committee, Delhi, dated 5 November 1874.

55. Letter from Captain Bartholomew, Sec. Local Committee, Delhi to I. Frizelle, Offg. Deputy Commissioner and President, Local Committee, Delhi, dated 5 November 1874.

56. Letter from the Deputy Commissioner, Delhi, to Lieutenant Colonel Cracroft, Commissioner and Superintendent, Delhi, dated 19 November 1873, Misc. 19/1876, DSA DCO.

57. Even as the municipality gradually attained the control and management of *nazul* properties, it was constantly entangled in disputes with authorities such as the government of India over its use. Urban planning was one such exercise, where the two would clash incessantly over the question of *nazul* land; see Chapter 5, this book.

58. Letter from Captain Bartholomew, Sec. Local Committee, Delhi to I. Frizelle, Offg. Deputy Commissioner and President, Local Committee, Delhi, dated 5 November 1874.

59. Letter from Captain Bartholomew, Sec. Local Committee, Delhi to I. Frizelle, Offg. Deputy Commissioner and President, Local Committee, Delhi, dated 5 November 1874.

60. Letter from W. Smith Esq. Deputy Commissioner, Delhi to G. Davies, Commissioner and Superintendent, Delhi, dated 7 August 1876, 15/1872 No. 167, Box 70, Vol. 2, DSA CO. In the end, after two more years of waiting and deliberation, a cash payment of Rs 3,310 was paid jointly from the coffers of the Delhi Municipality and provincial authorities towards settling the compensation claims of those *Sardarakhtidars* who refused to accept *nazul* land in exchange for their entitlements inside the Roshanara.

61. Letter from A. C. C. De Renzy, Sanitary Commissioner, Punjab to the Secretary to Government, Punjab, dated 4 December 1873, No. 2 A, December 1873, Vol. 5, CSA Punjab Home Proceedings.

62. Letter from Major Tighe, Deputy Commissioner, Delhi, to Lt. Colonel Cracroft, Commissioner and Superintendent, Delhi, dated 23 November 1873, Misc. 19/1876, DSA DCO.

63. Letter from Major Tighe, Deputy Commissioner, Delhi, to Lt. Colonel Cracroft, Commissioner and Superintendent, Delhi, dated 2 January 1874, Misc. 19/1876, DSA DCO.

64. Letter from A. C. C. De Renzy, Sanitary Commissioner, Punjab to the Secretary to Government, Punjab, dated 4 December 1873, No. 2A, December 1873, Vol. 5, CSA Punjab Home Proceedings.

65. Letter from Lt. Col. Cracroft, Commissioner and Superintendent, Delhi to R. Maclagan, Sec. to the Government, Department of Public Works, Punjab, dated 24 October 1872, 15/1872 No. 167, Box 70, Vol. 1, DSA DCO.

66. Letter from A. C. C. De Renzy, Sanitary Commissioner, Punjab to the Secretary to Government, Punjab, dated 4 December 1873.

67. Letter from A. C. C. De Renzy, Sanitary Commissioner, Punjab to the Secretary to Government, Punjab, dated 4 December 1873.

68. Letter from A. C. C. De Renzy, Sanitary Commissioner, Punjab to the Secretary to Government, Punjab, dated 4 December 1873.

69. Bengal Military Department, *Report on Water Analysis in Bengal in 1866–67 and Dr Sheppard's Report on the Analysis of Delhi Water* (Calcutta: Miscellaneous Official Publications, 1867), 34.

70. Letter from A. C. C. De Renzy, Sanitary Commissioner, Punjab to the Secretary to Government, Punjab, dated 4 December 1873.

71. Letter from Major Tighe, the Deputy Commissioner, Delhi to Lt. Col. Cracroft, Commissioner and Superintendent, Delhi, dated 23 November 1873.

72. Letter from Lt. Col. Cracroft, Commissioner and Superintendent, Delhi to R. Maclagan, Sec. to the Government, Department of Public Works, Punjab, dated 24 October 1872.

73. Stephen Carr, *The Archaeological and Monumental Remains of Delhi* (New Delhi: Aryan Books International, 2002), 150–51.

74. C. M. Villiers Stuart, *Gardens of the Great Mughals* (London: Adam and Charles Black, 1913), 112.

75. Stuart, *Gardens of the Great Mughals*, 111–13.

76. G. R. Hearn, *The Seven Cities of Delhi* (London: W. Thacker & Co., 1906), 30.

77. A *bigha* is the unit for the measurement of land; 6.4 *bigha*s equals to 1 acre.

78. Letter from the Assistant Conservator of Forests, Punjab to Major McMahon, Deputy Commissioner, Delhi, dated 18 May 1869, 3/1882, DSA DCO.

79. Letter from the Deputy Commissioner, Delhi to the Commissioner and Superintendent, Delhi, n.d., 3/1882, DSA DCO.

80. Melon cultivation on the banks of the Yamuna was encouraged by the Mughals, and when the East India Company wanted to eject 'insanitary' trades from the vicinity of the city, Bahadur Shah Zafar, the last emperor, even petitioned in support of the melon cultivators. See *India Political Extracts*, dated 16 January 1850, OIOC E/4/803, P/290-1.

81. Cited in Narayani Gupta, *Delhi Between Two Empires: 1803–1931: Society, Government and Urban Growth* (New Delhi: Oxford University Press, 1981), 167.

82. Narayani Gupta, 'The Indomitable City', in *Shahjahanabad/Old Delhi:*

Tradition and Social Change, ed. E. Ehlers and T. Krafft (New Delhi: Manohar Books, 2003), 34.

83. Letter from Cap. W. Stenhouse, Offg. Conservator of Forests, Punjab, to the Officiating Secretary to the Government, Punjab, dated 7 July 1874, No. 4 A, OIOC P/135, Punjab Forest Proceedings.

84. For studies on the impact of the railways on Indian forests, see, for example, R. Guha, 'Forestry in British and Post-British India: An Historical Analysis', *Economic and Political Weekly* XVII, no. 44, 1983, 1882–96; and Pallavi V. Das, 'Railway Fuel and its Impact on the Forests in Colonial India: The Case of the Punjab, 1860–1884', *Modern Asian Studies* 47, no. 4, 2013, 1283–1309.

85. Das, 'Railway Fuel and its Impact', 1290–95.

86. Das, 'Railway Fuel and its Impact', 1290–95.

87. Letter from Cap. W. Stenhouse, Offg. Conservator of Forests, Punjab, to the Officiating Secretary to the Government, Punjab, dated 7 July 1874.

88. Letter from B. H. Powell, Conservator of Forests to the Secretary to Government of Punjab, dated 14 June 1872, No. 1A, December 1875, OIOC P/135: Punjab Forest Proceedings.

89. Letter from Lt. Col. Cracroft, Commissioner and Superintendent, Delhi to the Secretary to the Government, Punjab, dated 22 March 1873, No. 1A, December 1875, OIOC P/135: Punjab Forest Proceedings.

90. Letter from Lt. Col. Cracroft, Commissioner and Superintendent, Delhi to the Secretary to the Government, Punjab, dated 22 March 1873.

91. Letter from the Deputy Commissioner, Delhi, to the Commissioner and Superintendent, Delhi, dated 18 May 1869, 3/1882, DSA DCO.

92. Letter from Lt. Col. Cracroft, Commissioner and Superintendent, Delhi to the Secretary to the Government, Punjab, dated 22 March 1873.

93. Conflicts between civil authorities and forest departments over the use of forested land were common in other parts of colonial India. These were exacerbated by the Forest Act, 1878, which was ironically meant to give more power to foresters. See Ravi Rajan, 'Imperial Environmentalism or Environmental Imperialism? European Forestry, Colonial Foresters and the Agendas of Forest Management in British India 1800–1900', in *Nature and the Orient: The Environmental History of South and Southeast Asia*, ed. Richard Grove, Vinita Damodran and Satpal Sangwan (Delhi: Oxford University Press, 1998), 354–55.

94. Letter from the Deputy Commissioner, Delhi to the Commissioner and Superintendent, Delhi, n.d., 3/1882, DSA DCO.

95. Letter from the Deputy Commissioner, Delhi to the Commissioner and Superintendent, Delhi, n.d.

96. Letter from the Deputy Commissioner, Delhi to the Commissioner and Superintendent, Delhi, n.d.

97. Letter from the Deputy Commissioner, Delhi to the Commissioner and Superintendent, Delhi, n.d.

98. Letter from the Deputy Commissioner, Delhi to the Commissioner and Superintendent, Delhi, n.d.

99. Letter from the Deputy Commissioner, Delhi to the Commissioner and Superintendent, Delhi, n.d.

100. Letter from B. B. Powell, Conservator of Forests, Punjab, to the Commissioner and Superintendent Delhi, dated 19 April 1872, OIOC P/135, Punjab Forest Proceedings.

101. Letter from B. B. Powell, Conservator of Forests, Punjab, to the Commissioner and Superintendent Delhi, dated 19 April 1872.

102. Letter from B. Ribbentrop, Deputy Conservator of Forests, Plantation Division, Punjab to the Deputy Commissioner, Delhi, dated 24 February 1873, 3/1882, DSA DCO.

103. Letter from Lt. Col. Cracroft, Commissioner and Superintendent, Delhi, to the Secretary to the Government, Punjab, dated 27 January 1874, 3/1882, DSA DCO.

104. Letter from Lt. Col. Cracroft, Commissioner and Superintendent, Delhi, to the Secretary to the Government, Punjab, dated 27 January 1874.

105. Letter from Lt. Col. Cracroft, Commissioner and Superintendent, Delhi Division, to Lt. Col. Young, Deputy Commissioner, Delhi, dated 16 May 1873, 3/1882, DSA DCO.

106. Letter from Lt. Col Cracroft, Commissioner and Superintendent, Delhi Division, to Lt. Col. Young, Deputy Commissioner, Delhi, dated 16 May 1873.

107. Letter from Lt. Col. Cracroft, Commissioner and Superintendent, Delhi Division, to the Secretary to the Government, Punjab, dated 27 January 1874, 3/1882, DSA DCO.

108. Letter from Lt. Col. Cracroft, Commissioner and Superintendent, Delhi Division, to the Secretary to the Government, Punjab, dated 27 January 1874.

109. Letter from J. E. Miller, Secretary to the Financial Commissioner, Punjab to the Officiating Secretary to the Government, Punjab, dated 6 November 1868, 610, B-29, Vol. 1, DSA CCO.

110. Letter from Lt. Col. Birch, Deputy Commissioner, Delhi to the Commissioner and Superintendent, Delhi, dated 14 October 1878, 610, B-29, Vol. 1, DSA CCO.

111. Report on the Delhi Plantation by the Forest Department—Letter from G. Minninkend, Assistant Conservator of Forests, Plantation Division, Punjab,

to the Conservator of Forests, Punjab, dated 25 June 1878, 610, B-29, Vol. 1, DSA CCO.

112. Report on the Delhi Plantation by the Forest Department—Letter from G. Minninkend, Assistant Conservator of Forests, Plantation Division, Punjab, to the Conservator of Forests, Punjab, dated 25 June 1878.

113. Letter from G. Smyth, Deputy Commissioner, Delhi to F. Birch, Commissioner and Superintendent, Delhi Division, dated 3 August 1880, 610, B-29, Vol. 1, DSA CCO.

114. Christopher Otter, 'Locating Matter: The Place of Materiality in Urban History', in *Material Powers: Cultural Studies, History and the Material Turn*, ed. Tony Bennett and Patrick Joyce (New York: Routledge, 2010), 46.

115. Proceedings of the Sanitary Board assembled at Delhi for the Purpose of Enquiring into the Sanitary Condition of the Environs of the Fort by Order of Col. W. Hunter, dated 14 May 1880, 3/1882, DSA DCO.

116. Proceedings of the Sanitary Board assembled at Delhi for the Purpose of Enquiring into the Sanitary Condition of the Environs of the Fort by Order of Col. W. Hunter, dated 14 May 1880.

117. Letter from G. Smyth, Deputy Commissioner, Delhi to F. Birch, Commissioner and Superintendent, Delhi Division, dated 3 August 1880, 610, B-29, Vol. 1, DSA CCO.

118. As suggested in Chapter 1, while there were tensions between civil and military authorities after the rebellion, the need for military security forced the two to cooperate, and it was in this context that an unwieldy system of compensation was created. From time to time, cooperation or lines of communication also broke down between the two departments, particularly over issues such as the removal of the city wall. See Narayani Gupta, 'Military Security and Urban Development: A Case Study of Delhi 1857–1912', *Modern Asian Studies* 5, no. 1, 1971, 61–77.

119. Letter from G. Smyth, Deputy Commissioner, Delhi to F. Birch, Commissioner and Superintendent, Delhi Division, dated 3 August 1880, 610, B-29, Vol. 1, DSA CCO.

120. Copy of a letter from the Conservator of Forests, Punjab to the Secretary to the Government, Punjab, dated 2 March 1881, 610, B-29, Vol. 1, DSA CCO.

121. Copy of a letter from the Conservator of Forests, Punjab to the Secretary to the Government, Punjab, dated 2 March 1881.

122. Copy of a letter from the Conservator of Forests, Punjab to the Secretary to the Government, Punjab, dated 2 March 1881.

123. Copy of a letter from the Conservator of Forests, Punjab to the Secretary to the Government, Punjab, dated 2 March 1881.

124. Copy of a letter from the Conservator of Forests, Punjab to the Secretary to the Government, Punjab, dated 2 March 1881.

125. Drayton, *Nature's Government*, 235.

126. Drayton, *Nature's Government*, 235–36.

127. Letter from the Sanitary Commissioner of Punjab to the Secretary to the Government, Punjab, dated 24 September 1880, 610, B-29, Vol. 1, DSA CCO.

128. Report on the Delhi Plantation by the Forest Department, Letter from G. Minninkend, Assistant Conservator of Forests, Plantation Division, Punjab, to the Conservator of Forests, Punjab, dated 25 June 1878, 610, B-29, Vol. 1, DSA CCO.

129. Letter from the Sanitary Commissioner of Punjab to the Secretary to the Government, Punjab, dated 24 September 1880, 610, B-29, Vol. 1, DSA CCO.

130. As K. Sivaramakrishnan has argued, these patterns of conflict and regional distinctions constituted the very domain of 'scientific forestry'. See K. Sivaramakrishnan, *Modern Forests: Statemaking and Environmental Change in Colonial Eastern India* (California: Stanford University Press, 1999).

131. Copy of a Letter from the Secretary to the Municipal Committee to T. Y. Smyth, Deputy Commissioner, Delhi, dated 20 April 1881, 610, B-29, Vol. 1, DSA CCO.

132. C. F. Andrews, *Zaka Ullah of Delhi* (Oxford: Oxford University Press, 2003), 25.

133. Proceedings of a Special Meeting of the Delhi Municipal Committee, dated 22 November 1897, 84-1897/8 Box 54, DSA CCO.

134. See T. R. Metcalf, 'Past and Present: Towards and Aesthetics of Colonialism', in *Paradigms of Indian Architecture: Space and Time in Representation and Design*, ed. G. H. R Tillotson (London: Curzon Press, 1998), 12–25.

135. Stuart, *Gardens of the Great Mughals*, viii.

136. Copy of a Letter from W. C. Rennouf, Director of Agriculture, Punjab, to the Secretary to the Government, Punjab, dated 10–11 November 1909, No. 4-11 A: No. 4, December 1909, OIOC P/8121 Punjab Revenue and Agriculture Proceedings, Agriculture.

137. Preliminary Note by W. C. Rennouf, Director of Agriculture, Punjab to Create and Train a Subordinate Gardening Service in the Punjab and to Transfer One or Two Members of the Existing Staff of European Gardeners in Punjab, n.d., No. 6, OIOC P/8121 Punjab Revenue and Agriculture Proceedings, Agriculture.

138. Stuart, *Gardens of the Great Mughals*, x.

139. Gupta, *Delhi Between Two Empires*, 167.

140. Letter from Major, C. J. Parsons, Deputy Commissioner, Delhi to A. Meredith,

Commissioner and Superintendent, Delhi Division, dated 3 June 1904, 610, B-29, 1872, Box 16, Vol. 2, DSA CCO.

141. Letter from Major, C. J. Parsons, Deputy Commissioner, Delhi to A. Meredith, Commissioner and Superintendent, Delhi Division, dated 3 June 1904.

142. Letter from Major, C. J. Parsons, Deputy Commissioner, Delhi to A. Meredith, Commissioner and Superintendent, Delhi Division, dated 3 June 1904.

143. Letter from Major, C. J. Parsons, Deputy Commissioner, Delhi to A. Meredith, Commissioner and Superintendent, Delhi Division, dated 3 June 1904.

144. Letter from Major, C. J. Parsons, Deputy Commissioner, Delhi to A. Meredith, Commissioner and Superintendent, Delhi Division, dated 3 June 1904.

145. Letter from Major, C. J. Parsons, Deputy Commissioner, Delhi to A. Meredith, Commissioner and Superintendent, Delhi Division, dated 3 June 1904.

146. Letter from Major, C. J. Parsons, Deputy Commissioner, Delhi to A. Meredith, Commissioner and Superintendent, Delhi Division, dated 3 June 1904.

147. Copy of a Letter from the Conservator of Punjab to the Secretary to the Government, Punjab, dated 2 March 1881, 610, B-29, 1872, Box 16, Vol. 1, DSA CCO.

148. Letter from Colonel Barnett, Officer Commanding Royal Engineers to the Deputy Commissioner of Delhi, dated 4 March 1905, 20/1905, DSA CCO.

149. Copy of a Letter from the Secretary of the Grass Farm Committee, Meerut, to the Assistant Adjutant General, Seventh Division, dated 24 May 1905, 20/1905, DSA CCO.

150. Note from J. Addison, Secretary of the Delhi Municipality, dated 13 March 1906, 20/1905, DSA CCO.

151. Note from J. Addison, Secretary of the Delhi Municipality, dated 13 March 1906.

152. Report on the *Bela* Plantation at Delhi, Report of the Committee Appointed to Investigate the Question of Sanitary Condition of the Fort at Delhi and its Surroundings, 6, 610, B-29, 1872, Box 16, Vol. II, DSA CCO.

153. Till the late-1890s, colonial medical practitioners in India tenaciously held onto the notion that the local environment and habits of Indians were responsible for its 'tropical' diseases. Attempts were even made to integrate newer perspectives on parasitology and bacteriological aetiologies into existing views of the Indian disease environment. See Mark Harrison, 'Tropical Medicine in Nineteenth Century India', *The British Journal for the History of Science* 25, no. 3, 1992, 299–318.

154. Report of the *Bela* Plantation at Delhi, Letter from A. Meredith, Commissioner, Delhi Division, to the Secretary to the Government, Punjab, dated 4 February 1910, 8, 610, B-29, 1872, Box 16, Vol. II, DSA CCO.

155. Report of the *Bela* Plantation at Delhi, Letter from A. Meredith, Commissioner, Delhi Division, to the Secretary to the Government, Punjab, dated 4 February 1910, 1.

156. Report of the *Bela* Plantation at Delhi, Letter from A. Meredith, Commissioner, Delhi Division, to the Secretary to the Government, Punjab, dated 4 February 1910.

157. Copy of an Inspection Note by Mr D. W. Aikman, Sanitary Engineer to the Government, Punjab, on the Sanitary Condition of the Ground known as '*Bela*' Near the Fort at Delhi, n.d., 610, B-29, 1872, Box 16, Vol. II, DSA CCO.

158. Copy of an Inspection Note by Mr D. W. Aikman, Sanitary Engineer to the Government, Punjab, on the Sanitary Condition of the Ground known as '*Bela*' Near the Fort at Delhi, n.d.

159. Gupta, *Delhi Between Two Empires*, 167.

4

Claiming the 'Queen's Highways'

The Street, Ritual Precedence and Public Order

INTRODUCTION

The street, as we have seen from the Delhi municipality's perspective, was a 'public' space, and this meant that a series of social activities and built structures were categorised as 'nuisances' or 'encroachments', and they came under the surveillance of the municipal staff and officials. Yet, the street was also a space of ritual and symbolic demonstration, as it had been so long before the arrival of the British. Festivals and processions were ways in which different social groups asserted themselves and contested one another's authority. Under colonial rule, the colonial government attempted to steer clear of interfering in 'public arena' activities like processions.[1] Colonial administrations did, of course, lay out the times and routes for such activities, and prepared policing arrangements for what were understood to be ostensibly 'religious' observances on the streets.[2] However, as this chapter shows, in the aftermath of the rebellion of 1857, there was a perceptible tension between such concerns for religious tolerance and public order on the streets. This was particularly acute when it came to the processions of social groups, which were previously marginal entities in the ceremonial and spatial structure of the city. The colonial paranoia of 'disorder' in the wake of the rebellion, and concerns of religious tolerance, it is suggested, was foundational to future struggles over the right to use the streets, as it hierarchised ceremonial precedence and spatial practices in Delhi.

Examining a series of petitions made between 1863 and 1875 by the Jain Saraogis in Delhi, this chapter traces how claims were made to overcome this ceremonial and spatial precedence. The Saraogis used their status as imperial subjects to appraise colonial power carefully and demonstrate the compatibility of their *rath yatra* with conceptions of public order and conduct. Their agency, this chapter suggests, was reflected in their judgement of particular colonial practices and policies, their ability to invert colonial categories and demand direct state interference in urban matters, and crucially, to shift to different registers of power, so that the actions of the local colonial government in Delhi could be critiqued effectively. The following section starts by delineating the hierarchies of ceremonial precedence, as they existed in cities like Delhi to suggest the importance of the street as a reason for mobilisation and action on behalf of contending social groups.

HIERARCHIES OF THE 'STREET': PROCESSIONS AND PRECEDENCE IN PRE-COLONIAL CITIES

Katherine Prior's work on how the early colonial codification of 'precedence' intensified rivalries between communities over public religious displays is useful to understand the spatiality of conflicts both before and during early colonial rule. Prior argues that towns and cities in pre-colonial India had a 'corporate tone' that reflected the political and economic strength of their inhabitants.[3] She gives several examples to suggest that one community's festival, monument or celebration stood out as the foremost in cities and that people were cognisant of this. This, however, did not necessarily mean that other communities were 'suppressed'; rather, it suggested that they knew that they could only use their public symbols and celebrate their festivals within acceptable limits. Thus, up until the time when the Mughal emperor ruled in cities like Delhi, for example, the corporate tone was largely Muslim, and *Id-ul-Fitr* was the ceremony that dominated the proceedings and in which both Hindus and Muslims participated.[4] Crucially, no written records were kept in order to allow for flexibility in local negotiations, that is, so that the corporate tone could be reworked according to a change in fortunes of contending social groups.[5]

Extending Prior's arguments about the corporate tone of public displays is extremely helpful at a spatial level in order bring back an emphasis on the street. If the ceremonies and processions of dominant social groups held sway in the city, they were performed in the largest streets or thoroughfares.[6] As Narayani Gupta suggests, when it came to formal processions in Delhi, the capital of the Mughal Empire, 'the use of the street was the privilege of the ruler'.[7] During major or dominant festivals like *Id-ul-Fitr* or *Muharram* in pre-colonial Delhi, processions took place in thoroughfares like Chandni Chowk, and those of other social groups were confined to smaller streets or neighbourhoods. Indeed, this explains why archival evidence suggests that in the aftermath of the rebellion of 1857, newer social groups wishing to capitalise on Queen Victoria's proclamation of 1858 petitioned the authorities for access to *particular* streets and thoroughfares for their processions.[8] Requests for new *rath yatras* to pass through Chandni Chowk, and the latter's categorisation as a 'public' street in petitions would indicate that spatial practices were hierarchised in the urban environment of Delhi. Moreover, post-1857, these instances were deemed as being compatible with new conceptions of 'public-ness'.[9] It must be stressed that once the dominant procession ended, the streets acquired different meanings, associated with work or other accustomed activities.[10] In other words, the street returned to its position as a social space once processions such as *Id-ul-Fitr* and *Muharram* were over.

The examples highlighted above attest to the fact that the street was as much a reason for mobilisation and action as the space upon which the action was performed.[11] In order to shape the corporate tone of a town or a city, it was the main streets or thoroughfares that had to be controlled by contending social groups through their processions. A focus on the street helps to contextualise the growing rivalries between contending social groups in the nineteenth century, and for the specific purpose of this chapter, contextualises the case of the Jain Saraogis in Delhi.

COLONIAL GOVERNANCE AND THE JAINS IN PRE-REBELLION DELHI

The Jains were one of many social groups that had a long history in Delhi. Jain migration to the city increased substantially under Mughal rule, particularly during the reign of Shah Jahan.[12] With the revitalisation of trade networks and connections during the eighteenth century, the Jains were able to establish a strong mercantile presence in Delhi, along with others like the Agarwals, Khatris and Punjabi Muslims.[13] As a visible manifestation of their increasing wealth, rich Jain merchants lavished huge sums on the construction of temples and other structures. C. A. Bayly suggests that between 1780 and 1820, for example, Jain merchants had spent more than Rs 25 lakh on religious edifices and urban facilities in Delhi.[14] This included the construction of the *Naya Mandir* (new temple) in the prosperous locality of Dharampura, not far from Chandni Chowk, in 1807, which came at the cost of Rs 8 lakh.[15] The contribution of the Jain merchants is even more significant during this period, as this was an era in which there was an overall decline in the construction of royal buildings in Delhi.[16]

It is important to mention here that in cities like Delhi, the Jains married into Vaishnavite Hindu families and maintained close personal and professional ties with them. As both Douglas Haynes and Bayly point out, in urban areas, Jains with their various sub-sects, could and did partake in the ritual activities, domestic observances and festivals of the Vaishnavite Hindus, both being of the same broad caste, that is, Bania grouping.[17] Indeed, at one level, the fluid nature of Jain identity allowed their participation in many shared local activities and ritual practices.[18] However, this accommodative character could be upset when it came to shaping the 'corporate tone' in towns and cities. As new arrivals from western India, rich Jain merchants did try to upset the balance of local ceremonial precedence in north Indian cities, and they certainly played a significant role in urban conflicts.[19] While struggles over ceremonial precedence were not simply of a material character, these were ways in which new social groups like the Jains could try and rework the 'corporate tone' of the city and announce their arrival in a new urban context.[20]

In Delhi, however, this area was also one in which the Jains were least successful. As mentioned earlier, any desire to make a statement in the city meant that new processions or demonstrations would have to pass through the grandest streets and thoroughfares of Delhi. Although the establishment of the British residency in 1803 and the waning power of the Mughals created opportunities for the Jains to push ahead with their processions, colonial fears of 'disorder' prevented the realisation of such actions. For example, in 1807, a Jain banker attempted to inaugurate the completion of the temple in Dharampura by holding a grand procession in Chandni Chowk. This sudden development was, however, thwarted by Muslim protesters who attacked the temple and occupied it.[21] In order to prevent reprisals, the then British resident of Delhi called his troops to take action and subsequently dispersed the rioters. In 1834, a similar attempt made by Jain merchants was only partially successful, as an inexperienced magistrate allowed the procession to pass through the main thoroughfares and streets, much to the consternation of Muslim protestors.[22] The procession, however, was eventually redirected to pass through smaller streets in the city.[23] On both occasions, thus, Jain attempts to rework the corporate tone were challenged by Muslim protestors to prevent the use of major streets and thoroughfares like Chandni Chowk from being used for processions other than *Id-ul-Fitr* and *Muharram*.

The role of the East India Company was no less significant in shaping these developments. As Michael Mann has argued, inexperienced officers and contradictory government orders created a climate of chaos for the British residency and contributed to the problems it faced in establishing law and order in early-nineteenth century Delhi.[24] Chapter 1 argued that official positions or administrative orders over the governance of urban property relations were shifting constantly, given the ideological predispositions of local officers before the rebellion. In the case of the Jain processions, a diffuse colonial apparatus represented by newly appointed magistrates with little knowledge of the hierarchy vis-à-vis street processions increased hostilities between social groups. As new authorities keen on governing through legal precedent, the officials invited social groups to come forward and prove their claims to the street.[25] In Prior's words, '[S]imply by their presence as a new authority, they opened up excellent opportunities for individuals and social groups to attempt to rework the public religious display in the favour of their community.'[26] If this triggered violence, the administration hastily reversed its decision to redirect processions to smaller streets. Eventually, the threat of violence was used to diffuse tensions.

The indeterminacy over the question of street processions continued after the rebellion of 1857. However, unlike the use of the rule of precedent, there were significant changes. Colonial fears of interfering in what were understood to be native rights, and in particular, 'religious' matters, led to the passing of resolutions such as Queen Victoria's Proclamation of 1858, which gave equal rights of religious observance to all. Crucially, this meant that in theory, all streets were open to the performance of 'religious' rituals, demonstrations and activities. However, with the rebellion still haunting the official mindset, a contradictory imperative, that is, the need to maintain urban 'order' on the streets, made way for heavy scrutiny of any activities that were thought to be dangerous to public security. As Thomas Metcalf suggests, after the rebellion of 1857, the British government found themselves in a reflection of contradiction, between vulnerability or anxiety, on the one hand, and mastery of India, on the other.[27] As will be suggested, these tensions affected practices of governance in Delhi and increased frictions with social groups like the Saraogi Jains for access to 'public' streets.

THE THREAT OF THE STREET AND THE PERFORMANCE OF 'RELIGION': COLONIAL RESPONSES TO SARAOGI PROCESSIONS

As we noted in Chapter 1, after the rebellion, once British forces captured the city, the Muslim population became a particular target of colonial reprisals. Muslim houses and religious structures were 'confiscated', and residents were kept from entering the city as a retributive measure.[28] An important shift linked to this was that established hierarchies with respect to the city streets were broken. In other words, the elimination of the Mughal elite and the ejection of almost the whole of the Muslim population meant that control over the major streets and thoroughfares of the city was thrown open to all groups for their processions. Moreover, this was reinforced by colonial ordinances proclaiming 'equal rights' of religious observance, a new political rationality predicated upon allowing natives to carry out their natural 'religious' functions.[29] One such group that sought to capitalise on the vacuum left by the absence of the Mughals were the Saraogi Jains.[30] The term 'Saraogi' would later be used by the British in censuses to ostensibly refer to the 'Digambara' sect of the Jains.[31] However, archival evidence of this period suggests that the category of the 'Saraogi' was used interchangeably with that of the 'Jain' in towns and cities of north India, and sometimes, was even preferred over it.[32]

The Saraogis, it has been suggested, were skilful at using colonial notions of citizenship and rights to demand their right to the use of public spaces after 1857. Also, interactions between them and the colonial government were marked by negotiations and dialogue, where the language of new colonial laws was applied in support.[33] Yet, when it came to allowing Saraogi *rath yatras*, local officials were themselves quite confused over whether permission was to be given, as questions of 'public order' *clashed* with understandings of 'religious tolerance'.[34] This increased conflicts between colonial authorities and the Saraogis, on the one hand, and between their rivals, on the other. We must understand the counter-claims of the Saraogis within this particular context.

In April 1863, Captain Miller, a newly appointed District Superintendent of Delhi, was approached by a group of Saraogis for permission to take their *rath yatra* through the 'principal streets' of the city.[35] After the rebellion, the authorities of Delhi decided that processions of an 'ordinary' character were to be allowed, and others were to be prohibited, given the ever-present colonial paranoia of disorder. Miller, in agreement with De Kantztow, the Magistrate of the city, decided to allow the Saraogi procession, convinced that it was 'unexceptional'. However, on the day of the procession, Mr Cooper, the Deputy Commissioner, was approached by a group of Brahmins in the city, who asked him to stop the Saraogi celebration by arguing that it was 'distasteful to their religious prejudices'. Cooper, fearing that the *rath yatra* had the potential to cause trouble, diverted it instead to a less-crowded route.[36] The hastiness with which the original decision was overturned suggests that there was much more ambiguity in the operations of the government. On the one hand, permission had been given to the Saraogis to conduct the *rath yatra* based on the fact that it was an ordinary religious ceremony. On the other hand, as soon as there were objections to the *yatra*, Cooper hurriedly changed its route to prevent any possible altercation. The local administration was caught in an awkward compromise between preserving public order and maintaining their avowed non-interference in religious events; and the outcome of this was a redirection of the *rath yatra* to an alternate route.

THE (UN)GOVERNABLE CITY

The Saraogis, for their part, had no doubt taken advantage of the situation by targetting Captain Miller, who was new to the city. Moreover, only a single day's notice was given to the administration to prepare for policing arrangements, and the *rath* was scheduled to proceed on the same day as another festival in the city.[37] Incensed by these findings, Commissioner Hamilton reiterated the need for 'strict discipline' in Delhi. Calling the whole event underhanded and aimed at causing 'public annoyance', Hamilton sought to end any future Saraogi *rath yatras* through the main streets of the city on grounds of security. He wrote in his report:

> Past experience has shown that the public exhibition of these ceremonies has ended in tumult, and although it is not probable that in the presence of a large military force and an effective police, and under the strict discipline which now prevails in the city, any popular outrage would take place, yet it cannot be doubted that the open performance of the proposed ceremonial processions would cause a bitter feeling of insult among the other and far more numerous sect of the population.[38]

As described by Gurpreet Bhasin, Hamilton and the local administration portrayed the Saraogis as 'cunning and unreasonable', and their celebrations were characterised as offensive to the customs of the Muslims and Hindus of the city.[39] In the interests of public order, Hamilton argued that any question of reopening the *rath yatra* case was to be 'authoritatively put down' in future, allowing no room for the Saraogis to represent their case.[40] However, a complete ban on the *rath yatra* could not be imposed without addressing the tricky question of the government's encroachment upon the 'religious' rights of the Saraogis. Hamilton's answer to this was tentative: he called the *rath yatra* an 'obsolete custom' and decreed that since it was only held on two occasions prior to 1863, it was not a part of the essential religious duties of the Saraogis. Only ceremonies of an 'ordinary' character, religious or otherwise, were to be allowed in future, unless of course, they were a threat to the peace and order of the city.[41]

Thus, Hamilton's categorisation of the Saraogi *rath yatra* as an 'obsolete custom' was a way to address the problems that arose from the contradictory practices of governance. We have already seen that the Jain *rath yatras* of 1807 and 1834 were a result of the pre-rebellion government's willingness that social groups come forward and demonstrate their claims to urban spaces. Hamilton's ban effectively reversed the previous policy and blocked access to places like Chandni Chowk for future Saraogi demonstration and processions.

The immediate spatial effect of this was to create a hierarchy or a tier of processional usages. Thoroughfares like Chandni Chowk and the streets passing through the Dariba, that is, the streets of primary importance for the processions of the Saraogis, were now restricted on grounds of 'public inconvenience'. In contrast, other celebrations like *Dussehra* and *Muharram*, for example, by virtue of being designated as purely 'religious' festivals, were given 'equal' access to the streets in contention. An example from a Tehsildari report in 1871 describes the hierarchised level of street processions and the position of the Saraogis within it. Sree Ram, a Tehsildar and Saraogi, was commissioned to write a detailed report on the grievances of the Saraogis. This move was in response to numerous petitions that had been received by the government in the years after the Saraogi *rath yatra* was banned. Sree Ram wrote in support of the petitioners:

> ... [T]he only ground for apprehending the alleged inconvenience is that crowds of people go to and from the Chandni Chowk and Dureeba where the Surrowgees wish to take their sacred idol, and this ground of public inconvenience, if it does really exist, exists in the case of the religious processions of all sects in general who are allowed to proceed in the above named streets without any restriction or disturbance especially on occasions of Mohurum and Dussera, festivals when a much greater concourse of people of all religions congregate to celebrate the processions.[42]

The Saraogis were, of course, permitted to host ceremonies or *rath yatras* in smaller streets and pass through smaller neighbourhoods, including where their perceived 'others' or rival groups lived. In other words, the point in contention became the Main Square. It was the desire to capture, as Sandria Freitag suggests, a 'maximum audience' for the display of power and strength, which was now denied to the Saraogis.[43] As Sree Ram eloquently summed up in his report to senior authorities:

> [The ban] relates only to the procession passing through a certain street of Delhi on a certain occasion, or in other words that it is not a general prohibition as

the Jainees or Surrowgees take their sacred car annually in one of the public streets of Delhi thickly inhabited by members of the Vaishnoo religion.[44]

For the Saraogis, colonial governance had thus created a spatial precedence quite similar to the pre-rebellion era. It was the contradictory practices of governance, and the result of competing understandings of 'public order' and 'religious rights' that were instrumental in creating a hierarchy of spatial practices. Labelled by the authorities as 'obsolete customs', the Saraogi processions were reduced to a marginal entity among public-arena activities. Moreover, in doing this, the colonial government's spatial interventions after the rebellion led to a breakdown of the relationships between the Saraogis and other social groups. Not only did spatial precedence embolden the Saraogis to challenge the government, but it also intensified the rivalry between them and other groups.

The Jains had married into Vaishnav households prior to the rebellion, and they maintained close personal and professional ties with Vaishnav families. At times, however, the relationship between the groups could also be strained, particularly as the competition to shape the corporate tone of the city intensified. A police report in Urdu that was filed regarding a confrontation between Jain and Vaishnav devotees in 1869, recalled that an outcome of the strained relationship between the two was that the Jains of the city of Delhi had stopped marrying their daughters into Vaishnav households, but had continued to receive Vaishnav brides.[45] With the ban on the Saraogi *rath yatras* and the subsequent creation of spatial precedence, the relationship between the two changed further. In 1870, for example, the Deputy Commissioner of Delhi would write that the Saraogis and Vaishnavs of the city had been at loggerheads with each other after the ban of the *rath yatra*. Significantly, he pointed out that the nature of the conflict had taken a 'religious' turn, unlike earlier. He wrote in his report:

> The bad feeling which exists between the vaishnus and saraogees, branches of the baniah caste exists in some towns and not others. It had its origin I believe in the report of one of the two sects to give their daughters in marriage to the members of the other sect but in the present day the enmity between the two parties is based on religious and not on social grounds.[46]

The colonial categorisation of the enmity between the Vaishnavs and the Saraogis as a 'religious' dispute thus highlights a new context after the ban on the *rath yatra*. Colonial officials often recorded tensions between rival groups in 'religious' or 'communal' terms.[47] Yet, colonial categorisations also provided the vocabularies to express grievances and address questions of access to public-arena activities.[48] The statement made by the Deputy Commissioner must also be put in the context of a changing vocabulary adopted by the Saraogis to voice their demands. The Saraogis' assertion of their presence had been through their processions or *rath yatras* through the city. However, as these began to be threatened, they increasingly framed their demands to access public spaces by suggesting that their 'religious' rights had been denied, while those of other groups had been upheld.[49] Saraogi claims to urban spaces, and in particular, the main streets of the city, are discussed in greater detail in the next section. However, it is important here to reiterate that the creation of spatial precedence directly shaped the content and form of the claims made by the Saraogis. For all its avowed neutrality in public-arena activities like processions, the colonial government instituted ceremonial precedence and spatial hierarchies in the aftermath of the rebellion.

VOCABULARIES OF THE STREET: COMPATIBILITY, PUBLIC ORDER AND POWER

The impasse between local authorities in Delhi and the Saraogis provides a window to examine the claims made by the latter to public spaces and the use of the street. To secure access to the main streets of the city, Saraogi petitioners not only appropriated new vocabularies to express their desire to engage in public-arena activities, but also used these vocabularies to appraise colonial power and authority.

Saraogis addressed numerous petitions to different levels of the colonial bureaucracy, ranging from provincial authorities to the imperial government in Calcutta after 1863. In this respect, an individual who became quite notorious for his petitioning was a man called Rickho Lal from Allahabad. Lal's petitions were made between 1863 and 1875 in both English and Urdu. Significantly, they carried a series of arguments demonstrating the compatibility of the Saraogi *rath yatra* with local arrangements, and stated the commonplace nature of their practices in other cities of India.[50] Lal stated on behalf of the Saraogi petitioners:

> We would take the liberty to state that our religious car the Rath of our God Parasnath, is paraded in every large town and city throughout India .... We had drawn our car even at Delhi through the several markets situated therein on different occasions and when the late king was residing in that city and had the practice which is prevalent among us been hurtful to the inhabitants the matter would have been forthwith brought to the notice of the authorities ...

He further stated:

> In the cities of Calcutta , Benares, Agra, Allahabad, Furrukabad, Allyghur, Ajmer, Sehrampore, Behar and others, the district officers often make the proper arrangements to prevent all unnecessary disputes and while this is done in those largest places we wonder how the commissioner of Dehlie [sic.] cannot make similar arrangements in his district where formerly his predecessors never hesitated to look after the very same affair.[51]

Significantly, Lal's petition points to the all-India character of the Saraogi *rath yatra* procession. Delhi is at once linked to administrative circuits across India, as part of a larger colonial domain. This regularity or 'ordinariness' of the celebration taking place in different cities challenges its prohibition by local authorities at Delhi by suggesting that they were deviating from official policies and practices.

The question of 'public convenience' was reiterated by colonial officials immediately after the Saraogi *rath yatra* of 1863, and it was constantly cited as a reason for why the *rath yatra* was not to pass through the streets and thoroughfares such as Chandni Chowk. Visions of 'disorderly' conduct and traffic bottlenecks haunted the colonial administration and were used as tactics to deter the Saraogis from asking for permission. Lal's petitions, however, show a willingness to engage with colonial conceptions of order and security on the streets. For example, in one of several petitions sent to the Under-Secretary to the government of India in November 1863, Lal argued:

> ... [T]he Rath is paraded in the city some two or three hours only, and this can interrupt no traffic, more especially when we keep our own arrangements

to guard against any accident. In the cities of Calcutta, Benares, Agra, and Allahabad, & c. the district officers often make the proper arrangement to prevent all unnecessary disputes, and while this is done in these largest places, we wonder how the Commissioner of Dehlie [*sic.*] cannot make similar arrangement in his district, where formerly, his predecessors never hesitated to look after the very same affairs.[52]

One of the ways in which the Saraogis tried to convey a new relationship with urban space was by arguing that their ceremonies were orderly and regulated movements. They had no problem incorporating notions of orderly traffic or movement, one of the tropes of colonial modernity; they provided a breakdown of the hours and security arrangements for their procession. Moreover, by adopting these categories, Saraogis like Lal attempted to challenge what they saw as an aberration or inconsistency in state practice in Delhi. From this statement, we find that conceptions of 'public order' and 'religious rights' are mobilised together to critique practices of colonial governance. Indeed, this was not a form of outright resistance to colonial rule; rather, it was a careful appraisal of certain practices and a dismissal of others.

A second petition sent a month later by Lal, in December 1863, highlighted this question about the accountability of local authorities more clearly. By using the Queen's Proclamation of 1858, Lal and the petitioners attempted to disavow the conduct of local officials in Delhi, but only in the particular context of the *rath yatra*. Lal wrote:

We beg [further] to state that where people of one denomination raise objections for the religious performances of another, the district officers should, after enquiry, do justice to both sects for their satisfaction .... We also beg to represent that the proclamation of Her Majesty does not direct interference on the part of the district officials with the religious ceremonies of the natives of India, but the authorities at Delhi have acted quite contrary to the dictates of her Majesty's Proclamation in this instance.[53]

Here, Lal and others cite the particular instance of the ban as going against Queen Victoria's proclamation. Imperial subjecthood is evoked and even extolled to challenge the stance of the local authorities in the case of access to the street. Moreover, if we recollect, Hamilton's rejection of the Saraogi *rath yatra* was on the basis of its 'obsoleteness', that is, its 'difference' from ceremonies of the Vaishnav Hindus. Here, colonial conceptions of justice were used to address the similarity of the Saraogi street procession with that of other 'sects'.[54] These responses show how Saraogis like Lal fashioned themselves as imperial subjects whose rights of equal access to the streets had been injured. Throughout the 1860s, their petitions stated the 'ordinary' nature of their *rath yatra* processions, and importantly, used this to state that their conduct was as expected of native celebrations on the streets.

Lal's petitions from 1863 also reveal an astute awareness of how the logic of numerical representation could be used to influence colonial authorities. Large demonstrations and processions, as mentioned earlier, were an integral part of the pre-colonial landscape, and a huge number of spectators participated in festive events in the city. Colonial rule, however, brought with it new systems of enumeration and a reliance on censuses, which were used to elucidate the 'cultural difference' of India.[55] As a tactic to underline the 'difference' of the Saraogis from other groups, Hamilton and other local authorities in Delhi argued that the majority of the population in Delhi did not want a Saraogi procession.[56] The fact that the Saraogis were a minority in the city was reason enough for Hamilton to forbid the *rath yatra* from passing through the main streets and thoroughfares like Chandni Chowk.[57] However, while Lal and other petitioners did not challenge that they were a minority in Delhi, they quantified their presence to suggest that they numbered 'several thousands' in the city.[58] This was significant, they argued, since their numerical presence in Delhi was more than in other smaller towns where Saraogis had been granted permission for a grand *rath yatra* through the main streets and squares.[59]

'Numbers', as argued in the earlier chapters, constituted a source of tension between the colonial government and its loyal supporters, particularly since they could be interpreted and deployed in many different ways.[60] In the case of the Saraogis, numbers were again used creatively to suggest that the Saraogis were indeed a minority, but a minority group that had the largest numerical presence in Delhi, as opposed to other areas where they had been given permission. The denial of the choice of their procession to this large a minority group was a carefully constructed argument and was used by the Saraogis to buttress their claims for the right to use the main streets of the city. In other words, they accepted their minority status but redeployed to lay claims to public spaces.

THE 'QUEEN'S HIGHWAYS': CONFRONTATIONS AND SARAOGI RESPONSES

By the early 1870s, evidence presented by the Saraogis to suggest that their *rath yatra* was compatible with notions of public order was partially successful in making local officials in Delhi change their opinion about the case. However, this also represented a shift in tactics on the part of local colonial authorities to address the challenges thrown up by the Saraogis. In 1872, for example, the Deputy Commissioner of Delhi was inundated with petitions from Saraogis like Lal, which were, in his words, becoming very 'loud and frequent'.[61] The ban on the Saraogi *rath yatra*s was significant as it increased hostilities between the Saraogis and the Vaishnav Hindus. The Saraogis had effectively severed all ties with the Vaishnav Hindus over the issue of being banned from using the main streets of the city for their *rath yatra*. Colonial officials in Delhi sought to use this tension to their advantage by suggesting that only when the Vaishnavs and the Saraogis would agree to discuss the details of the *rath yatra* together, would it be feasible to allow it. In the words of the Deputy Commissioner, it was perhaps best to have

> ... [a] meeting of the heads of the two contending sects but only about half a dozen of each so as not to have a noisy rabble and after listening to the arguments of each side to attempt a simple 'give and take solution' i.e. to make each party withdraw some of their objections for after all if the procession is allowed in other large cities there seems to be no reason why the same should not be allowed here.[62]

This was, of course, an attempt for the authorities to stand above the fray. By suggesting that questions of religion were *private* matters and if an agreement for the *rath* had to be reached, compromises had to be made between disputing parties and not arbitrated by the colonial government. For all intents and purposes, mediation in such cases was entrusted to those deemed to be 'natural leaders' of their religious groupings, and it was preferred that agencies like *panchayat*s (village councils, here with possible reference to those in the Delhi district) resolve what were assumed to be intra-caste disputes.[63] This was a measure that Saraogis like Lal were uncomfortable with.[64] There is little archival detail to suggest why exactly the Saraogis were reluctant to take up their case in the *panchayat*s, except that this was where they felt they lacked influence.[65] Perhaps on the basis of their relatively smaller numerical presence in the city, the Saraogis felt incapable of representing themselves in *panchayat* associations.

However, Saraogi refusals to participate in the *panchayat* discussions were turned around strategically to reinforce the need of the colonial government to intervene directly in the case of the *rath yatra*. For example, in 1871, Lal, who had been championing the Saraogi cause since 1863, was informed by the Secretary of State for India that the Saraogi case was one for the *panchayat*s to settle and that the government would not side with any party on the *rath yatra* issue. Lal responded by petitioning to the Deputy Commissioner of Delhi. He wrote:

> I can't say that this case will be settled in the Punchait because both parties are not equal, as the Baishnavies and Khutries are at liberty to hold their religious matters at any time they like while we are deprived of our right which pleases them as it is a custom to hate to see the religious rites of others .... Therefore, I hope you will do something yourself in this case then it may be settled easily, as on the public road no one has such power to interfere in religious matters as the local authorities.[66]

It is significant here how Lal represents the authority over the 'public road'. William J. Glover suggests that 'public space', a novel concept that only appeared with colonialism in India, was used as a medium by Indians to translate longer-standing spatial practices and traditions. He cites examples from Punjab to show that unlike conceptions of 'public good' in British legal traditions, Indian petitioners translated authority over the 'public' as accruing from superior might rather than from benevolent governance when making claims against the colonial government.[67] In the case of the Saraogis, we have a similar example, but where the petitioners in Delhi advanced the authority of colonial government over the 'public road' as absolute in order to delegitimise the working of associations where they had little influence. The petitioners took on a subordinate position with respect to their rivals in the case of the *panchayat*s. This was similar to when they called themselves a large minority in 1863. However, in doing so, they called upon the government to protect their rights since only the government possessed outright power and superiority over 'public' road. 'Difference' from other groups was again evoked, but the colonial government was called upon as the supreme arbitrator that could police such differences.

Not only do colonial records provide petitions of Saraogi representatives like Lal, but they also contain traces of counter-claims made by the Vaishnav Hindus of Delhi. The growing confidence of the Saraogis and the ongoing struggle between the two parties made the Vaishnav Hindus challenge Saraogi attempts to attain ritual precedence. A sophisticated use of interpretations of public conduct is also to be seen in their arguments. For example, in 1870, Vaishnav petitioners voiced their own grievances to government authorities. They argued that a future Saraogi procession would undoubtedly bring numerous devotees to Delhi, and this had the potential to spread diseases in the city.[68] Presumably knowing the concerns that colonial officials had concerning sanitation, this argument was used to discredit any large Saraogi processions.

In a similar fashion, a second charge levied by the Vaishnav petitioners was that the Saraogi idol was 'indecent' and to parade it in the main streets would greatly offend them. The petitioners deemed that the only way the parade of the Saraogi idol, *Parasnath*, would be accepted in their *rath yatra* was if 'suitable arrangements' were made to dress the naked figure of the god.[69] It becomes clear from these petitions that they were willing to reach an agreement on the *rath yatra*, but on terms that were difficult for the Saraogis to accept.[70] To call the Saraogi idol and their procession 'indecent' was a way of appropriating understandings of public conduct and dismissing threats.

The response of the Saraogi petitioners to the charge levied by the Vaishnavs is equally significant as it highlights the way questions of 'difference' were redeployed by them for access to public spaces. For example, in 1872, two Saraogi petitioners called Jy Singh and Dhoom Singh sent a letter to the Deputy Commissioner in Delhi.[71] Their petition was sent a few days before the annual Ramlila celebrations were to take place. Both petitioners claimed that the festival of Ramlila, patronised by the Vaishnavs, was accompanied by fireworks and it brought a large number of people into the city. Significantly, they argued that this also had the potential to spread sickness and that the Saraogi *rath yatra* would thus not be out of the ordinary if it were allowed.[72]

By arguing that disease and sickness could result when people came to the city to take part in other ceremonies, the Saraogis accepted the colonial position that religious celebrations in India had the potential to spread diseases. However, since the Vaishnavs were allowed to host their potentially threatening ceremonies, the Saraogis demanded that they, too, should be given 'equal indulgence' to hold their *rath yatra*.[73] In other words, the celebrations of both parties had equal potential to spread disease in the city, and thus, the Saraogis needed to be given permission for their *yatra*. Conversely, if a ban on the *rath yatra* was to continue, the Vaishnav celebrations also had to be stopped.[74] By skilfully redeploying colonial arguments, the Saraogis made a bid for equal rights and challenged the Vaishnav petitioners.

Between 1871 and 1875, Saraogi petitioners like Lal continued petitioning to different branches of the colonial government. They positioned themselves as imperial subjects, redeployed colonial constructions of 'difference' to show that their celebrations were compatible with public order, and demanded that the authorities guarantee their access to the main streets of Delhi. In 1871, the Punjab government's orders for local impartiality in matters of Indian religious observance provided further opportunities for the Saraogis to highlight their grievances. The Lieutenant Governor of Punjab issued a declaration that upheld the colonial government's position on religious tolerance and even-handedness when arbitrating matters of religious observance. The Governor declared:

> The British Government has in no way changed or abandoned the principles upon which it declared on the annexation of Punjab, should govern its policy. That policy has been and is today to consider all creeds and religions equal before law; to secure to each individual the right of following the undisturbed practices enjoined by his faith and to impose upon all no further restraint than is demanded by the convenience and welfare of the entire community.[75]

This declaration was another revealing example of the contradiction between the imperatives of religious tolerance and public order. We have already seen the awkward balancing act that the local authorities performed in 1863 and the creation of ceremonial precedence that it resulted in. The authorities in Delhi steadfastly hung on to the notion that public order in the city had to be prioritised after the rebellion. To deal with the problem of injuring the religious practices of the Saraogis, Hamilton issued the proclamation that their procession was an 'obsolete' custom. Now, the fault lines within the government were exposed once again as the Governor made this proclamation. Saraogi petitioners were quick to use this tension between the Punjab government's proclamation and the practices of the local authorities. For example, in 1873, appeals were made by Lal directly to the Secretary of State for India to dismiss the ban placed by local authorities and demand equal rights for their *rath yatra*. Lal wrote:

> It is respectfully submitted that to disallow the said procession would appear in the estimation of those concerned, and the public generally, a departure from that policy of toleration which is eminently the policy of the British Government, and would also appear to be the introduction of what the natives of this country have been taught was impossible, under the British rule; viz., *a policy that does not consider all creeds and religionists equal to secure to each individual the right of the above mentioned undisturbed practices enjoined by his faith* (emphasis in original).[76]

Again, as Lal's petitions suggest, the Saraogis wanted colonial rule to live up to its promise of equal access to public spaces even as they were critical of the conduct of local officers in the case of the *rath yatra*. Yet, despite the proclamation, local authorities in Delhi clung on to Hamilton's original ban claiming that the procession still had the potential to cause upheaval in the city. In turn, the government of India responded to Lal's petition by suggesting that the orders of the local authorities could not be withdrawn.[77] In the subsequent petitions, the Saraogis grew more boisterous in their claims for the use of public spaces in Delhi and upped the ante in dismissing local authorities. In 1875, for example, Lal wrote a scathing petition to the government of India, castigating the failure of the local authorities to govern the city effectively. He wrote:

> The Jainies submit that if the avoidance of affrays and riots be the only object of the local (district) authorities in putting a stop to the issue of the Jainies

procession in the bazaars of Dehlie [*sic.*] that object could be accomplished without the deprivation of the privileges all along enjoyed by the Jainies sect ...

The petition further stated:

As when the Jainies celebrate every year their rath jatra festival in the streets of Delhi where the houses of the sects of Bashnavas and Brahmins are situated they fail to perceive the reason, then why the Jainies are debarred from enjoying the same privilege in the Queen's highways .... The Jainies sect is confident that by judicious police arrangement and the enforcement of the law all sects could be bound down to avoid disturbances ... [78]

Indeed, as Bhasin suggests, by referring to the Queen's highways, the Saraogis were making explicit spatial claims to the city.[79] However, Lal's petition taps into a distinct framework of authority and power. The failure of the local government to live up to the promise of equal rights of religious tolerance after the proclamation of 1871 made the Saraogis reassess their position vis-à-vis the colonial government. The subtle change, that is, invoking the Queen's highways, is particularly significant in this case. The 'public' road was represented as a sovereign space, quite literally, as the Queen's highways, and was used to delegitimise the claims of local colonial authorities to control that space. Till now, the Saraogis had carefully appraised colonial practices and stated the 'ordinary' nature of their ceremonies across north India. Now an overlapping geography of power, that is, the basic association of sovereignty with territory was invoked to gain access to the city's public streets.[80] If this form of outright authority over the 'public road' was earlier used to delegitimise institutions like the *panchayat*s, now it was deployed directly against the local authorities because of its perceived failure to maintain law and order. This attempt by the Saraogis to shift to a different register of authority was a way of affirming their imperial subjecthood without outright resistance to colonial power.

Of course, colonial authorities were also caught in a bind because of the tensions between the two contradictory impulses of 'public order' and 'religious tolerance'. Neither here nor there, the silence over the question of the Saraogi *rath yatra* became increasingly difficult to maintain. In light of the sustained critiques and petitions sent by the Saraogis, the government of India finally revoked the local ban on the *rath yatra* in 1877. In May 1877, a petition sent by the Saraogis, seeking permission to hold a *rath yatra* during *Dussehra* (a major Hindu festival) in September, was forwarded to the Secretary to the government of Punjab.[81] In what was now understood as an 'entirely harmless' and 'unobjectionable' ceremony, Lepel Griffin, the Secretary of State, acknowledged the need to review and revoke the local ban. He wrote in a reappraisal of the *rath yatra*:

> After the fullest consideration, and giving due weight to the arguments advanced by able and distinguished officers of government on the other side of the question, Mr Egerton is of the opinion that the Saraogi procession is of such a character that the opposition of Brahmanical Hindus is fanciful and only made in a spirit of intolerance and bigotry. The present commissioner of Delhi reports that the cry of indecency set up by the Vaishnavs is absolutely without foundation. He has himself seen the idol, and there is nothing whatever to object to on this ground.

In the same spirit, the reappraisal continued further to argue in favour of the Saraogi *rath yatra*:

> If this be so, the lieutenant governor fails to see why the saraogi sect should not have as much right to the protection of the British Government in the performance of their religious ceremonial as the Brahmanical Hindus themselves. Their own procession of the Ramlila which is commonly celebrated with much pomp, is far more open to objection on the score of impeding traffic and collecting crowds than the Rath Jatra procession of the saraogis, whose society being small, the size of their procession is necessarily confined within moderate limits.[82]

This statement was a stunning endorsement of the arguments made by the Saraogis over the course of the years. The Lieutenant Governor of Punjab dismissed the caricature of the Saraogi *rath yatra* as an 'infinitesimal grievance' and suggested that in a period of 'absolute tranquillity', there was no need for it to be banned.[83] The removal of the ban marked the end of years of lobbying by the Saraogis and their campaign for access to the main streets of the city. Yet, it should also be highlighted that what made it conducive for the authorities to accept Saraogi demands at this juncture was the creation of a separate arena of state rituals, which reached its climax in the form of the Delhi Durbar of 1877.[84] One of the arguments made by the Lieutenant Governor was that any hostilities between the Saraogis and the Vaishnavs could now be effectively dealt with by striking off the names of the leaders of the two groups from the divisional Durbar lists.[85] In other words, as a new terrain of political practice was laid down, the acceptance of the Saraogi *rath yatra* became tenable. It seemed, at least to the higher authorities at the time, that the entry of the 'natural leaders' of their respective 'communities' and religious groups into public politics would effectively act as a buffer between the Raj and its subjects.[86]

CONCLUSION

Access to the street, then, was a source of bitter competition and rivalry between social groups during times of ritual processions and displays. Hierarchised in terms of ceremonial precedence, the street became a focal point for social groups that were seeking to change the corporate tone of the city. Colonial rule after the rebellion of 1857 marked a significant departure in the governance of the street. At one level, streets were accessible to all those who wished to celebrate their processions based on the rationale that they were performing 'religious' activities. This was based on a new political rationality, which allowed natives to partake in their religious observances with little restriction. On the other hand, the rebellion also left a deep-seated fear of 'public disturbances' and colonial paranoia of 'disorder' on the streets.

It was at the intersection of these two contradictory imperatives that the governance of the street was located. This idea, it has been suggested, was foundational to future struggles over the streets as it effectively re-hierarchised urban spaces for some groups, such as the Jain Saraogis in Delhi. As wealthy but ritually insignificant actors in the public arena prior to the rebellion, the Saraogis wished to express their growing influence and power via grand processions in large thoroughfares and through streets like Chandni Chowk. However, the contradictions in colonial governance led to the ban of their grand *rath yatra* on grounds of public security, and they were reduced to a minor entity in public-arena activities. This context, as has been observed, shaped the Saraogis' demand for access to the main streets and thoroughfares of Delhi for their *rath yatra*.

The Saraogis fashioned themselves as imperial subjects and demonstrated the compatibility of their *rath yatra* procession by interpreting and using notions of public conduct and behaviour to their advantage. If they assumed that the colonial government categorised them as a minority in the city, they turned this around to suggest that they formed the largest minority in Delhi. When colonial authorities tried to steer clear of urban disputes by suggesting that the Saraogis take their case to the *panchayats*, they used their minority position to argue that they needed the authorities to intervene directly in their matters. They used the proclamation of the provincial authorities in 1871 to challenge the ban that the local authorities had imposed. When all else seemed lost, the Saraogis shifted the registers of authority, invoking sovereign power as the absolute arbitrator over the territory to dismiss the claims of local authorities in Delhi. These examples show that Saraogi claims to access public spaces were a product of the government's decision to withhold the main streets of the city from their processions. Moreover, they carefully appraised colonial power, which was judged for its justness or unjustness, partiality or impartiality, or even dismissed outright by the invocation of the power of the sovereign as a higher authority.

NOTES

1. See Sandria Freitag, *Collective Action and Community: Public Arenas and the Emergence of Communalism in North India* (Berkeley: University of California Press, 1989).

2. Colonial urban policing per se is a growing research area in the study of South Asian cities. Broadly, questions have ranged over the extent to which the colonial police force was an instrument of social control. David Arnold's pioneering work on the Madras constabulary, for example, argues that the police functioned as an authoritarian and violent agent of the state, which allowed the colonial government to maintain its dominance. See David Arnold, *Police Power and Colonial Rule: Madras, 1859–1947* (New Delhi: Oxford University Press, 1986). On the other hand, in opposition to Arnold, Rajnarayan Chandavarkar, in his work on Bombay, has argued that in its everyday operations, the colonial police was hardly a cohesive or monolithic force. In support, Chandavarkar highlights the structural weaknesses of the police organisation and its need for alliances in urban neighbourhoods to

carry out policing operations. See Rajnarayan Chandavarkar, *Imperial Power and Popular Politics: Class, Resistance and the State in India, c. 1580-1950* (Cambridge: Cambridge University Press, 1998), 180-233. For another study which looks at how the growing regulatory powers of the police force itself increased clashes with local populations in colonial Bombay, see Prashant Kidambi, *The Making of an Indian Metropolis: Colonial Governance and Public Culture in Bombay, 1890-1920* (Aldershot: Ashgate Publishing, 2007), 115-56. On the development of disciplinary models that attempted to internalise and pre-empt resistance in late-colonial Delhi, see Stephen Legg, *Spaces of Colonialism: Delhi's Urban Governmentalities* (New Delhi: Wiley-Blackwell, 2007), 82-147.

3. Katherine Prior, 'The State's Intervention in Urban Religious Disputes in the North-Western Provinces in the Early Nineteenth Century', *Modern Asian Studies* 27, no. 1, 1993, 173-203.

4. Prior, 'The State's Intervention', 186.

5. Prior, 'The State's Intervention', 186.

6. I use the category of 'social groups' instead of 'community' in order to avoid the reification of Jain identity in this chapter.

7. Narayani Gupta, 'The Management of Urban Public Spaces, Shahjahanabad, New Delhi, Greater Delhi, 1851-1997', in *Urban Governance: Britain and Beyond Since 1750*, ed. Robert J. Morris and Richard H. Trainer (London: Ashgate Publishing, 2000), 245.

8. Sree Ram Tehsildar's Petition in the Case of the Surrowgees Procession, dated 20 December 1871, 1/1863, DSA DCO.

9. Sree Ram Tehsildar's Petition in the Case of the Surrowgees Procession, dated 20 December 1871. For examples of how Indian concepts of space interacted with European notions of the 'public', see Sudipta Kaviraj, 'Filth and the Public Sphere: Concepts and Practices about Space in Calcutta', *Public Culture* 10, no. 1, 1997, 83-113; and William J. Glover, 'Constructing Urban Space as Public in Colonial India: Some Notes from the Punjab', *Journal of Punjab Studies* 14, no. 2, 2007, 211-24.

10. As Jim Masselos suggests in his study of colonial Bombay, people used 'mental maps' or 'templates' in order to navigate the city. Moreover, perceptions of space as familiar or unfamiliar were derived through accustomed activities and times. See Jim Masselos, 'Appropriating Urban Space: Social Constructs of Bombay in the Time of the Raj', in *The City in Action: Bombay Struggles for Power*, ed. Jim Masselos (New Delhi: Oxford University Press, 2007), 284-318.

11. As philosopher Henri Lefebvre explains, space should not be seen simply as inert or as a container in which action takes place, but it should rather

be understood as a series of unequal relationships. See Henri Lefebvre, *The Production of Space*, trans. Donald Nicholson-Smith (Oxford: Blackwell Publishers, 1991).

12. Mai Dayal Jain, *Jain Rath Yatra: Dehli ka Itihas* (New Delhi: Rising Sun Press), 1.

13. Michael Mann, 'Turbulent Delhi: Religious Strife, Social Tension and Political Conflicts, 1803–1857', *Journal of South Asian Studies* XXVIII, no. 1, 2005, 18.

14. C. A. Bayly, *Rulers, Townsmen and Bazaars: North Indian Society in the Age of British Expansion, 1770–1870* (Cambridge: Cambridge University Press, 1983), 141–42.

15. Lala Harsukh Rai financed the construction of the Dharampura Naya Mandir. The Lala wore many hats; he was the Royal Treasurer of Delhi, a *jagirdar* (an official of the king acting given rights to collected revenue of the land allotted to him) as well as a Councillor in the Bharatpur Durbar. See Lala Pannalal Jain Aggarwal, *Jain Institutions in Delhi* (Delhi: The Jain Mitra Mandal, 1947), 1.

16. Bayly, *Rulers, Townsmen and Bazaars*. 141–42. On the basis of his research, Bayly records that between 1790 and 1800, there was a large-scale migration of Jains from the nearby towns to Delhi.

17. See, for example, Douglas Haynes's account of the Vaishnav and Jain ties in the city of Surat. Douglas Haynes, *Rhetoric and Ritual in Colonial India: The Shaping of a Public Culture in Surat City, 1852–1928* (Berkeley: University of California Press, 1991), 55. See also C. A. Bayly's description of the Jagat Seth merchants of Calcutta; Bayly, *Rulers, Townsmen and Bazaars*, 390.

18. There is a small but growing amount of literature on Jain identity, although, as Paul Dundas notes, the history of the Jains in the nineteenth century has 'hardly begun to be written'. See Paul Dundas, *The Jains* (London: Routledge, 1992), 4. For a collection of essays that examine the construction of 'Jain-ness' and the contested nature of Jain identity in early and medieval India, see John E. Cort (ed.), *Open Boundaries: Jain Communities and Cultures in Indian History* (New York: State University of New York Press, 1998). On contemporary anthropological works on Jain identity in India and in the global context, see Michael Carrithers and Caroline Humphrey (eds), *The Assembly of Listeners: Jains in Indian Society* (Cambridge: Cambridge University Press, 1991). See also James Laidlaw, *Riches and Renunciation: Religion, Economy and Society Among the Jains* (Oxford: Clarendon Press, 1995).

19. See C. A. Bayly, 'The Pre-History of "Communalism"? Religious Conflict in India, 1700–1860', in *Origins of Nationalism in South Asia: Patriotism and Ethical Government in the Making of Modern India*, ed. C. A. Bayly (New Delhi: Oxford University Press, 1998), 229–30.

20. Prior, 'The State's Intervention', 188.

21. Memorial by Rickho Lal to the Secretary of State for India, dated 31 January 1873, No. 585-586 A, NAI Home Public, January 1873.

22. Memorial by Rickho Lal to the Secretary of State for India, dated 31 January 1873.

23. Note of the Commissioner of Delhi Division: Claims of Certain Persons of Surowgee Sect to Convey their Idol in Procession through the Principal Streets of Delhi, dated 28 May 1863, 1/1878, DSA DCO.

24. Mann, 'Turbulent Delhi', 21–22.

25. Prior, 'The State's Intervention'.

26. Prior, 'The State's Intervention', 201.

27. T. R. Metcalf, *Ideologies of the Raj* (Cambridge: Cambridge University Press, 1994), 160.

28. See Chapter 1, this book, and Narayani Gupta, *Delhi Between Two Empires: 1803–1931: Society, Government and Urban Growth* (New Delhi: Oxford University Press, 1981), 24–27.

29. I am in disagreement with Katherine Prior's argument that the colonial state extended an unequivocal grant to all groups to conduct their religious observances after the rebellion of 1857. The evidence from the Saraogi files points to the fact that questions on whether to allow the Saraogis to have their processions was debated as arbitrarily as earlier. In this scenario, the Saraogis had to *demonstrate* the compatibility of their ceremonies and practices within the new political framework established by the state.

30. It should be pointed out here that there is a lack of mention in the source material regarding 'Hindu–Muslim' tension during this period. An explanation for this, and this links up with the rising demands of the Saraogis, is that there was both a spatial and ceremonial vacuum left in the city as Muslims were evicted wholesale. With the absence of one set of competitors for spatial precedence, the rivalries between the Saraogis and Vaishnavs took centre-stage.

31. H. A. Rose, D. Ibbetson and E. D. Maclagan, *Glossary of the Castes and Tribes of the Punjab and North West Frontier Province* (Lahore: Government Printing Press, 1911), 105.

32. Letter from the Deputy Commissioner Dehlie to the Magistrate of Mathura, dated 10 June 1868, 1/1863, DSA DCO.

33. Gurpreet Bhasin's excellent PhD dissertation discusses the 'discursive networks' used by the Saraogis to make their claims to the public spaces of Delhi. See Gurpreet Bhasin, *Public Spaces and Discursive Practices in Colonial Delhi, 1860–1915*, Unpublished PhD Thesis, Open University, England, 2009.

34. Bhasin points to the multi-layered nature of the colonial state and suggests that at different levels of the colonial apparatus, opinions varied about 'rights of access to public spaces for religious celebrations'. She also suggests that in Delhi, 'religious tolerance was superseded by considerations for public order'; Bhasin, *Public Spaces and Discursive Practices*, 88, 92. However, I differ with Bhasin to the extent that when discussing how different discourses of access and use existed within the state, it is not elaborated how they could complicate the role of colonial governance in the city. Such contradictions, I would suggest, were foundational to future struggles over the right to use the streets by hierarchising ceremonial precedence.

35. Report by G. Hamilton on the Claim of the Surrowgee Sect to Carry their Idol through the Principal Streets of Delhi, dated 28 May 1863, No. 101-108A: No. 103, NAI Foreign Dept. Genl., November 1863.

36. Report by G. Hamilton on the Claim of the Surrowgee Sect to Carry their Idol through the Principal Streets of Delhi, dated 28 May 1863.

37. Report by G. Hamilton on the Claim of the Surrowgee Sect to Carry their Idol through the Principal Streets of Delhi, dated 28 May 1863.

38. Report by G. Hamilton on the Claim of the Surrowgee Sect to Carry their Idol through the Principal Streets of Delhi, dated 28 May 1863.

39. Bhasin, *Public Spaces and Discursive Practices*, 88.

40. Report by G. Hamilton on the Claim of the Surrowgee Sect to Carry their Idol through the Principal Streets of Delhi, dated 28 May 1863.

41. Report by G. Hamilton on the Claim of the Surrowgee Sect to Carry their Idol through the Principal Streets of Delhi, dated 28 May 1863.

42. Sree Ram Tehsildar's Petition in the Case of the Surrowgees Procession, dated 20 December 1871.

43. Although Sandria Freitag carefully points to the significance of the 'main streets' for collective action and the fact that space could act as a 'divisive as well as integrative' agent during performances of religious rituals, she does not extend her examination to the spatial hierarchisation of processions in the urban environment. For her brief discussion on the significance of 'main streets' and the general importance of space during procession times, see Freitag, *Collective Action and Community*, 133–35.

44. Sree Ram Tehsildar's Petition in the Case of the Surrowgees Procession, dated 20 December 1871.

45. ' ... *jab saraogiyon ka tamval jyada hua unhone ye tajviz ki ke dena apni dukhtaran ka baishnu ko band kiya magar dukhtaran lete rahe ...* ' (' ... As the influence of the Saraogis rose, they resolved to stop marrying their daughters into Vaishnav households but continued to receive Vaishnav

brides ... '); Case Regarding the Saraogis, dated 14 April 1869, 23(A), Misc. File, DSA DCO.

46. Letter from the Magistrate of Delhi to the Deputy Commissioner of Delhi, dated 2 January 1870, 23(A), Misc. File, DSA DCO.

47. Gyanendra Pandey, *The Construction of Communalism in Colonial North India* (New Delhi: Oxford University Press, 1990).

48. Sandria Freitag, 'Contesting in Public: Colonial Legacies and Contemporary Communalism', in *Making India Hindu: Religion, Community and the Politics of Democracy in India*, ed. David Ludden (New Delhi: Oxford University Press, 1996), 219.

49. Letter to the Private Secretary to the Government of India from Rickho Lal, dated 11 December 1870, 1/1863, DSA DCO.

50. Petition from Rickho Lal and Others, Inhabitants of Dehlie to the Right Hon'ble Sir Charles Wood, Secretary State for India in London, dated 13 November 1863, Allahabad, 1/1863, DSA DCO.

51. Petition from Rickho Lal and Others, Inhabitants of Dehlie to the Right Hon'ble Sir Charles Wood, Secretary State for India in London, dated 13 November 1863.

52. Petition from Rickho Lal and Others to the Under-Secretary to the Government of India, dated 12 November 1863, No. 1-3A: No. 1, NAI Foreign Dept. Genl., December 1863.

53. Petition from Rickho Lal, Kunhyah Lal and Jhoona Lal and Others, Residents of Allahabad, to the Secretary to the Government of India, dated 12 December 1863, No. 101-108A: No. 105, NAI Foreign Dept. Genl., November 1863.

54. Bhasin also makes this point regarding the Saraogi claims of 'similarity to' and 'difference from' their rivals. See Bhasin, *Public Spaces and Discursive Practices*, 92–96, 221–22.

55. As Arjun Appadurai has argued, the difference between the Mughals and the British was that while the former *acknowledged* the presence of group identities, the latter *enumerated* them. See Arjun Appadurai, 'Number in the Colonial Imagination', in *Modernity at Large: Cultural Dimensions of Globalisation* (Minnesota: University of Minnesota Press, 1996), 129. See also Bernard Cohn, 'The Census, Social Structure and Objectification in South Asia', in *An Anthropologist Among the Historians and Other Essays*, ed. Bernard Cohn (New Delhi: Oxford University Press, 1987), 224–54.

56. Petition from Rickho Lal and Others, Inhabitants of Dehlie to the Right Hon'ble Sir Charles Wood, Secretary State for India in London, dated 13 November 1863, Allahabad, 1/1863, DSA DCO.

57. Petition from Rickho Lal and Others, Inhabitants of Dehlie to the Right

Hon'ble Sir Charles Wood, Secretary State for India in London, dated 13 November 1863.

58. Petition from Rickho Lal and Others, Inhabitants of Dehlie to the Right Hon'ble Sir Charles Wood, Secretary State for India in London, dated 13 November 1863.

59. Petition from Rickho Lal and Others, Inhabitants of Dehlie to the Right Hon'ble Sir Charles Wood, Secretary State for India in London, dated 13 November 1863.

60. See Chapter 1, this book.

61. Letter from the Deputy Commissioner of Delhi to the Magistrate of Delhi, dated 29 February 1872, 1/1863, DSA DCO.

62. Letter from the Deputy Commissioner of Delhi to the Magistrate of Delhi, dated 29 February 1872.

63. In the case of the Saraogis and Vaishnav devotees, the need for urban *panchayat*s to resolve these problems was resorted to because the disputes were between members of the same *Jati* or endogamous units. For a description of this relationship in another colonial city, see Haynes, *Rhetoric and Ritual,* 55–58.

64. Petition from Rickho Lal to the Deputy Commissioner of Delhi, dated 14 March 1871, 1/1863, DSA DCO.

65. Petition from Rickho Lal to the Deputy Commissioner of Delhi, dated 14 March 1871.

66. Petition from Rickho Lal to the Deputy Commissioner of Delhi, dated 14 March 1871.

67. Glover, 'Constructing Urban Space as Public', 213–15.

68. Letter from the Deputy Commissioner of Delhi to the District Superintendent of Police in Delhi, dated 3 December 1870, 1/1863, DSA DCO.

69. Letter from the Deputy Commissioner of Delhi to the Commissioner and Superintendent of Delhi, dated 31 May 1871, 1/1863, DSA DCO.

70. Letter from the Deputy Commissioner of Delhi to the Commissioner and Superintendent of Delhi, dated 31 May 1871.

71. Petition from Jy Singh and Dhoom Singh to the Deputy Commissioner of Delhi, dated 2 October 1872, 1/1863, DSA DCO.

72. Petition from Jy Singh and Dhoom Singh to the Deputy Commissioner of Delhi, dated 2 October 1872.

73. Petition from Jy Singh and Dhoom Singh to the Deputy Commissioner of Delhi.

74. Petition from Jy Singh and Dhoom Singh to the Deputy Commissioner of Delhi.

75. 'On Religious Liberty': A Series of Extracts Collated by Rickho Lal, n.d., 1/1863, DSA DCO.

76. Letter from A. Thornton, Secretary to the Government, Punjab to A. C. Lyall, Offg. Secretary to the Government of India, Home Department, dated 15 April 1873, No. 283-87 B: No. 283, NAI Home Public, May 1873.

77. Letter from A. Thornton, Secretary to the Government, Punjab to A. C. Lyall, Offg. Secretary to the Government of India, Home Department, dated 15 April 1873.

78. Petition from Rickho Lal Agent to the Jaines Sect of Delhi, to the Under-Secretary to the Government of India, dated 16 March 1875, 1/1878, DSA DCO.

79. Bhasin, *Public Spaces and Discursive Practices*, 106.

80. For an explanation of the linkage between sovereignty and territory, and its operation in a distinct form, that is, 'railway space', see Chapter 5, this book.

81. Letter from Lepel Griffin, Officiating Secretary to the Government of Punjab to the Lt. Colonel W. G. Davies, Commissioner and Superintendent of Delhi, dated 22 May 1877, 3/1877, DSA DCO.

82. Letter from Lepel Griffin, Officiating Secretary to the Government of Punjab to the Lt. Colonel W. G. Davies, Commissioner and Superintendent of Delhi, dated 22 May 1877.

83. Letter from Lepel Griffin, Officiating Secretary to the Government of Punjab to the Lt. Colonel W. G. Davies, Commissioner and Superintendent of Delhi, dated 22 May 1877.

84. See B. Cohn, 'Representing Authority in Victorian India', in *The Invention of Tradition*, ed. Eric Hobsbawm and Terrence Ranger (New Delhi: Oxford University Press, 1996), 165–210.

85. Letter from Lepel Griffin, Offg. Secretary to the Government of Punjab to the Lt. Colonel W. G. Davies, Commissioner and Superintendent of Delhi, dated 22 May 1877, 3/1877, DSA DCO.

86. For a detailed study on how Indian elites negotiated their roles as both 'natural leaders' and representatives of public opinion, see Haynes, *Rhetoric and Ritual.*

5

The Railways, Traffic Management and Commercial Growth

Re-imagining Colonial Delhi

INTRODUCTION

In 1889, Robert Clarke, the Deputy Commissioner of the city and President of the Delhi municipality, addressed an audience over the state of municipal affairs. On the one hand, Clarke's address was full of praise for how much trade and new industries had grown in Delhi since the formation of the municipality in 1863. The railways, he felt, had directly contributed to this, and this had resulted in commercial wealth and prosperity to the city and its growing suburbs.[1] But herein lay the problem for Clarke. Commercial growth had brought with it the problem of traffic and its circulation. Although goods carts as well as pedestrian traffic had grown between the city and its suburbs, the material fabric of the old city was beginning to stifle commerce. Delhi's old Mughal walls and pathways were represented as 'intolerable obstructions' and were blamed for blocking the flow of cart and pedestrian traffic heading into and outside the city.[2] For Clarke, if the material prosperity of the city was to continue and the unbounded potential of infrastructure like the railways was to be harnessed, a concerted effort had to be made to encourage smooth flows of traffic through the city.

This chapter discusses how the management of traffic gained a new resonance in municipal activities from the 1880s. It highlights the material impacts of a city becoming a transport node and the spatial imaginaries that sought to facilitate commerce and flows of capital.[3] Two interlinked arguments about municipal planning in this period are suggested here. First, this chapter shows how the question of urban traffic management gained resonance for municipal officials with the expansion of railway networks in north India from the 1880s onwards. Municipal heads, in particular, Robert Clarke, began drafting proposals to ensure that if Delhi was to become a major commercial centre in north India, it was essential to regulate the flow of goods and pedestrian traffic and reconstitute the spaces of the city, where traffic moved. As we shall see, while municipal schemes were formulated to construct large thoroughfares, build city extensions, high-level overbridges, new localities and picturesque gardens, they were distinctly 'colonial' in their orientation. Municipal plans were built upon specific understandings of what constituted the 'natural' behaviour of the natives, and they continued to reflect anxieties over security and policing in the Indian city.

Second, the chapter sheds light on how railway-inspired urban planning in the colonial city was actually driven by the contestation between different scales of the state.[4] If the Delhi municipality's moves were aimed at fostering commercial growth and boosting circulation in a colonial context, the interests of this body intersected with the government of India's designs for the city. The latter occurred in the form of infrastructural works meant to absorb Delhi into larger rail networks, a method of inscribing its power through an India-wide project of territorial consolidation. Between 1889 and 1910, the clashes and contestation between such scales of the state could fuel urban planning in the city and its outskirts.

THE RAILWAYS, TRAFFIC AND THE CITY

As we know from Clarke's aforementioned address, by the late-1880s, the question of commercial traffic and its circulation in Delhi was becoming a significant concern for municipal officials. This was so was because of the growing network of railway lines running through the city and Delhi's position as a terminus for major railway systems.[5] Marian Aguiar has highlighted the significance of the railways in state policy, suggesting that on the one hand, the railways promoted the promise of modernity through movement, but on the other, it also allowed the colonial state to control the bodies of Indians through the workings of capitalism and the ideologies of colonial rule.[6] Significantly, moreover, the construction and management of the railways and other 'state works' was itself a form of extension of control, whereby the sovereign power of the government of India consolidated its territory and bound India into a 'colonial state space'.[7]

In connection with these factors, the desire for security was ubiquitous in the strategic construction of India-wide railway networks. After the rebellion of 1857, for example, in north Indian cities like Delhi, railway lines were purposefully constructed to run right through the heart of the city and divide it into two as an act of punishment. The elite and predominantly white area of the Civil Lines to the north of Delhi was protected by railway lines, and the station acted as a defensive frontier, which could be used to mobilise and transport troops in case of another threat from the south (see Figure 5.1).[8] Therefore, the creation of the railway station and lines in and around cities like Delhi was underpinned by a host of economic and political considerations. This fit with the

Figure 5.1: The Delhi Railway Station c. 1900

Source: This postcard was provided by the author.

THE (UN)GOVERNABLE CITY

government's larger project of consolidating its authority over India's territory by the end of the nineteenth century.

Under the aegis of the government of India, the construction of railway sidings and goods stations was rapid, and by the early-1880s, colonial gazetteers boasted that Delhi had become 'exceedingly well-provided' with railway communications, with no less than three major railways entering the city.[9] In 1911, this would rise to six, with the Delhi station becoming the largest junction station in north India.[10] Such construction was accompanied by a growing preference of railway usage in both goods and passenger traffic after the 1880s, as the railways were slowly beginning to dominate, but not replace, other forms of transport.[11] However, rail traffic brought with it additional questions of circulation, particularly about how the city itself was to be made conducive to flows of people, goods and commerce. As bulk goods headed to and from the railway station, passenger traffic and other modes of transport competed for road space; municipalities such as those in Delhi grew increasingly concerned about bottlenecks in passages of flows and movement within the city.

Indeed, the influx of railway traffic was at once a sign of healthy circulation of commerce as well as a source of anxiety. As David Arnold suggests, this was the 'problem' of traffic in India, which was typified both by its dynamism and energy and the threat of disorder. The bustle of Indian street life, its perceived irregularity, and its indiscipline gave the impression of a chaotic pre-modern temporality coexisting with the excitement of modern traffic. It was this discourse of traffic that became the basis for thinking about new forms of governance, policing and relationship between machines and bodies.[12] Clearly, if Delhi was to grow as a large rail terminus and commercial centre, then the rate at which goods and passenger traffic circulated in the city needed regulation with planned interventions to minimise obstacles, both human as well as those of the built environment. It was at this scale of planning that the Delhi municipality was to play an important role.

MUNICIPAL 'EXTENSION' SCHEMES AND THE OUTSKIRTS OF DELHI

In 1889, when Clarke laid out his first comprehensive plan for the needs of traffic and commercial growth, there was no special agency responsible for the formulation of urban plans, and senior municipal officials remained in charge of designing improvement projects till the shift of the capital in 1911.[13] Clarke, who had made various assessments to see how the circulation of commercial traffic was being affected, pointed out to other members of the municipality that the Lahore Gate, one of the old Mughal entrances into the city, was increasingly becoming a source of traffic problems. He felt that military orders to preserve the old Mughal walls and gates after 1863 had stifled commercial traffic, and this problem had grown particularly acute near the Lahore Gate. Building operations or alterations in the area had been prohibited on security grounds after the rebellion. Thus, not only did traffic move slowly, but the grain trade of the Khari Baoli *bazaar* inside the city were also cut off from the suburban markets of Saddar *bazaar* and Teliwara, which lay outside the city. For Clarke, these developments had checked the 'natural expansion' of the city and had impeded commercial traffic so badly that only a single grain cart could pass through the Lahore Gate at a time.[14]

As Indian railway operations were expanding northwards to places like Shimla and Ambala, and new industries were springing around Delhi in connection with growing railway commerce, Clarke felt that this was an opportune moment to shape the future of the city. Serendipitous in this regard was also a recent order by military authorities that lifted the ban on the removal of Lahore Gate.[15] The Western Gate or Lahore Gate of the city and the city walls had proved to be the thorn in municipal plans for years. When demands were made from time to time for its removal, either for ventilation or for commerce, the government of India dismissed these demands swiftly on the pretext of maintaining security.[16] The removal of the Gate at this juncture therefore was no doubt quite fortunate for the likes of Clarke. However, while permission for the removal of the Gate itself was acceded to, the government of India decreed that the old Mughal walls around the city had to be retained; and this was something the municipality simply had to contend with.[17] Thus, sovereign power represented by the government of India's control over the walls stood in contrast to municipal demands to enable the circulation of commercial traffic.[18] Therefore, any plans to encourage commercial growth in Delhi had to be creative when it came to the question of the city walls.

Significantly, by retaining the walls, the government of India found unlikely allies in some Indian members of the municipality, who also agreed that the walls should remain *in situ*. Clarke felt that the Indian members of the council would not be convinced to give up what he felt were their 'sentimental attachments' to the city wall.[19] Thus while the municipality began conceiving of urban planning from the perspective of commercial expansion and circulation of goods and traffic, it could not inveigh against the security prescriptions of the government nor tread on 'native sentiment' in its own ranks. The latter would be counter-productive, especially since it was only recently, in the 1880s, that the participation of local elites into the colonial project had been secured as part of the local self-government scheme. Traffic plans for the city therefore had to be innovative. The end result was Clarke's extension scheme: a plan to create a new quarter (later known as 'Clarke*ganj*') outside the Lahore Gate on *nazul* land, which was managed by the municipality. As per Clarke's plan, the circulation of commercial traffic could be facilitated if a new quarter was placed between the famed Chandni Chowk and the Pahari in Saddar *bazaar* by leasing out plots of land. This would connect the two commercial areas 'without break of continuity' by the means of a straight road and would also ensure that commerce circulated in an unimpeded manner.[20]

Along with the generation of wealth, Clarke also envisaged the new quarter as a model of health and salubrity, 'constructed systematically with due regard to ventilation, drainage and communications', which would bring some semblance of order to what were perceived to be the haphazard suburban settlements.[21] The scheme of improvement that Clarke envisioned was not intended to develop the outlying suburban settlements on their own terms, but rather, it was meant to be a receptacle for the extension of the city. Clarke's emphasis on the quarters being connected 'without break of continuity' was vital to the smooth movement of goods and commodities between the city, new *bazaar*s and railway lines.

Notably, Clarke's scheme ensured that too much interference did not take place with the city wall, and that only sections near the Lahore Gate would be removed. In a statement to the municipality, Clarke outlined his plan:

As an example of an extension scheme I mean there is the Lahore gate improvement project. This involves the removal of the gate for which sanction has already been received and a piece of wall on either side, the covering in of the ditch and the levelling of the glacis so as to allow of the construction of a square or *gunj* with a Mosque in the centre and shops all round.

The *ganj* was described thus:

> The *gunj* would be about 400 feet square one side where the wall is now and the opposite side on the circular road. The north and South sides would connect these at equal distances from the present gate, and the frontages on the circular road would be extended as far as there was a good demand for sites.[22]

As Jyoti Hosagrahar has suggested, Clarke's plan, although sharing the ideals of a pre-planned and orderly urban scheme similar to European practices at the time, also featured mixed-use structures such as houses with residences above and shops below, which were common to Indian cities.[23] This mixed-use feature was also evident when Clarke argued for the mosque to be placed at the centre of the market with shops all around. 'Class' was to be the new basis for organisation of neighbourhoods in the area, but it went hand in hand with the moralising presence of a mosque, a visual symbol that had a longer precedent in the city.[24] While Hosagrahar points out the 'hybrid' nature of Clarke's plan, Clarke's model was at the same time a specimen geared towards promoting circulation in the city. Commercial traffic had to move fast through the new quarter, and as a result the streets were cut up at right angles and shops were planned at the centre. Wide-planned streets would ensure the circulation of air along with traffic, and thus, were also an answer to health concerns.

It can also be said that such plans were oriented towards future developments. For example, by suggesting that frontages on the circular road could be extended as and when there was a 'good demand' for sites, his plan made provisions for the forces of demand and supply to be incorporated within it. In other words, as circulation of commerce would increase, the sites could be developed and given out on leases. If this model was followed, then Clarke felt that the municipality would be able to generate Rs 2 lakh, out of which Rs 50,000 could be reinvested for more roads, drains and bridges, and the rest of the reduction of municipal debt or investment, as the government might decide.[25] This was a wait-and-watch game where plots of the 'greatest demand' would be given out first and the municipality would wait for other plots to appreciate in value.[26] Clarke proudly declared that the plan would guarantee financial benefits to the municipality, 'relieve congestion, furnish facilities for trade and add a handsome quarter to the city'.[27] Commerce would be invigorated, and the street that would then run continuously from the fort-end till the Chandni Chowk and ultimately to the Pahari 'would be without any equal in the city or Northern India'.[28]

As we know from Clarke's statement above, one of the main features of his plan was the mosque at the centre of what later became known as the 'Grand Parade Road'. Hosagrahar writes that the presence of the mosque was a concession to the population, and although it projected an image of moral order, in reality this was a veneer, as the scheme marked a shift from religious power to secular power, or the power of the market.[29] However, we should see the presence of the mosque not simply as external to the forces of commerce, but also as integral to it. Placed at the centre of the *ganj*, and thereby central to the project itself, the mosque with shops all round was based on an understanding of the centrality of religion to the 'natural' behaviour of urban life and commerce in Oriental cities. This was indeed a moralising presence, and one that highlighted the importance of religion to the success of flows and commerce in the Oriental city. Simply put, Clarke's instincts dictated that religion was central to the success of a new commercial quarter. In the end, therefore, Clarke's plan incorporated a variety of political concerns, ranging from managing security needs to basing urban designs on a colonial sociology, underpinned by an understanding of what constituted commercial behaviour in an Indian city.

In its realisation, however, Clarke's plan had several unintended effects, which proved to be challenging for the municipality. In 1905, 16 years after the scheme was instituted, it was realised that neither was there the provision of a time plan to recover the *nazul* lands if the municipality needed them for 'public' purposes, nor had there been a clause to prevent subletting.[30] After Clarke's proposals were submitted, the municipality agreed to allow capitalists to secure several adjacent plots and distribute their buildings as they saw fit, rather than regulate the dimensions of plots at 15 feet apart.[31] This was again based on the assumption that economic activity would take root as per commercial behaviour in the Indian city. The owners of the plots not only built dwellings, but also sublet sections to tenants who set up their own shops and businesses. When the municipality realised that it needed to raise money and capitalise on its investments, it was left to fight long-winding legal cases as ejected tenants took the fight to the courts. This became a financial burden for the municipality and added to its never-ending fiscal worries.[32] Indeed, the owners of the sites transformed the original plans beyond recognition. They modified their plots and buildings at their own initiative; these were re-converted, partitioned, and given on subleases to increase commercial prospects. It was only when finances became a concern that the municipality tried to re-establish its control by directing its focus on inspecting the leases.

There were also other unintended ways in which the plan was transformed. Every effort had been made to ensure that those sites that were in the greatest demand would be sold off first, and the most valuable sites, that is, the Grand Parade Road plots, were bought almost entirely by wealthy Punjabi Muslim merchants from an area near the Sadar *bazaar* called Kishen*ganj*. These merchants were willing to construct shops on the Grand Parade Road plots because of their proximity to the city, and thus, avail the benefits of a grid of commerce.[33] However, this move went slightly contrary to Clarke's plan, who was hopeful that the grain merchants of Khari Baoli, just inside the city walls, would move into the new area, set up warehouses and shops, and therefore, also relieve the city from what could become a centre of plague contagion.[34] In refusing to move from their business quarters, the Khari Baoli merchants resisted municipal designs. However, they remained on Clarke's grid, on the street running from Chandni Chowk to Saddar *bazaar*. The benefits of commerce were just as great, and the ties that were built through a long association with the city could be nurtured in this way.[35]

It is important to note that along with local resistance and negotiation, the influence of other agencies was also a crucial factor in how the Clarke*ganj* scheme was shaped. As we have seen, the demands made by the military authorities to remain in control of the walls required the modification of Clarke's scheme and necessitated a situation where, instead of the removal of the walls, a straight road leading from the Saddar *bazaar* to Khari Baoli was planned and was eventually created by the municipality. But as the municipality began its project, the railway authorities under the government of India also objected to Clarke's designs, arguing that the *nazul* land over which Clarke hoped to build, needed to be reserved for either the Bombay Baroda and Central India Railway, or the India Midland Railway.[36] The government of India believed that such plots were ideally suited for the construction of goods sidings and that either of the two railway companies would soon apply for their transfer.[37]

If we recall, although the municipality assumed the trusteeship of the *nazul* lands, they formed a part of colonial 'state space' and the government of India reserved the right to alienate them. In the case of the *bela* plantation, for example, from time to time, colonial agencies like the forest department and military authorities were allocated sections of the *bela*, which irked the civil authorities since it impeded their designs for 'improvement'. From the late-1880s, the creation of track placements and goods sidings along the city wall and the transformation of the city into a 'railway space' would again shape how plans for the city were implemented. Railway construction was one of the most powerful expressions of 'state works' in colonial India. As Manu Goswami has argued, for the government of India, claims to sovereignty were closely tied to the centralisation of authority over territory after 1857, when power was transferred from the East India Company to the Crown.[38] Through the control of lands and the encouragement of 'state works', the colonial government created a territorially bounded entity, which represented its interventionist or managerial impulse.[39] As a result, the government of India kept a close watch over the activities of railway companies in matters of land allocation and supervised transfers of railway land.[40]

In Delhi, the advances of the government of India in the late-1880s meant that the proposed railway line divided Clarke's scheme into two halves, with some plots lying on the side of the Saddar *bazaar* and others in a cul-de-sac between the siding and city wall. While much of Clarke's original layout had to be altered, what proved to be a silver lining for the municipality was that the plots in the cul-de-sac were expected to fetch Rs 10,000 in future ground rents because they were close to the station. The municipality took advantage of the developments in this case, and now began to wait for the cul-de-sac plots to increase in value.[41] This 'wait-and-watch' approach, then, nudged the municipality towards a more assiduous management of its propertied assets.

The railways were thus drawn into a politics of planning in which the municipality as well as the government of India featured. Clarke's new settlement or extension scheme was intended to encourage the circulation of commercial traffic on a well-planned grid extending from Saddar *bazaar* to Chandni Chowk. This would be close to not only the commercial centres, but also the new railway facilities and lines outside the city walls. However, the very railway facilities that Clarke hoped would provide for the growing needs of commercial traffic had altered the character of his plans. The land planned for the extension of the city overlapped with the government of India's railway operations and its plans to extend and control railway land around the Lahore Gate.

The unintended result of this was a reshaped plan in which the municipality began to closely monitor the value of its plots between the railway siding and the city wall, which were expected to increase in value as a result of the railway reclamations. As we shall see, the interaction between the government of India and the municipality over questions of improvement of commercial traffic and its circulation was also productive in terms of inspiring planning for the interiors of the city. By the mid-1890s, the government of India focused its attention on transforming the junction arrangements at the central station inside the city to transform Delhi into the 'Charing Cross' of north India.[42] The renewed emphasis on the railways, however, brought with it further questions of circulation, particularly about how the interiors of the city were to be made conducive to the needs of increased rail traffic. At this level of planning, the municipality and Clarke were to play an important role once again.

PRODUCING RAILWAY SPACE: MANAGING TRAFFIC AND FLOWS INSIDE THE CITY

On 18 February 1899, Clarke, who was now an old hand and had been overseeing municipal operations for over 14 years, delivered another memorandum to the municipality. Delhi, he said, had 'risen from the ashes' after the rebellion and could proclaim to be the capital of India once again because it was now a terminus for the major railway systems in northern India.[43] However, he went on to explain, it was as a result of this very status that 'the interchange of traffic' inside the city had become a problem, and while 'constant extensions and improvements' had been carried out, a solid plan for the regulation of railway traffic was required.[44] While no mention of the eponymous Clarke*ganj* extension project was made, Clarke did want to press on other members the fact that previous plans like the extension scheme needed to be complemented by an appraisal of passenger and goods traffic facilities between the city and the central station.[45]

Clarke's proclamations were in anticipation of the government of India's proposal to redesign the central station or the East India station so as to accommodate the needs of different railway lines.[46] In a meeting held between the government of India and the railway companies the previous year, the central or the East India station was considered suitable to host the coaching traffic of all lines.[47] For goods traffic, the debate remained open, the government declaring that the representatives of the different lines needed to 'formulate detailed proposals for giving adequate facilities for goods traffic at Delhi and its suburbs to each of the railways concerned'.[48] This meeting was an attempt to not only delineate that the government of India was the final arbitrator of the way in which business was conducted at the station, but also to reinforce the fact that the East India station was, for all intents and purposes, a joint station.[49]

The centralisation of authority over railway works, and as in this particular case, over the main station, was not an isolated move. Since the 1880s, land for railway sidings was sanctioned near the city wall, and as we have seen, this was a process tied to how the government of India understood its own power. By 1895, with seven major railway lines projected to run in and around the city within 10 years, the government of India tightened its control over land allocation even further by insisting that only by special sanction could land be given to a railway company that wanted to construct its lines within a five-mile radius of the city.[50] A second action was aimed at resolving the nature of interests at the central station, and the Joint Station Proposal of 1898 was in response to this.

For Clarke and the municipality, the prospect of multiple lines entering the city again brought forward questions of how traffic circulation was to be managed. However, if in the 1880s, traffic entering the city was a cause for concern, now the regulation of flows within garnered attention. In this regard, two issues became glaringly clear. First, traffic within the city had to, of course, move fast in order to avoid delays. Indeed, a delay in reaching the station meant that merchants would have to pay more in freight charges, and this was an anathema to trade and the commercial success of the city. However, Clarke and the municipality were also aware that fast-moving streams of traffic had a downside since accidents and collisions could cost the municipality dearly. These had to be avoided at any cost and would have to be factored within a plan. The other consideration was that all of this meant that the interiors of the city had to be reconstituted if railway-associated commerce was to flourish. It was in this light that Clarke delivered his scheme for the improvement of the Delhi railway station in 1899.

Significantly, the concern was to remedy 'traffic congestion'—the intermingling of pedestrian and heavy goods traffic coming to and from the city—which became the basis of traffic plans in the 1890s. Clarke felt that as traffic from the city approached the railway station, it had two roads to traverse, the Kauria Pul and Nai Sarak, both of which were on either side of the Town Hall, the headquarters of the municipality and its municipal buildings. These two roads were far apart, and all traffic had to use either one or the other to get to the station. He wrote:

> From the railway station gate to the Clock tower, in the Chandni Chauk, the distance is 1,600 feet, but for a passenger to get from one point to the other, either on foot or driving, a distance of 3,200 feet, or exactly double, has got to be traversed, and the only routes are by the Kouria pul and Nai sarak, both of which are at all hours of the day crammed with goods traffic ... [51]

Clarke felt that congestion could be relieved by creating four arterial approach roads to the station instead of the two that were in use. New roads would cut open the city to ensure that traffic moved seamlessly in straight lines, avoiding what were lamented as the narrow and tortuous paths of the old Mughal city. In this way the frequently used but ill-suited lanes through localities like the Dariba would be freed and rendered suitable for pedestrian-only traffic. [52]

Traffic congestion was then problematised at two points of entry into the city, the Ajmeri Gate and Delhi Gate. The proposals identified that traffic from Paharganj, which was then a suburb of 10,000 inhabitants, entered through the Ajmeri Gate of the city, but converged with goods

THE (UN)GOVERNABLE CITY

and pedestrian traffic coming from the Qutub and Gurgaon directions outside the city. Clarke lamented that goods carriages were confronted with narrow roads immediately passing through the Ajmeri Gate and this prevented them from seeing what lay ahead. A similar case was made for the Delhi Gate, which was claimed to require a 'tolerable' approach road of about 20–30 yards after the gate.[53] Clearly, new roads promised to make the space of the city and its traffic 'legible' under the gaze of the municipality while finally putting an end to the physical and material constraints of the Mughal city.

In segregating forms of traffic, a conviction present in the municipal scheme was that the urban fabric had the potential to discipline pedestrianised activity in the city. For example, Clarke pushed for the creation of high footpaths on the new roads, which would keep 'heavy traffic from coming on to light roads'.[54] Footpaths, of course, were not altogether new as a municipal enterprise. Yet, in the context of railway traffic management, they had a particular resonance. Not only would rail passengers and pedestrians be able to access the station faster, but they would also avoid accidents if they were out of the way of carts and goods traffic. The fact that infrastructural technology could modify human capacity (in this case, normalise movement) was a belief that Clarke shared with planners in the metropolis.[55] From this perspective, roads were best kept for carriages, goods carts and animals, that is, non-human circulation or to borrow Clarke's term, 'heavy' traffic.

At specific points, these footpaths would cut across the municipal gardens or the 'Queens Gardens', which lay in between the railway station and municipal buildings. In effect, the gardens were to draw in pedestrian traffic, and thus, make circulation problems less acute (See Figure 5.2). Reduced in size, the gardens were to be kept adorned with open flowerbeds and benches along with a mock ruin in the form of an old Mughal *burj* or tower.[56] Thus, in conjunction with easing congestion and ensuring that pedestrian traffic would be diverted and disciplined to walk on pavements, Clarke's plans also had a pedagogical quality. Pedestrian traffic moving in and around the municipal gardens would instruct and adjust their gaze to admire a picturesque ruin in a garden setting. As William Glover has argued, across the Anglo-European and colonial world in the nineteenth century, there was a growing belief that material 'objects' had the potential to actively shape urban society and mould the sentiments and faculties of individuals.[57] Material environments, he suggests, served as object lessons to induce proper behaviour in colonised subjects, 'tirelessly and persuasively'.[58] If we recall, in the late-1880s, the placement of the mosque in the extension scheme was a similar endeavour in regulating circulation. The mosque was placed on a traffic grid and this allowed people to alight for worship. This was a careful method of redistributing flows, managing sentiments and engineering bodily movements.

In examining the placement of the *burj* in Figure 5.2, it can be seen that Clarke's 'ruin in a garden' setting shows similar concerns. The lesson performed by such an 'object' here was to enable the pedestrian to pause, and thus, regulate her/his movement and enjoy a scene that was based on the seemingly 'natural' characteristics of its own environment. This 'object lesson' was therefore to regulate the flow of traffic near the railway station and it meant that direct interference of municipal authorities in disciplining traffic could be reduced. These attributes of the municipal plan focused on turning the existing arrangements near the station and the Queens Gardens into 'the greatest thoroughfare in Delhi, open at all hours of the day and night'.[59]

Along with the orderly circulation of traffic, the municipal plan appealed to commercial sections of the city by linking their interests to the land market. A fundamental incentive in Clarke's scheme was to allow owners of houses on the route to the station to convert sections of their buildings into business premises. The major commercial markets in Delhi were located either directly in Chandni Chowk or just beyond the Lahore Gate of the city to the west. Clarke's plan was twofold: first, to widen streets at strategic points in *mohallas* that were near to the station, and second, to stimulate commerce in those lanes just off Chandni Chowk which had benefitted from railway expansion in terms of commercial development. By clearing out 30-foot roads in areas like *Kucha* Kabuli Attar and *Kucha* Lattu Shah, two localities on either side of the municipal buildings in the city (See Figure 5.3), for example, it was hoped that the owners of houses would convert some sections of the newly freed area into business premises. In the case of opening out *Kucha* Lattu Shah, Clarke explained that while business premises were already extending into the lane, they were hampered by the narrowness of the roadway. As an 'effect',

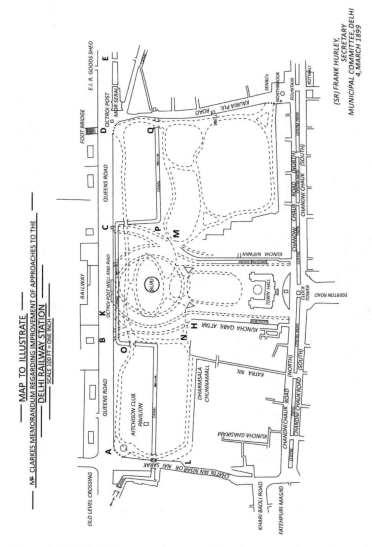

Figure 5.2: Clarke's Memorandum Regarding the Approaches to the Delhi Railway Station, 1899

Note: The dotted lines show the foothpaths cutting through the Queens Gardens with the *burj* at the centre. The image has been modified by the author.

Source: F.No. 98/1899, CO, Delhi Archives, Government of NCT of Delhi, India.

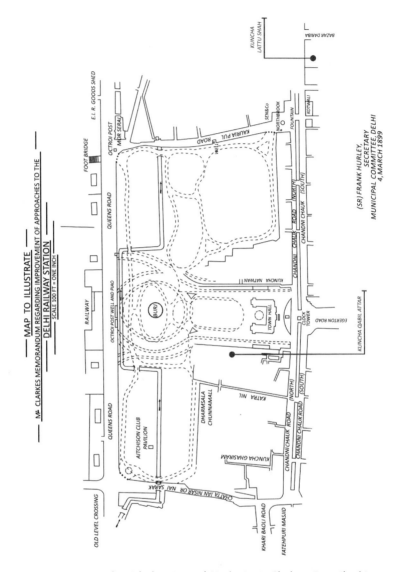

Figure 5.3: *Kucha* Kabuli Attar and *Kucha* Lattu Shah as Described in Clarke's Plans

Note: The image has been modified by the author.
Source: No. 98/1899, CO, Delhi Archives, Government of NCT of Delhi, India.

the clearances would 'increase the value of all property facing the new road, and make a frontage of 700 feet as a valuable as an equal length to the frontage in Chandni Chouk [sic.]'.[60]

Finally, Clarke's scheme turned towards resolving the problem of congestion inside the city gates. Commercial traffic and its movement around the margins of the city had been a source of anxiety even earlier, and we know that the Lahore Gate extension project was meant to facilitate commercial circulation by connecting Saddar *bazaar* with Chandni Chowk. Clarke's attention now turned to two other points of entry into the city, the Ajmeri Gate and Delhi Gate. Clarke felt that traffic from Paharganj, a suburb of 10,000 inhabitants, entered through the Ajmeri Gate of the city but converged with goods and pedestrian traffic coming from the Qutub and Gurgaon directions.[61] In this way, carriages were confronted with narrow roads and high walls inside the city immediately after passing through the Ajmeri Gate, and this prevented them from seeing what lay ahead. Clarke castigated the perceived lack of order of Mughal pathways, and their curvature and irregularity was cited as inimical to the flow of goods carts and passengers. The remedy for this was the creation of straight geometrical roads, aligned to ensure that no obstacles would face commercial traffic. A similar sentiment was espoused when the Delhi Gate was considered. This gate had been used as an exit route for livestock heading for pasture grounds near Firozabad, which was outside the city, but it was also used by carriage traffic coming into the city from areas like Ballabgarh, Palwal and Mathura.[62] Congestion in the city was seen as an intermingling of all kinds of traffic at the source of entry, and thus, the plan was to make approach roads more 'tolerable' by constructing straight roads for about 20–30 yards beyond the gates.[63]

It has been argued that by drawing maps and plans, the Delhi municipality sought to freeze the built form of the city, allowing minimum deviation from municipal norms and intentions.[64] Yet, the evidence suggests that such arguments of 'total' control need to be scrutinised further. At one level, the plans *did* allow smooth flows of traffic and forms of circulation to stimulate commercial activity in the city with a view towards the future. There were high-level footpaths to divide traffic and ensure that passengers and pedestrians were able to move smoothly. New localities were earmarked for construction, and gardens were included as places of aesthetic reflection where flows were managed through 'object lessons'. However, a close reading of the archive suggests that concerns with policing and security in the Indian city continued to shape the official imagination in plans oriented towards flows and circulation. Thus, in a manner similar to colonial notions of the 'naturalness' of traffic flows in Indian cities, be it framed by the religious presence of the mosque or the aesthetics of the Mughal *burj*, there were other distinctly 'colonial' imaginaries at work in the plan. These worked not to stifle *all* movement but rather to qualify them.[65]

In the first instance, Clarke's designs clearly envisaged 'who' could move through the newly transformed gardens. In this regard, the continued surveillance of those characterised as 'thieves and disreputable characters more generally' finds a mention in the plans.[66] For long, the municipality had simply locked the Queens Gardens at night to prevent them from being frequented, and therefore, had sidestepped any concerns over crime and policing. Further, the entry, opening and closing times were previously restricted since the gardens adjoined a wing of municipal buildings, including an assembly room for Europeans.[67] Now, since plans for a municipal garden open all day and night were suggested, policing concerns in the vicinity of the busy railway station gained a new significance. The emphasis on 'thieves and disreputable characters more generally' is particularly suggestive here, in the colonial context, since it touches upon broader colonial anxieties over public order as well as the place of the urban poor in the Indian city and their mobility.[68]

The urban poor, categorised as an undifferentiated mass, were understood as sharing dangerous traits, and thus, a threatening presence in the city.[69] Indeed, the same Clarke had himself argued a few years earlier that policing, and particularly military presence was of a high priority in Delhi in order to keep communication lines open. This was because the city's symbolic status still had the potential to attract dangerous elements prepared to stir another rebellion. The argument went that the railway lines and the station had to be protected to enable a European military garrison station in the fort to drop down and defend the European population residing in the northern half of the city.[70] Thus, despite a shift in the understanding of Delhi as a commercially viable transport hub, there remained fears of dangerous elements eager to cause trouble, particularly in the vicinity of the railway station. One can suggest, then, as Stephen Legg does, that the colonial government was unsure of moving away from a form of government that focused on 'dispositions' of people to one entirely focused on self-regulating and semi-autonomous processes.[71] Clarke's railway plan would offer spatial remedies for such issues in the newly transformed gardens.

One measure was to hasten the shift of the assembly room to a 'new club' at Ludlow Castle, a centre for European exclusiveness and sociability. Evidence suggests that this was already agreed upon, and Clarke indicated that this would benefit the scheme overall.[72] This relocation would eventually remove fears of a native intrusion into European spaces of sociability on a near-permanent basis. A second solution was to take the railings and gates lifted from the central *patri* (pavement) on Chandni Chowk and use them in the transformed gardens. The railing-free Chandni Chowk would then be able to accommodate a range of sundry trades, such as the growing number of cap-sellers, whose business had grown as a result of the railways. The borrowed railings, in turn, would be installed at strategic points in the new gardens.[73] With railings all around and gates at certain points enclosing a smaller version of Queens Gardens, ingress and egress would become more predictable. Indeed, not only would traffic flow smoothly, but a smaller version of Queens Gardens also made it easier to bring the area under observation with renewed hopes of achieving proper surveillance of so-called dangerous and untrustworthy elements.

The predictability of movement towards the railway station was again important, but it should be highlighted that the function of railings and gates differed from that of the *burj*. While the latter enabled pedestrians to pause and admire a ruin in a garden-setting, the strategic placement of railings and gates ensured that colonial concerns about security and the itinerancy of the urban poor were managed. The use of space in Clarke's plans thus constructed and enabled a differentiation of the *legitimate* users of the gardens and railways from the *illegitimate* users, such as the commercially inclined native rail users from the likes of 'thieves and disreputable characters more generally'. Thus, as has been suggested the vision of a commercially rich city with smooth and orderly traffic flows in Clarke's plan was framed in relation to distinctly colonial imaginaries and a variety of concerns around political security.

CONTESTING RAILWAY SPACE: EXTRA-MURAL PROPERTIES AND THE CITY

While Clarke's plan for the interiors of the city evoked a vision of pinpoint precision ushered to separate forms of traffic and ensure commercial profitability while keeping in mind the needs of security, there was a predictable gap between intent and effect. This became all too clear when Clarke left the city at the end of his tenure in 1900. The municipality was found wanting when it came to disbursing funds, and at first, only attempted to alter the width of the city gates. Wide approach roads were created for the Ajmeri Gate and Turkoman Gate of the city, and a separate entrance for cattle was constructed near the Delhi Gate.[74] However, plans for the much-desired straight roads leading from the railway station to Chandni Chowk were shelved initially and were only given a new lease of life as the *Durbar* celebrations of 1902 approached.[75] Rather than from the point of view of a long-term benefit to the city, the straight roads from the railway station were built for immediate purposes of imperial power in the spectacle of the *Durbar*. The realisation of the plan was a disjointed affair and might, in hindsight, be deemed a 'failure'.

Nevertheless, we should not forget that Clarke's scheme reveals how the interaction between the government of India and the municipality could fuel the planning process in Delhi to reorganise the city as railway space. As an agency that encouraged circulation, albeit in a distinctly colonial framework, the municipality was able to channel the demands of the government of India and transform the interiors of the city for the smooth flow of commercial traffic. However, at times, this relationship between the two authorities was fraught with tensions, particularly as urban planning became a site for competing visions of circulation and political jurisdiction. These tensions erupted when the government of India proposed the question of expansion of railway facilities outside the city. As we shall see, while the municipality had earlier negotiated with and redesigned its plans to suit the central government's railway activities around the Lahore Gate, by the 1900s, it explicitly resisted the shift of circulatory infrastructure to extra-mural properties outside the city.

If we recall, in Chapter 3, under the rhetoric of 'improvement', the municipality had begun reclaiming garden lands and alluvial tracts in the suburbs of Delhi after the 1870s. Numerous aims and objectives were envisaged in 'improving' the natural landscape, such as the health of the agricultural population residing in the *Sabzi Mandi*. However, compared to the city, the outlying areas had been much neglected in terms of provision of civic amenities. For example, even when expensive schemes for water purification like the water works were implemented in the city, areas like Saddar *bazaar*, the *Sabzi Mandi* and Paharganj were ignored.[76] Suburban *nazul*, however, continued to be used for the collection of *nazul* and *teh-bazari* rents, the allocation of land to private businesses, and to house some government departments.[77] In 1900, the impulse to transform *nazul* lands outside the city came not from the municipality but from the government of India, when it proposed to shift the transhipping arrangements and construct goods sheds in the *Sabzi Mandi*. The municipal authorities opposed this on the grounds that commerce would be stifled if the goods sheds were located far away from burgeoning commercial centres like the Lahore Gate. The government of India, which saw Delhi's railway space as connected to networks of circulation and territorial consolidation at a much larger scale, competed with municipal visions of the city as remaining a localised centre of commercial circulation.

In the late-1890s, the central railway station of Delhi became the focus of a series of debates between the government of India and the railway companies about how the existing goods and passenger traffic facilities could be expanded.[78] With a range of railway interests using Delhi as a terminus, there was an increased need for sidings, transhipping stations and goods depots. Moreover, there was the additional question regarding the sort of railway facilities that could be provided to serve the cotton ginning and flour mills that were springing up on the outskirts of Delhi.[79] In 1898, it was decided that coaching traffic of all the railway lines was to be managed at the central station, and the government of India shifted its attention to the construction of goods depots both within and outside of the city. In 1900, a plan called the 'Railway Extension Project of Delhi' was finalised. The government of India passed a resolution that a part of traffic in goods and transhipping arrangements could be shifted near the *Sabzi Mandi* so as to free the central railway from congestion. Two proposals were put forward, which would place either a station in the *Sabzi Mandi* proper or one in Saddar *bazaar*. The first expounded that the East Indian

Railway Line (which was also responsible for the central station) could construct a goods station in the *Sabzi Mandi* about two miles from the city.[80] The second was that the Sindh Punjab Railway could construct a suburban station between the *Sabzi Mandi* and Saddar *bazaar*.[81] Unlike the proposed East India Line, the latter was closer to the Lahore Gate and its burgeoning trade centres. However, there was a caveat if this option was preferred. The government expected the Rajputana Malwa Railway to vacate their sidings at the Lahore Gate, moving all goods traffic to the new goods station. It was anticipated that this process would take place gradually over time and could involve delays.[82] The Delhi municipality was asked to provide its opinion on which proposal best suited the traders of the city.[83]

Like Clarke before him, the Deputy Commissioner of the city argued that the commercial fortunes of the city were inextricably linked to the railways and the development of its railway traffic. He also felt that since the question was about changing goods stations, the leading traders and manufacturers of Delhi needed to be involved in the decision-making process.[84] Once appointed, a majority in the consortium of Indian and European merchants appealed to the municipality to reject the transfer of goods traffic from the central station to anywhere other than the Lahore Gate. This was actually in opposition to the government of India's preferred option of creating railway facilities at the *Sabzi Mandi* proper. The East India Railway's site in the *Sabzi Mandi* was listed as too far from the burgeoning trade centres of the city and it was said to be 'prejudicial to local interests'.[85] Rather, the stress was entirely on developing the Lahore Gate area further by shifting the entire goods traffic to a new station there. It was argued that if private capital could be invested in constructing warehouses for the storage of non-hazardous goods based on the same principle as that of the port trusts of Bombay and Karachi, it would give the merchants enhanced facilities to expand and profit from trade.[86]

Certainly, there were some dissenting voices from within the trader's consortium, which saw potential in the *Sabzi Mandi* as a lucrative market. Some of the members appointed in a select committee felt that plans could include future development of the area. Some select measures, such as the removal of transhipping arrangements and the creation of sleeper depots, could be implemented for the time-being. For example, municipal members like Ram Kishen Das argued that the potential markets for *gur* (jaggery), *shakkar* (sugar) and vegetables in the *Sabzi Mandi* could be developed to supply future down-country markets and the East Indian Railway could be instituted for the purpose.[87] Others like the merchant Bishnoo Das had mixed opinions, claiming that while the station could benefit the *Sabzi Mandi*, there was not much business there; and if the 'public' was really to benefit from banking and clearing their goods, then the station needed to be closer to the city.[88] As a space of circulation, flows and commerce, the city, for Bishnoo Das, was therefore qualitatively different from outlying areas like the *Sabzi Mandi*.

Since the municipal report was overwhelmingly against relocation to the *Sabzi Mandi*, the government of India reconsidered its proposals. Later a different plan was drafted, underlying little desire to remove the goods station from within the city or the Lahore Gate in the short term. It simply suggested moving transhipping arrangements, and creating a metre gauge locomotive yard and a sleeper depot in the *Sabzi Mandi*. No other shift was suggested until there were further requirements to extend the broad gauge arrangements of all stations, or until other companies needed space to construct new lines, goods stations or passenger arrangements.[89] Thus, we see how an understanding of the city as a localised centre of commercial circulation distinct from outlying areas like the *Sabzi Mandi* was championed by the municipality and was used to contest the government of India's plans to integrate the city into a wider project of territorial consolidation and centralisation of authority. The logics of circulation and territorialisation overlapped with conceptions of colonial power represented by the municipality and government of India, respectively. At times, the planning process was driven by the interaction of the two forces, and on other occasions, they clashed with each other, as in the case of the location of the railway facilities.

As we will see, between 1903 and 1909, such clashes between the authorities would again take place over the allocation of land just outside the city walls. While the municipality wanted a central goods depot to be located near the Lahore Gate for purposes of commercial circulation, it was also opposed to too much railway involvement in the area because of a loss of *nazul* property that was required for the construction of overbridges, ventilation, and the lease of land to private companies to create tramway lines and electric lighting stations. Plots along the wall were deemed suitable for the construction of infrastructure, so that traffic moving into the city could flow smoothly. Conflicts between the authorities highlighted the unstable boundaries between 'city space' and 'railway space', as much as they reflected the distinctions between the municipality and the government of India's authority.

CLASHES AT THE MARGINS: THE CITY GATES AND INFRASTRUCTURES OF CIRCULATION

In 1903, the Agra–Delhi Chord (ADC) railway applied to the government of India for permission to acquire a plot along the Lahore and Ajmeri gates. After some consideration, under the aegis of the government of India, the railway authorities recognised that the plot was needed for permanent acquisition at a future date and agreed to the request. The municipality of Delhi, however, intervened to stop the allocation. Instead, it argued that the area in question needed to remain under their jurisdiction since it was *nazul* property and was needed for the construction of high-level bridges.[90] The reason cited for this was that the municipality wanted to construct bridges, owing to the sheer volume of traffic entering the city through its Farashkhana (between the Ajmeri and Lahore gates) and Lahore gates. Along with pedestrian and railway traffic, *ekkas* (two-wheeled horse carts), municipal filth carts, goods carts driven by bullocks, and new modes of transport like bicycles and tramways were now competing for space on the roads. The *Durbar* of 1902 was significant in this regard, as it became a platform through which the supposed benefits of colonial rule in terms of newer technologies like the motorcar and the electric tramway were launched in Delhi.[91] Eventually, many officials touring Delhi, such as the Lieutenant Governor of the Punjab, Louis Dane, would do so by motorcar and meet municipal members in the Town Hall, one of the few spaces that was soon illuminated by electric lighting.[92]

The influx and indeed intermingling of different forms of traffic once again piqued municipal anxieties, and the ADC railway allocation clashed with municipal plans for the redevelopment of the smaller Farashkhana and Ajmeri gates. While the Lahore Gate had been included in municipal plans from time to time and had become a bone of contention between the government of India and the municipality, the Farashkhana Gate and the Ajmeri Gate would now take centre-stage. Significantly, the area between the Lahore and Ajmeri gates teemed with all kinds of traffic, including religious processions. These were funerary processions heading to and from Muslim burial grounds to the south-west of the city, which used the Ajmeri Gate for egress and ingress.[93] The Ajmeri Gate was therefore also configured in a sacral topography that overlapped with the regulation of the flows of commercial activity, which was its relatively newer municipal configuration.

Conscious of a variety of flows, commercial or otherwise, being hampered by the dense network of level-crossings outside the city gates, the municipality made demands for the construction of overbridges and appealed to the government against the erection of more railway sidings. E. D. Maclagan, the Chief Secretary of Punjab, was informed in 1908 that traffic had to face long waiting times at the Farashkhana level-crossing, and that this had the potential for accidents since people were simply walking across the railway tracks to avoid being burdened by delays.[94] Within a span of 24 hours, local authorities recorded a mix of traffic, including 447 bullock carts, 355 *ekka*s, 98 country carts, 123 municipal filth carts, 29 bicycles, 115 spring carts, 14 *doli*s (carriages), 2,157 animals and 18,325 persons passing over the crossing. The report listed that this traffic had to pass through the crossing when the gates closed 31 times and the average period of closure was 11 minutes. Seven closures were so long that traffic had to wait for 20 minutes, and the longest closure at one time was 28 minutes.[95] All this was presented as detrimental to the municipality's attempts to encourage the smooth movement of traffic and commercial growth in the city. It was clear that circulation would be impeded if further railway construction, and thus, 'state works' were allowed, injuring the city's long-term economic prospects.

As a remedy, overbridges were planned as an effective means of creating unrestricted connections between burgeoning trade centres and bypassing the grid of railway sidings and level crossings. Iron grids of urban infrastructure like cart and footbridges were similar to Clarke's creation of high pavements, which could separate heavy goods from pedestrian traffic. The conviction here was again that colonial technologies and infrastructure had the potential to reduce the constant monitoring, maintenance and financial liabilities of the municipality. Therefore, they were an important factor when it came to asking the government of India to rethink the allocation to the ADC railway near the city walls.

Interestingly, the pursuit of technology itself was another reason why the municipality resisted the allocation of *nazul* lands near the walls. A resolution passed by municipal members in 1902 stated that a plot of land measuring 600 feet by 300 feet should be reserved for the construction of an electric power station, and there should be a provision in place so that more land could be taken for future construction of tramway lines.[96] Not only were these infrastructures important for circulation in the city, but as Jyoti Hosagrahar has argued, electric lighting and the tramway were also 'visible markers of improvement' meant to assert the superior authority of the British government over its native subjects.[97] In 1902, private companies were promised leases to construct such services as 'a matter of considerable importance to the municipality and consequently to the public'.[98] Major Douglas, the Deputy Commissioner at the time, summed up the municipal problem with the ADC railway proposals to his superiors by referring a map of the area:

> The firm responsible for those lights obtained a site for their power station at the point B on plan A. The Railway Company, whose plans have been in complete abeyance since 1897, have in the meantime reappeared and in accordance with the scheme now submitted their line will pass through the Electric power station at B.[99]

Finally, the question of ventilation added additional weight to municipal arguments against the ADC land allocation. Indeed, such an argument went hand in hand with the need for traffic management. The municipality had for long sought to check the preponderance of activities that were considered 'nuisances' to air flows and circulation. Also, an excessive state regulation of everyday street activities existed in India unlike in the metropolis, giving rise to what has been called a 'discriminatory sanitary order'.[100] By 1902, the growing network of railways lines had drastically changed perceptions of sanitation and ventilation in the city. With a dense network of railway lines to the north and to the west of the city in place, and the Yamuna River to its east, the municipality contended that Delhi was being 'hemmed in'.[101] It argued that 'ample space' was urgently needed for future plans, including a roadway scheme, electric tramway extension scheme, and the creation of a sewage farm to the south-west of the Ajmeri Gate.[102]

The outcome of such tensions between state authorities was profound. In 1908, the government of India backtracked on its plans and gave way for the municipality to create overbridges. Predictably, however, and as is now a familiar story, when it came to the actual execution of the overbridge projects the municipality felt pinched when considering the financial outlays.[103] Yet, if in this particular exercise efforts came to a nought, this was not a total loss. Over the years, the wrangling between the municipality and government of India enabled the former to bolster its legal credentials. Ultimately, this purposeful digression was effective inasmuch as it secured for the municipality the future right to 'reopen the case of the Farashkhana or the provision of other roads or streets calculated to facilitate communications and traffic in this quarter of the city'.[104] Therefore, if the original plans faltered, now the plan itself was to keep the area earmarked for future needs protected by increased regulatory powers.

In the early 1900s, then, the density of railway traffic and the desire for the government of India to acquire land along the city wall made it an extremely contested area as the municipality battled railway authorities to stay in control of its *nazul* lands. Such conflicts over territory highlighted the tensions between overlapping but at times distinct conceptions of authority. Planning the city for circulation, particularly for the smooth flow of commercial traffic, was a claim to authority for the municipality. Moreover, in the 1900s, this clashed with demands for control over territory by the government of India, whose increased interference in land allocation and management of the railways, in turn, led to plans for the city being reshaped along with increased regulatory powers for the municipality. These clashes also reveal the constant process of redefinition, where the boundaries of railway space, on the one hand, and Delhi's space, on the other, were not fixed but renegotiated under the claims of the two authorities.

CONCLUSION

This chapter has shown how, from the late-1880s, the Delhi municipality began to take an active interest in managing the circulation of commercial traffic in the city. In this regard, the growth of the railways was crucial to the reimagination of Delhi as a transport node. Municipal plans drafted by senior officials began focusing on how the spaces of the city could be reconstituted so that the smooth flows of goods and commodities could be facilitated. The urban fabric was to play a key part in this endeavour with extension schemes, new garden projects, redesigned localities, large pavements and overbridges relieving traffic congestion by separating forms of traffic and disciplining or modifying movement in the city. Indeed, by 1905, the Punjab Chamber of Commerce showered praise upon the Delhi municipality for the efforts it had undertaken to 'develop traffic', popularise the railways, and the 'great saving in time' brought by the railway facilities in Delhi.[105] It should be no surprise that mercantile interests and commercial growth were at the forefront of the plans. As Sandip Hazareesingh has argued, the colonial model of urban citizenship relied on 'class' and property rights to frame the state's relationship with the residents of the city and restricted mass material entitlements and participation.[106]

Indeed, we can find examples of how this colonial model of urban citizenship won out even as echoes of 'town planning' could be heard as early as 1908. In the same year, for example, a settlement officer of the Delhi district wrote to the Deputy Commissioner and President of the municipality that a comprehensive plan needed to be laid out so that benefits of health, sanitation and leisure facilities could be extended to Delhi's outlying areas. He was critical of how narrowly previous plans were conceived by the municipality, inasmuch as they took into consideration the need of a select mercantile and European elite, and were based on the simple desire to accumulate profit from *nazul* rents. It is worth quoting here a handwritten note from the settlement officer's report on a *nazul* survey, which was underway. The officer wrote of a proposed southward expansion in the following manner:

> Would it not be possible to lay out a new suburb on the existing nazul land of Khandarat Kalan, Ferozabad Banger and perhaps take in Narhaula and Raisena as well? I mean a really respectable sanitary suburb in which the ADC railway would open a station, with proper boulevards and wide-open spaces. Our present proposed improvements are unsympathetic, leaving no open spaces

or resort and recreation, in spite of the subject lesson of the Queen's gardens and its perpetual crowd ...

The proposal further continued:

> ... What a treat it would be to have that miserable Khandarat land extending down to Nizam-din's [sic.] tomb land out in blocks, systematically arranged for future building sites, with a purpose allowance for roads and hygienic recreation! Surely it is better to tackle the question now and to ensure orderly expansion than to allow the city to expand according to the taste and fancy of individual land owners?[107]

While in one sense the official echoed the oft-repeated colonial trope of orderly development of the 'miserable' 'waste' lands, his attempt signalled how the imaginary of planning had the potential to embrace both the city and the suburbs by incorporating the elements of sanitation, recreation and leisure for the population. This direction, that is, focusing on the benefit of the 'population' at large was qualitatively different from planning for the sake of profitability or for the interests of commercial sections and landowners, of which the municipality was the largest. This expansion to the south of the city, however, entailed a costly shift in direction in terms of both resources and extending the benefits of commercial circulation; and this would only come to pass for very different reasons after the *Durbar* of 1911.[108]

Second, this chapter suggests that if the desire for a commercially rich and congestion-free city caught the fancy of municipal heads like Clarke, his plans were also distinctly colonial in the way they foregrounded policing needs and drew upon colonial imaginaries of what constituted 'natural' features of the urban environment of Indian cities. The presence of a mosque in the extension scheme of the 1880s was therefore based on the understanding of the necessity of religion in a commercially vibrant north Indian city. This was not a faux installation, masking in reality a shift from the religious to the secular power of the market. Instead, it was understood as essential to, and embedded within, market realities and therefore necessary for future commercial growth in Indian cities. Moreover, the re-development of the Queens Gardens was imagined as moving hand in hand with the relocation of European spaces of sociability and the policing of traffic heading to the railway station. The memory of the rebellion still provoked fears of 'dangerous' elements, and carefully placed gates and railings in garden plans were meant to isolate and monitor traffic so that the station could be guarded effectively. Indeed, this evidence suggests that a politics of difference continued to underpin municipal calculations even as the city was being imagined as the 'Charring Cross' of north India.

Finally, this chapter demonstrates how a 'scalar politics' between state agencies could be constitutive of urban planning in colonial Delhi. It has revealed how the colonial project of territorial consolidation, and thus, the inscription of state sovereignty intersected with centrifugal processes of circulation at the level of the city. For the government of India, the city and its outskirts were conceived as part of 'state works', and this territorialisation of power led it to intervene more directly in urban affairs, such as the allocation of land to different railway companies, especially from the 1880s. The claims of local urban agencies like the Delhi municipality, however, rested on managing circulation, flows and movement, albeit, as we have seen, from a distinctly colonial orientation. The interaction between the two authorities often came in the form of clashes such as that over the placement of railway facilities outside the city walls over *nazul* lands.

Contending logics at work in the Delhi municipality and government of India's actions were revealed by disputes over space for the Bombay Baroda and the Central India Railway or the India Midland Railway in the 1880s, the *Sabzi Mandi* station relocation in the 1890s, and the ADC land allocation question in the early-1900s. Along with local negotiation, resistance and financial conservatism, such clashes did affect the realisation of urban plans. Of course, it is also important to be aware that simply concluding that urban plans 'failed' obscures how the interlocking claims of the two aforementioned agencies could be productive in terms of reorganising the city as railway space in various ways. Municipal planning was spurred on by the demands of the government of India for the management of bodies and goods traffic. Its capacity for planning also increased, such as its assiduous management of lucrative cul-de-sac plots near the station or the legal credentials it unintentionally strengthened in the process of staving the government of India's ADC railway allocation.

Therefore, it was as a result of the contradictions within the state that urban planning was bolstered.

NOTES

1. Letter from Robert Clarke, Deputy Commissioner, Delhi, to the Commissioner and Superintendent, Delhi, dated 18 April 1888, No. 43, 10 A, Box 41, 1888, DSA CCO.

2. Letter from Robert Clarke, Deputy Commissioner, Delhi to the Commissioner and Superintendent, Delhi, dated 3 January 1893, No. 43, 10 A, Box 41, 1888, DSA CCO.

3. For a comparative study on how material changes shaped and remade Paris in the nineteenth century, see David Harvey, *Paris, Capital of Modernity* (London: Routledge, 2006).

4. I have taken inspiration from Manu Goswami's scalar approach that examines how political–economic processes shaped the formation of a distinctly 'colonial', and later, 'national' space in India. I have borrowed her notion of the 'territorialisation' of sovereign power, part of larger political and economic processes; but I examine how this worked in tension with other state agencies encouraging circulatory modalities at the level of the city. See Manu Goswami, *Producing India: From Colonial Economy to National Space* (Chicago: University of Chicago Press, 2004). For another perspective that considers spatial scalar politics in colonial Delhi, see Stephen Legg, *Prostitution and the Ends of Empire: Scale, Governmentalities and Interwar India* (Durham: Duke University Press, 2014).

5. Although an extensive amount of work has been produced on the railways, as Ian Kerr points out, the relationship between urban cities and the railways has received 'little direct attention'. See Ian J. Kerr, 'Introduction', in *27 Down: New Departures in Indian Railway Studies*, ed. Ian J. Kerr (New Delhi: Orient BlackSwan, 2007), xxi–xxii. Kerr himself has tried to rectify this shortcoming by assessing the impact of railway development on the urbanisation of Bombay and Lahore. See Ian J. Kerr, 'Bombay and Lahore: Colonial Railways and Colonial Cities: Some Urban Consequences of the Development and Operation of the Railways in India, c. 1850–1947', available at http://www.docutren.com/HistoriaFerroviaria/Aranjuez2001/pdf/07.pdf (accessed 15 June 2020). A similar perspective that examines how new modes of communication like the railways shaped commercial and political relationships between Bombay and Deccan towns is Ellen Macdonald

Gumprez, 'City–Hinterland Relations and the Development of a Regional Elite in Nineteenth Century Bombay', in *Railways in Modern India*, ed. Ian J. Kerr (New Delhi: Oxford University Press, 2001), 97–125.

6. Marian Aguiar, *Tracking Modernity: India's Railway and the Culture of Mobility* (Minnesota: University of Minnesota Press, 2011), xviii.

7. Goswami, *Producing India*, 6–8.

8. Jyoti Hosagrahar, *Indigenous Modernities: Negotiating Architecture and Urbanism* (London: Routledge, 2005), 59.

9. Government of Punjab, *Gazetteer of the Delhi District: 1883–84* (Gurgaon: Vintage Books, 1988), 143.

10. Government of Punjab, *Gazetteer of Delhi (1912)* (Gurgaon: Vintage Books, 1992), 164.

11. In his case study of Uttar Pradesh, Ian Derbyshire points out that rail usage only started gaining momentum in north India after the 1880s. As reason behind this, he cites that there was an overall reduction in freight rates per *maund*, which is an Indian unit of measuring weight (from 0.4 pies in the mid-1860s to 0.25 pies by the mid-1880s) and a decrease in the average rates per passenger mile (from 3.5 pies to 2.5 pies in the same period) in the north Indian plains. See Ian D. Derbyshire, 'Competition and Adaptation: The Operation of Railways in Northern India: Uttar Pradesh 1860–1914', in *Our Indian Railway: Themes in India's Railway History*, ed. E. Srinivasan, M. Tiwari and S. Silas (New Delhi: Foundation Books), 50–76.

12. David Arnold, 'The Problem of Traffic: The Street Life of Modernity in Late Colonial India', *Modern Asian Studies* 46, no. 1, 2012, 119–41.

13. Independent of the municipality, separate agencies instituted for civic restructuring and urban renewal in the form of 'Improvement Trusts' in India would only take root after the 1890s. The Bombay Improvement Trust, the first of its kind, was created a decade later in 1898 to address the question of sanitation and public health, which had arisen in the light of the plague. For a detailed study of the trust and its activities, see Prashant Kidambi, 'Housing the Poor in a Colonial City: The Bombay Improvement Trust, 1898–1918', *Studies in History* 17, no. 57, 2001, 57–79.

14. Letter from Robert Clarke, Deputy Commissioner, Delhi, to the Commissioner and Superintendent, Delhi, dated 18 April 1888.

15. Letter from Robert Clarke, Deputy Commissioner, Delhi, to the Commissioner and Superintendent, Delhi.

16. See Narayani Gupta, 'Military Security and Urban Development: A Case Study of Delhi 1857–1912', *Modern Asian Studies* 5, no. 1, 1971, 61–77.

17. Letter from Robert Clarke, Deputy Commissioner, Delhi, to Colonel Grey,

Commissioner and Superintendent, Delhi, dated 25 March 1889, No. 43, 10 A, Box 41, 1888, DSA CCO.

18. For another example of how sovereign power triumphed over the logic of circulation and the disciplinary apparatus of the state, albeit in the context of post-colonial urban planning, See Marcus Daechsel, 'Sovereignty, Governmentality and Development in Ayub's Pakistan: The Case of Korangi Township', *Modern Asian Studies* 45, no. 1, 2011, 131–57.

19. Letter from Robert Clarke, Deputy Commissioner, Delhi, to Colonel Grey, Commissioner and Superintendent, Delhi, dated 25 March 1889.

20. Letter from Robert Clarke, Deputy Commissioner, Delhi, to Colonel Grey, Commissioner and Superintendent, Delhi, dated 25 March 1889.

21. Note to the Members of the Delhi Municipality by Robert Clarke, Deputy Commissioner and President, Municipal Committee, n.d., No. 43, 10 A, Box 41, 1888, DSA CCO.

22. Note to the Members of the Delhi Municipality by Robert Clarke, Deputy Commissioner and President, Municipal Committee, n.d.

23. Hosagrahar, *Indigenous Modernities*, 123–26.

24. Hosagrahar, *Indigenous Modernities*, 123–26.

25. Note to the Members of the Delhi Municipality by Robert Clarke, Deputy Commissioner and President, Municipal Committee, n.d.

26. Copy of a Letter from the Secretary, Municipal Committee, Delhi, to the Deputy Commissioner, Delhi, dated 15 August 1893, No. 43, 10 A, Box 41, 1888, DSA CCO.

27. Note to the Members of the Delhi Municipality by Robert Clarke, Deputy Commissioner and President, Municipal Committee, n.d.

28. Note to the Members of the Delhi Municipality by Robert Clarke, Deputy Commissioner and President, Municipal Committee, n.d.

29. Hosagrahar, *Indigenous Modernities*, 125.

30. Report on the Administration of the Delhi Crown Lands, Lahore, 1910, 33, No. 13-II, Box 64, 1908, DSA CCO.

31. Letter from Robert Clarke, Deputy Commissioner, Delhi, to the Col. T. H. Grey, Commissioner and Supt. Delhi Division, dated 15 July 1890, No. 43, 10 A, 1888, Box 41, DSA CCO.

32. Letter from Robert Clarke, Deputy Commissioner, Delhi, to the Col. T. H. Grey, Commissioner and Supt. Delhi Division, dated 15 July 1890.

33. Report on the Administration of the Delhi Crown Lands, Lahore, 1910, 30–31.

34. Hosagrahar, *Indigenous Modernities*, 129.

35. Report on the Administration of the Delhi Crown Lands, Lahore, 1910, 32.

86. Letter from Robert Clarke, Deputy Commissioner, Delhi, to Col. T. H. Grey, Commissioner and Supt. Delhi Division, dated 15 July 1890.

87. Letter from Robert Clarke, Deputy Commissioner, Delhi, to Col. T. H. Grey, Commissioner and Supt. Delhi Division, dated 15 July 1890.

38. Goswami, *Producing India*, 45.

39. Goswami, *Producing India*, 56–58.

40. In conjunction with these, Goswami writes that the accounts of railway companies were kept under tight scrutiny, and on the board of each company, a state official was appointed, who had the right of ultimate veto; Goswami, *Producing India*, 52.

41. Letter from Robert Clarke, Deputy Commissioner, Delhi, to Col. T. H. Grey, Commissioner and Supt. Delhi Division, dated 15 July 1890.

42. Narayani Gupta, *Delhi Between Two Empires: 1803–1931: Society, Government and Urban Growth* (New Delhi: Oxford University Press, 1981), 171–72.

43. Note Recorded by Mr Clarke Commissioner of Delhi, Under Section 176 (1) of the Municipal Act and Submitted for the Consideration of the Municipal Committee of Delhi, dated 18 February 1899, S. No. 50, B-10, Box 56, 1899, DSA CCO.

44. Note Recorded by Mr Clarke Commissioner of Delhi, Under Section 176 (1) of the Municipal Act and Submitted for the Consideration of the Municipal Committee of Delhi, dated 18 February 1899.

45. Letter from Robert Clarke, Commissioner and Superintendent, Delhi, to the Deputy Commissioner, Delhi, dated 22 February1899, S. No. 50, B-10, Box 56, 1899, DSA CCO.

46. The central station was created in the aftermath of the rebellion of 1857. It formed a part of a larger project to turn Delhi into a distribution centre between Punjab and Calcutta. See Gupta, *Delhi Between Two Empires*, 43.

47. Copy of a Letter from the Secretary to Government of India, PWD, to the Secretary to the Government of Bombay, PWD, Railway Branch, and the Consulting Engineer, the Government of India for Railways, Calcutta and Lucknow, dated 3 August 1899, S. No. 50, B-8, Box 56, 1899, DSA CCO.

48. Copy of a Letter from the Secretary to Government of India, PWD, to the Secretary to the Government of Bombay, PWD, Railway Branch, and the Consulting Engineer, the Government of India for Railways, Calcutta and Lucknow, dated 3 August 1899.

49. Copy of a Letter from the Secretary to Government of India, PWD, to the Secretary to the Government of Bombay, PWD, Railway Branch, and the Consulting Engineer, the Government of India for Railways, Calcutta and Lucknow, dated 3 August 1899.

50. Letter from the Government of India, PWD to the Secretary to the Government, Punjab, dated 24 July 1895, No. 429-230 A: No. 429, NAI PWD, Railway Construction.

51. Note Recorded by Mr Clarke, Commissioner of Delhi, Under Section 176 (1) of the Municipal Act and Submitted for the Consideration of the Municipal Committee of Delhi, dated 18 February 1899, S. No. 50, B-10, Box 56, 1899, DSA CCO.

52. Note Recorded by Mr Clarke, Commissioner of Delhi, Under Section 176 (1) of the Municipal Act and Submitted for the Consideration of the Municipal Committee of Delhi, dated 18 February 1899.

53. Note Recorded for the Consideration of the Municipal Committee by the Commissioner of Delhi Under Section 176 (1) (D) of the Municipal Act, dated 4 March 1899, S. No. 50, B-10, Box 56, 1899, DSA CCO.

54. Note Recorded for the Consideration of the Municipal Committee by the Commissioner of Delhi Under Section 176 (1) (D) of the Municipal Act, dated 4 March 1899.

55. For a discussion on how technology was used to mould subjectivities in the metropolis, see Christopher Otter, 'Cleansing and Clarifying: Technology and Perception in Nineteenth-Century London', *Journal of British Studies* 43, no. 1, 2004, 40–64.

56. Note Recorded by Mr Clarke, Commissioner of Delhi, Under Section 176 (1) of the Municipal Act and Submitted for the Consideration of the Municipal Committee of Delhi, dated 18 February 1899.

57. William J. Glover, *Making Lahore Modern: Constructing and Imagining a Colonial City* (Minneapolis: University of Minnesota Press, 2007), xx–xxi.

58. Glover, *Making Lahore Modern*, xxv.

59. Note Recorded by Mr Clarke, Commissioner of Delhi, Under Section 176 (1) of the Municipal Act and Submitted for the Consideration of the Municipal Committee of Delhi, dated 18 February 1899.

60. Note Recorded by Mr Clarke, Commissioner of Delhi, Under Section 176 (1) of the Municipal Act and Submitted for the Consideration of the Municipal Committee of Delhi, dated 18 February 1899.

61. Note Recorded for Consideration of the Municipal Committee by the Commissioner of Delhi under Section 176 (1) (D) of the Municipal Act, dated 4 March 1899.

62. Note Recorded for Consideration of the Municipal Committee by the Commissioner of Delhi under Section 176 (1) (D) of the Municipal Act, dated 4 March 1899.

63. Note Recorded for Consideration of the Municipal Committee by the

Commissioner of Delhi under Section 176 (1) (D) of the Municipal Act, dated 4 March 1899.

64. Hosagrahar, *Indigenous Modernities*, 140.

65. What I suggest here on the qualification of movement has parallels with arguments made by historians in other parts of the colonial world, where the creation of circulatory infrastructures in the late-nineteenth century did not imply either the encouragement of unregulated flows or a complete clampdown of mobilities. As Valeska Huber suggests, for example, this rather meant the initiation of a third path, that is, through 'the differentiation, bureaucratisation and regulation of different kinds of movement'. Valeska Huber, *Channelling Mobilities, Migration and Mobilisation in the Suez Canal Region and Beyond, 1869–1914* (Cambridge, Massachusetts: Cambridge University Press, 2013), 3.

66. Note Recorded for Consideration of the Municipal Committee by the Commissioner of Delhi Under Section 176 (1) (D) of the Municipal Act, dated 4 March 1899.

67. Note Recorded for Consideration of the Municipal Committee by the Commissioner of Delhi Under Section 176 (1) (D) of the Municipal Act, dated 4 March 1899.

68. As Nandini Gooptu suggests, it was the urban poor much more than the rural poor who were viewed as a threat to public order and social stability by both the British administration and the Indian elites. This process of demonisation of the urban poor intensified during the interwar period. Nandini Gooptu, *The Politics of the Urban Poor in Early Twentieth-century India* (Cambridge, Massachusetts: Cambridge University Press, 2004), 12–14.

69. Gooptu, *Politics of the Urban Poor*, 12–14.

70. Copy of a Letter from H. C. Fanshawe, Commissioner and Superintendent Delhi, to the Secretary to the Government of Punjab, Judicial and General Department, dated 7 April 1901, S. No. 33, CB-42, Box 42, 1888, DSA CCO.

71. Stephen Legg, *Spaces of Colonialism: Delhi's Urban Governmentalities* (New Delhi: Wiley-Blackwell, 2007), 25.

72. Note Recorded for Consideration of the Municipal Committee by the Commissioner of Delhi Under Section 176 (1) (D) of the Municipal Act, dated 4 March 1899.

73. Note Recorded for Consideration of the Municipal Committee by the Commissioner of Delhi Under Section 176 (1) (D) of the Municipal Act, dated 4 March 1899.

74. Copy of a Letter from Captain W. M. Douglas, Deputy Commissioner, Delhi, to Gordon Walker, Commissioner and Superintendent, Delhi, dated 5 February 1902, S. No. 50, B-10, Box 56, 1899, DSA CCO.

75. Rai Sahib Madho Pershad, *The History of the Delhi Municipality: 1863–1921* (Allahabad: Pioneer Press, 1921), 141.

76. Letter from the Secretary, Municipal Committee, Delhi, to the Deputy Commissioner, Delhi, dated 22 June 1898, S. No. 67, W-2, Box 51, 1894, DSA CCO.

77. Hosagrahar, *Indigenous Modernities*, 135.

78. Copy of a Letter from the Secretary to the Government of India, PWD, to the Secretary to the Government of Punjab, PWD, dated 2 July 1900, 8/1899, DSA DCO.

79. Statement of Traffic to North Western Railway and Southern Punjab Railway and of that to and from North Western Railway and Southern Punjab Railway for the Half Year Ended 30 June 1901, No. 35-45A: No. 38/2, February 1902, NAI PWD, Railway Construction.

80. Copy of a Letter from the Secretary to the Government of India, to the Deputy Commissioner, Delhi, dated 17 March 1900, 8/1899, DSA DCO.

81. Letter from Hardhian Singh to the Deputy Commissioner, Delhi, dated 19 December 1900, 8/1899, DSA DCO.

82. Copy of a Letter from the Secretary to the Government of India, to the Deputy Commissioner, Delhi, dated 17 March 1900.

83. Copy of a Letter from the Secretary to the Government of India, to the Deputy Commissioner, dated 17 March 1900; and Copy of a letter No. 1486 R. C. from the Secretary to the Government of India, PWD, to the Secretary to the Government Punjab, dated 2 November 1900.

84. Copy of a Letter from the Deputy Commissioner, Delhi, to the Secretary to the Railways, PWD, Buildings and Roads Branch, dated 17 April 1900, S. No. 50, B-10, Box 56, 1899, DSA CCO.

85. Letter from James Currie Esq. to the Deputy Commissioner, Delhi, dated 12 April 1900, 8/1899, DSA DCO.

86. Letter from James Currie Esq. to the Deputy Commissioner, Delhi, dated 12 April 1900.

87. Letter from Ram Kishen Das to the Deputy Commissioner, Delhi, dated 17 December 1900, 8/1899, DSA DCO.

88. Letter from Bishnoo Das to the Deputy Commissioner, Delhi, dated 19 December 1900, 8/1899, DSA DCO.

89. Copy of a Letter from the Secretary to the Government of India, PWD, Railway Construction, to the Secretary to the Government, Punjab, PWD, Buildings and Roads Branch, dated 29 August 1901, 3/1901, DSA DCO.

90. Letter from Major M. W. Douglas, Deputy Commissioner, Delhi, to T. Gordon Walker, Commissioner and Superintendent, Delhi Division, dated 18 February 1903, 50-B (8), Box 56, 1899, DSA CCO.

91. Delhi's tryst with motorcar traffic began as early as 1905 when 33 vehicles took off from the city to drive through to Bombay. These 'motor car trials' were organised by members of private motor clubs across India. See Special Correspondent, 'Motor Trials in India: Lessons of the Trials', *The Times of India*, 4 January 1905, 6.

92. Reuter's Agency, 'Progress of Delhi: A Model Punjab City', *The Times of India*, 11 January 1909, 7.

93. Letter from the Hon. Mr E. D. Maclagan, Chief Secretary to the Government, Punjab to the Secretary, Railway Board, dated 3 June 1908, No. 128-151A: No. 128, November 1909, NAI PWD, Railway Construction.

94. Letter from the Hon. Mr E. D. Maclagan, Chief Secretary to the Government, Punjab to the Secretary, Railway Board, dated 3 June 1908. Making a case for space to be reserved for overbridges, the Commissioner stated:

> It is a matter of common knowledge in the city that people coming to and going from the city by this route in hackney vehicles find it more convenient and expeditious to pay off their conveyance at the level crossing when the gates are shut, walk across and reengage another vehicle from the crowd waiting at the other side.

95. Letter from the Hon. Mr E. D. Maclagan, Chief Secretary to the Government, Punjab to the Secretary, Railway Board, dated 3 June 1908.

96. Letter from Major M. W. Douglas, Deputy Commissioner, Delhi, to T. Gordon Walker, Commissioner and Superintendent, Delhi Division, dated 18 February 1903.

97. Hosagrahar, *Indigenous Modernities*, 100–01.

98. Letter from Major M. W. Douglas, Deputy Commissioner, Delhi, to T. Gordon Walker, Commissioner and Superintendent, Delhi Division, dated 18 February 1903.

99. Letter from Major M. W. Douglas, Deputy Commissioner, Delhi, to T. Gordon Walker, Commissioner and Superintendent, Delhi Division, dated 18 February 1903.

100. Historian Gyan Prakash has coined this expression. See Gyan Prakash, *Another Reason: Science and the Imagination of Modern India* (Princeton: Princeton University Press, 1999), 132.

101. Letter from Major M. W. Douglas, Deputy Commissioner, Delhi, to T. Gordon Walker, Commissioner and Superintendent, Delhi Division, dated 18 February 1903.

102. Letter from Major M. W. Douglas, Deputy Commissioner, Delhi, to T. Gordon Walker, Commissioner and Superintendent, Delhi Division, dated 18 February 1903.

103. Letter from the Deputy Commissioner and President, Municipal Committee, Delhi to the Agent, Great Indian Peninsular Railways, dated 2 August 1909, No. 128-151A: No. 146, November 1909, NAI PWD, Railway Construction.

104. Letter from the Deputy Commissioner and President, Municipal Committee, Delhi to the Agent, Great Indian Peninsular Railways, dated 2 August 1909.

105. Anonymous, 'Punjab Chamber of Commerce', *The Tribune*, 14 February 1906, 4.

106. Sandip Hazareesingh suggests that this would not change until a new discourse of inclusive urban citizenship was initiated by Patrick Geddes in India. See Sandip Hazareesingh, *The Colonial City and the Challenge of Modernity: Urban Hegemonies and Civic Contestations in Bombay City 1900–1925* (New Delhi: Orient BlackSwan, 2007), 167–216.

107. Note by the Settlement Officer, Delhi, dated 4 May 1908, 18/1908, DSA DCO.

108. The Khandarat, Ferozabad and Raisena lands were incorporated into urban plans after the shift of the capital from Calcutta to Delhi in 1911. However, when the landscapes of 'old' and 'new' Delhi were entwined, it was not through any idea of benevolent planning, but again because the territorialisation of sovereign power worked in tension with and shaped processes of circulation. While New Delhi was to be a symbolic capital, distinct from the 'old' city, policing and sanitation priorities, for example, made it essential to interlock the two through grids of governance. See Legg, *Spaces of Colonialism*, 82–209.

Conclusion

This book has highlighted a distinct time frame, which is significant for the ways in which colonial power was organised and developed. Indeed, we have seen how overlapping visions, practices and knowledges intersected with one another in unexpected ways between 1858 and 1911, and how they were instrumental for the constitution of colonial power. It is possible to suggest, then, that the 'High Noon of Empire' (1858–1914), broadly coinciding with the time period of this book, was an era when the 'consolidation' of colonial power was linked to its 'instability' and not the other way around. Yet, how might one reflect on the legacies of such a formative period in the history of the city? In 1911, it was announced that a 'New' Delhi would be built, which would serve as the capital of British India instead of Calcutta. This 'transfer of the capital' corresponded with an intense reorganisation of urban agencies and bureaucracy in line with administrative requirements. Yet, policy contradictions, competing priorities of, and among, government agencies, along with clashes among different scales of the state apparatus persisted, as did the resistance towards failed promises of urban renewal. A consequence of this was the systematic neglect of 'Old' Delhi, which stood in contrast to its newer and more pampered cousin.

Stephen Legg's research on Delhi between 1911 and 1947 provides rich insights into how crucial sanitary initiatives and decongestion measures were marginalised by the priorities of the imperial government, to the detriment of Old Delhi and its inhabitants. Thus, the 'Western Extension scheme', perhaps one of the most significant measures drawn up to relieve congestion in 'Old' Delhi by the Delhi Municipality after 1911, languished as a result of the central government's apathy and unwillingness to sanction funds till the late-1930s.[1] New Delhi, the seat of sovereign power, with its wide spaces and better-equipped 'New Delhi Municipal Corporation' (NDMC), had less problems with congestion, and thereby, fared better in health and medical statistics.[2] Moreover, despite the Delhi municipality's constant pleading and its loss of lucrative *nazul* lands to the government of India, the latter failed to provide adequate funding to either cover the costs of municipal losses or issue extra capital to house poor families displaced by the new capital project.[3] Even after 1937, when the Delhi Improvement Trust (DIT), a forerunner of the post-Independence Delhi Development Authority (DDA), was created, urban sanitation and decongestion measures took a backseat to other priorities. As Jyoti Hosagrahar suggests, the DIT's tenure was marked by hidden agendas such as 'institutional interests in profiteering', which conflicted with its goals to provide urban sanitary services.[4] As an arm of the imperial government, it would protect the latter's interests by refusing to sell the government lands that it was developing, and instead, it would retain proprietary titles by issuing long-term leases.[5]

Significantly, after the DIT undertook haphazard 'Slum Clearance' projects, in the 1940s, it began rehousing the dispossessed urban poor as tenants on rental properties that they could little afford; this compounded congestion problems.[6] Such colonial legacies would influence the practices of the DIT and the DDA (established in 1957) in the postcolonial era.[7] Both would continue, for example, to pursue other priorities such as institutional 'speculation' of property at a time when Delhi was engulfed by larger crises such as the Partition of India and the influx of Hindu and Sikh refugees from the new state of Pakistan.[8] Since the 1960s, the DDA 'masterplan', in its various avatars, has been the preferred mode for urban management of the city. Yet, historical and contemporary research on urban Delhi has also highlighted how the pursuit of order through master planning has intensified, instead of alleviating, the markers of urban distress, particularly for the urban poor.[9]

While the history of Indian cities like Delhi can thus be read as a reminder of the trials of planning or perhaps of the 'failure' of urban development, there is another story here, which needs to be recounted. In the cases outlined, particular attempts to promote urban renewal may have failed; yet, the agencies of the state, and their regulatory and bureaucratic powers found new means of expression. Thus, Legg suggests, for example, that even as the Delhi municipality failed to realise its stated objectives in the 1930s, its focus changed as a result of funding crises. This was, as Legg subtly puts it, a 'partial transformation of purpose'; no longer was the municipality intent on creating poor-class dwellings to accommodate those forced out by slum clearances, but its energies were devoted to making 'financially remunerative' middle-class dwellings.[10] The failed project of providing dwellings for the poor, then, had inadvertently morphed into something altogether new. A new sense of purpose was complemented by a redirection of resources and manpower. This is something we have seen time and again in the previous chapters.

Indeed, if we take up the recent trajectory of the Delhi municipality for closer examination, I hope this will drive home the connections between 'failure' and state power, as legacies of the colonial that live on even in our postcolonial present. The MCD or the Delhi Nagar Nigam has, of course, undergone much change in recent years.[11] Yet, it is a prime candidate when exploring some of the concerns raised about the arbitrary and contingent nature of state power and its effects. In March 2017, the Indian National Congress party drafted a proposal to restructure the MCD.[12] The aim was strategic: the Congress had hoped to win the Delhi assembly elections from the incumbent Hindu nationalist Bharatiya Janata Party (BJP) and wrest control over the trifurcated MCD (an abortive effort as each of its three divisions continue to remain under the BJP).

Notably, earlier in the year, sanitation workers employed by one division, the east MCD, had gone on strike protesting against their dire pecuniary conditions, particularly the fact that their salaries had not been paid by the MCD for over two months. As a result, garbage piled up on the streets of east Delhi, reported quite conspicuously by the media.[13] This created an opportune moment for political point-scoring. P. Chidambaram, a senior Congress leader, took this opportunity to offer his thoughts on planning for a 'world-class city' of the future. 'World-classness' implied an aspirational global future for Delhi, underpinned by an idealised aesthetic as a grid for the delineation of state policy and practice.[14] In order to attain this, it was clear that administrative restructuring was required to reshape the existing municipal enterprise since its three divisions were profligate and inefficient. Chidambaram would suggest a radical path for municipal success in this light, not simply having the 'same tired bureaucracy' once again, but an a open initiative with the involvement of 'experts' and the 'public': 'I invite experts and layman, both to be part of this exercise as we plan to radically restructure Delhi (MCD). Ultimately the plan must be something the people must adopt and accept .... And, in 10 years through this plan, we will make Delhi a world-class city.'[15]

Significantly, it was only a few years earlier, in 2011, that the Congress government, the then ruling party in the National Capital Region (NCR) of Delhi, had itself initiated a trifurcation of the MCD, a way of ensuring 'proper administration' in the city.[16] Better municipal services, and thereby, urban development, the then Chief Minister Sheila Dixit suggested, would come with the decentralisation of the MCD into subdivisions (three which came into effect from the five that were originally planned), each responsible for its own operations.[17] The salient point here is that in 2011, the solution proposed was the reorganisation of the municipal regulatory capabilities in new directions, such as the trifurcation of its services. This was carried out with the expectation that all the difficulties hitherto experienced would finally abate, be it to do with the MCD's fiscal woes or its inefficient service provision. Distinct entities serving different areas of the city were envisaged as the answer to the needs of Delhi's citizens.

However, there is no suggestion that the problem of civic administration and service provision was resolved. Indeed, we have seen how structural inequalities persisted, manifested in the resistance that came in the strike action followed by the sanitation workers a few years later. It can also be suggested that the 'failure' in carrying out its responsibilities and the subversion of its original intentions made the need for newer proposals felt in 2017. A *further* reorganisation of the body was called for, on the pretext of satiating world-class city aspirations. Presumably, the desire to restructure the municipality 'radically', if pursued, will result in the allocation of manpower and resources and will generate a wide variety of bureaucratic procedures and regulations—all creating worlds of their own. This shows, then, how the expansion of regulatory and bureaucratic powers of urban agencies like the municipalities, and along with it, the state, continues, but not necessarily with any concomitant effect on their originally stated plans. This is not to suggest that there are *no* consequences of such processes. It is the *desired* effects that escape it. And we have seen this time and again between 1858 and 1911, to return to the historical frame for this book.

Indeed, colonial governance had transformed Delhi's economic, political, social and cultural life during this period. As early as the 1860s, policy interventions had created a market in private property and urban space had been commoditised for circulation. At the same time, new modes of 'public' governance and models of environmental 'improvement' had been established, and Delhi's *nazul* lands were brought under the management of civic agencies like the Delhi municipality. Along with new regimes of health and sanitation, urban planning had turned its focus towards enhancing the benefits of commercial circulation brought by the railways after the 1880s. Alongside this, new ways of measuring and describing urban space were accompanied by a proliferation of colonial laws over its appropriation and use by imperial subjects. These multiple interventions, as we have seen, did in turn influence the conduct of the population, who negotiated these changes.

Yet, the entrenchment of the state, its laws, regulations and bureaucratic procedures was not a straightforward process, but one rife with tensions and contradictions, which were characteristic of colonial governance. Several examples have been highlighted in the earlier chapters. We have seen how a new regime of property was a product of internal tensions and negotiations, where a nascent colonial administration was caught in the midst of a variety of competing demands. Similarly, when examining the municipality's actions using a historical lens, we know that as it carried out its operations to reorganise 'public' spaces, its intentions were subverted by the growth of its own power and its interaction with other colonial agencies. As evident in Chapter 4, the local administration in the city was caught in a bind over whether new celebrations were to be allowed on the basis of a new logic of 'religious' tolerance or prohibited on accord of 'public order'. Often, the answers to these questions were inconsistent, and brought new complications for colonial governance and contestations with local residents. Competing logics of 'improvement' or understandings of native 'rights and entitlements', all revealed the ambiguities of colonial rule.

Crucially, such ambiguities and tensions within the government, although never fully resolved, were productive inasmuch as they legitimised particular brands of colonial knowledge, expanded bureaucratic capabilities, facilitated control over territory, and drove colonial urban planning. In other words, the myriad internal tensions and competing priorities provided opportunities for the colonial government to further its own ends. Indeed, the experience of the city demonstrates how this inchoate process took root, where tense negotiations between authorities, contradictory claims of colonial governance, and overlapping jurisdictions all intersected to produce unexpected results. In concrete terms, we saw, for example, how the scheme of compensation elaborated in Chapter 1 was a bricolage of multiple demands, competing claims and priorities, and was constitutive of modern property relations.

Similarly, solutions to resolve the 'failures' of municipal interventions to govern 'public' spaces came in the form of the augmentation of its power. Proposals for comprehensive surveys of the city, along with demands for a larger bureaucracy, were an outcome of the municipality's everyday dealings in the city and its perceived weaknesses in removing 'encroachments'. Its clashes with other departments and government officials led to the creation of investigative bodies and commissions, spawning an increase in its bureaucratic responsibilities and functions. When considering the question of 'improvements' to the natural landscape, we have seen how disagreements between civil and forest authorities over the nature and direction of 'improvement' plans fuelled the takeover of *bela* lands by the former. When sanitary specialists dismissed local 'improvement' initiatives by citing that they were profligate and based on erroneous sanitary principles, they also legitimised and sanctioned particular brands of colonial knowledge and 'scientific' expertise. These 'failures' were really, then, using the words of one scholar, 'productive failures'.[18]

'Productive failures' as contingent and arbitrary outcomes that extended the bureaucratic and regulatory capacities of the colonial government were also seen in the context of the Saraogi *rath yatras*.[19] In order to maintain the ban on the former (itself a result of the contradictory positions between 'public order' and 'religious tolerance'), a new category of 'obsolete custom' was created, and this guided the policies of the local authorities until the ban was revoked. In effect, the process of exclusion (of the Saraogi *rath yatras*) required much work and effort, leading to a new discursive and regulatory framework to guide local policing. Finally, the question of 'failure' was dealt with most explicitly in the context of the railways. Urban planning was a product of the overlapping claims of the imperial and municipal government, and was shaped by such rivalries and contestations. The municipality became more assidous with regard to its management of lucrative *nazul* poperties, and despite lacking funds for urban reconstruction, honed its legal skills to prevent spaces from being reallocated to railway companies. Moreover, a 'wait and watch' policy replaced the original municipal goals to become the mainstay of planning. Thus, through highlighting these examples of 'productive failures', this book has presented ambiguity, contradiction and failure as constitutive of colonial governance.

Yet, as the book makes abundantly clear, the contradictions and tensions of colonial policy must also be seen as 'productive' in other ways, inasmuch as they provided opportunities for different sections of Delhi's population. Thus, in the immediate aftermath of the rebellion, we saw how 'loyal' ticket-holders used their status as allies of the Raj to negotiate for a better share of profits from the auctions. The municipalisation of space and the contradictions within also offered possibilities, albeit limited, for sweepers employed by the Delhi municipality, who turned a blind eye towards encroachments, given their unfair treatment at the hands of the former. Similarly, local cultivators and *Sardarakhtidar*s used the confusion over the assessment of compensation claims by suggesting that the plots that the government wanted to exchange were inferior, and instead, demanded cash payments. The Saraogis, too, made use of overlapping levels and jurisdictions of power at work in the city when staking their claims as imperial subjects. This book has thus presented several examples of the ways in which the contradictions of power, and policies and their 'failures' fuelled possibilities for the inhabitants of the city as much as the growth of bureaucratic power. In fact, such legacies continue to shape urban life to this day.

NOTES

1. Stephen Legg, *Spaces of Colonialism: Delhi's Urban Governmentalities* (New Delhi: Wiley-Blackwell, 2007), 183–90.
2. Legg, *Spaces of Colonialism*, 186.

3. Legg, *Spaces of Colonialism*, 186–87.

4. Jyoti Hosagrahar, *Indigenous Modernities: Negotiating Architecture and Urbanism* (London: Routledge, 2005), 170.

5. Hosagrahar, *Indigenous Modernities*, 171.

6. Hosagrahar, *Indigenous Modernities*, 170–71.

7. On the legacies of the DIT that lived on in the DDA, see Stephen Legg, 'Postcolonial Developmentalities from the Delhi Improvement Trust to the Delhi Development Authority', in *Colonial and Postcolonial Indian Geographies*, ed. S. Corbridge, S. Kumar and S. Raju (London: SAGE Publications, 2006), 182–204.

8. Diya Mehra, 'Planning Delhi ca. 1936–1959', *South Asia: Journal of South Asian Studies* 36, no. 3, 2013, 354–74.

9. See, for example, A. Sharan, *In the City, Out of Place: Nuisance, Pollution, and Dwelling in Delhi, c. 1850–2000* (New Delhi: Oxford University Press, 2014); R. Sundaram, *Pirate Modernity: Delhi's Media Urbanism* (London: Routledge, 2009); and Amita Baviskar, 'Between Violence and Desire: Space, Power and Identity in the Making of Metropolitan Delhi', *International Journal of Social Science* 55, no. 175, 2003, 89–98. See also Gautam Bhan's essay on twentieth-century planning in Delhi, which makes suggestive arguments about the production of 'illegality' through planning; Gautam Bhan, 'Planned Illegalities: Housing and the "Failure" of Planning in Delhi: 1947–2010', *Economic and Political Weekly* XLV III, no. 24, 2013, 58–70.

10. Legg, *Spaces of Colonialism*, 186–87.

11. Useful accounts on the MCD's changing composition and regulatory activities, and the forms of contestation it engenders can be found in the following books: Veronique Dupont, Emma Tarlo and Denis Vidal (eds), *Delhi: Urban Space and Human Destinies* (New Delhi: Manohar Books, 2000); Bharati Chaturvedi, *Finding Delhi: Loss and Renewal in the Megacity* (New Delhi: Penguin Books, 2010); and Surajit Chakravarty and Rohit Negi (eds), *Space, Planning and Everyday Contestations in Delhi (Exploring Urban Change in South Asia)* (New Delhi: Springer India, 2016).

12. Anonymous, 'Cong Unveils Plan to Restructure MCD, Bigwigs Attack BJP', *Outlook India*, 6 March 2017. Available at https://www.outlookindia.com/newsscroll/cong-unveils-plan-to-restructure-mcd-bigwigs-attack-bjp/1001906 (accessed 15 June 2020).

13. Abhishek Dey, 'With Municipal Polls Coming Up Later this Year, Garbage Politics Stinks Up the City: The AAP-led State Government is Trading Barbs with BJP-led Delhi Municipal Corporations', *Scroll.in*, 11 January 2017. Available at https://scroll.in/article/826295/with-municipal-polls-in-delhi-

coming-up-later-this-year-garbage-politics-stinks-up-the-city (accessed 15 June 2020).

14. 'World-classness' has been studied in the context of an emergent and contested inter-Asian urbanism that attempts to redefine globality from the vantage point of cities in the region. See Ananya Roy and Aihwa Ong (eds), *Worlding Cities: Asian Experiments and the Art of Being Global* (Malden, MA: Wiley-Blackwell, 2011). See also David Asher Ghertner's monograph on aesthetic as a guiding force for urban governance in Delhi; David Asher Ghertner, *Rule by Aesthetics: World-Class City Making in Delhi* (Oxford: Oxford University Press, 2015).

15. Anonymous, 'Cong Unveils Plan to Restructure MCD'.

16. Special Correspondent, 'MCD May be Divided into Five Corporations with 408 Wards', *The Hindu*, 3 April 2011. Available at http://www.thehindu.com/todays-paper/tp-national/tp-newdelhi/MCD-may-be-divided-into-five-corporations-with-408-wards/article14668947.ece (accessed 15 June 2020).

17. PTI, 'Delhi Government Decides to Split MCD into Three Parts', *The Hindu*, 30 May 2011. Available at http://www.thehindu.com/news/cities/Delhi/delhi-govt-decides-to-split-mcd-into-three-parts/article2062613.ece (accessed 15 June 2020).

18. Peter Redfield, *Foucault in the Tropics: Displacing the Panopticon*, in *Anthropologies of Modernity: Foucault, Governmentality and Life Politics*, ed. Jonathan Xavier Inda (Oxford: Wiley-Blackwell, 2005).

19. All these examples validate that colonial bureaucratic and regulatory capabilities were forged in a 'patchwork' manner, where policies and plans took different directions from originally stated technocratic intentions and objectives. See W. Walters, *Governmentality: Critical Encounters* (London: Routledge, 2012), 74–76.

Bibliography

CHANDIGARH STATE ARCHIVES

Punjab Home Proceedings

DELHI STATE ARCHIVES

Chief Commissioner's Office Files, 1863–1910
Deputy Commissioner's Office Files, 1863–1910
Residency Records (1):

- Ellenborough Tank Clearances (Box 5)
- Chandni Chowk Clearances (Box 5)
- Hamid Ali Khan Clearances (Box 2)

Residency Records (2) Miscellaneous Records

EMAIL CORRESPONDENCE

Shamsur Rahman Faruqi, Email Correspondence, 13 April 2010

NATIONAL ARCHIVES OF INDIA

Foreign Department Records (Political and General)
Home Department Records (Public, Sanitary and Municipalities)
PWD, Railway Construction Records

NEWSPAPERS

Friend of India
Native Newspaper Reports (of Punjab and North-western Provinces)

The Mofussilite
The Times of India
The Tribune

ONLINE ARTICLES AND NEWSPAPERS

Anonymous. 'Cong Unveils Plan to Restructure MCD, Bigwigs Attack BJP', *Outlook India*, 6 March 2017. Available at https://www.outlookindia.com/newsscroll/cong-unveils-plan-to-restructure-mcd-bigwigs-attack-bjp/1001906 (accessed 10 December 2017).

Dey, Abhishek. 'With Municipal Polls in Delhi Coming Up Later this Year, Garbage Politics Stinks Up the City', *Scroll.in*, 11 January 2017. Available at https://scroll.in/article/826295/with-municipal-polls-in-delhi-coming-up-later-this-year-garbage-politics-stinks-up-the-city (accessed 10 December 2017).

Kerr, Ian J. *Bombay and Lahore: Colonial Railways and Colonial Cities: Some Urban Consequences of the Development and Operation of the Railways in India, c. 1850–1947.* Available at http://www.docutren.com/HistoriaFerroviaria/Aranjuez2001/pdf/07.pdf (accessed 13 December 2017).

PTI. 'Delhi Government Decides to Split MCD into Three Parts', *The Hindu*, 30 May 2011. Available at http://www.thehindu.com/news/cities/Delhi/delhi-govt-decides-to-split-mcd-into-three-parts/article2062613.ece (accessed 10 December 2017).

Special Correspondent. 'MCD May be Divided into Five Corporations with 408 Wards', *The Hindu*, 3 April 2011. Available at http://www.thehindu.com/todays-paper/tp-national/tp-newdelhi/MCD-may-be-divided-into-five-corporations-with-408-wards/article14668947.ece (accessed 10 December 2017).

ORIENTAL INDIA OFFICE COLLECTIONS, BRITISH LIBRARY, LONDON

Series: E/, F/, L/PJ, P/

PUBLISHED PRIMARY SOURCES

Aggarwal, Lala Pannalal Jain. *Jain Institutions in Delhi*. Delhi: The Jain Mitra Mandal, 1947.

Andrews, C. F. *Zaka Ullah of Delhi*. Oxford: Oxford University Press, 2003.

Anonymous. *The Tourists Guide from Delhi to Kurrachee: Describing the Various Towns Commerce: Railways: River Communications: & C: & C: With a Map.* London: British Library, 2011 [1865].

Bahadur, Rai Jeewan Lal. *A Short Account of the Life and Family of Rai Jeewan Lal Bahadur, Late Honorary Magistrate Delhi, with Extracts from his Diary Relating to the Time of Rebellion, 1857.* Lahore: The Tribune Steam Press, 1911.

Beg, Mirza Sangin. *Sair ul Manazil*, trans. (from Persian) Sharif Hussain Qasmi. New Delhi: Ghalib Institute, 1982.

Bengal Military Department. *Report on Water Analysis in Bengal in 1866–67 and Dr Sheppard's Special Report on the Analysis of Delhi Waters.* Calcutta: Miscellaneous Official Publications, 1867.

Bernier, Francois. *Travels in the Mogul Empire: A.D. 1656–1668.* Delhi: Low Price Publications, 2005.

Beverley, H. *The Land Acquisition Acts (Act X of 1870 and Act XVIII of 1885) with Introduction and Notes.* Calcutta: Thacker, Spink and Co., 1888.

Carr, Stephen. *The Archaeological and Monumental Remains of Delhi.* New Delhi: Aryan Books International, 2002 [1876].

Cooper, Frederick. C. *The Handbook for Delhi: With Index and Two Maps, Illustrating the Historic Remains of Old Delhi and the Position of the British Army Before the Assault in 1857 & c. & c.* Lahore: T. C. McCarthy, Lahore Chronicle Press, 1865.

Forbes, James. *Oriental Memoirs: A Narrative of Seventeen Years Residence in India. Second Edition by his Daughter, the Countess of Montalembert*, 2 Vols. London: R. Bentley, 1834.

Government of Punjab. *Gazetteer of the Delhi District: 1883–84.* Gurgaon: Vintage Books, 1988.

———. *Gazetteer of Delhi (1912).* Gurgaon: Vintage Books, 1992.

Greathed, Wilberforce H. *Report on the Drainage of the City of Delhi and on the Means of Improving It.* Agra: Secundra Orphan Press, 1852.

Hearn, Gordon Risley. *The Seven Cities of Delhi.* London: W. Thacker & Co., 1906.

Jain, Mai Dayal. *Jain Rath Yatra Dehli ka Itihas.* New Delhi: Rising Sun Press, 1963.

Kaye, M. M. (ed.), *The Golden Calm: An English Lady's Life in Moghul Delhi. Reminisces by Emily, Lady Clive Bayly, and her Father, Sir Thomas Metcalf.* Exeter: Webb and Bower, 1980.

Khan, Syed Ahmad. *Aassaar us Sanaadeed.* Delhi: Urdu Academy, 2006.

Metcalfe, Charles Theophilus. *Two Native Narratives of the Rebellion in Delhi, Translated from the Originals by the Late Charles Theophilus Metcalfe, C. S. I.* London: Archibald Constable & Co., 1898.

Pershad, Rai Sahib Madho. *The History of the Delhi Municipality: 1863–1921*. Allahabad: Pioneer Press, 1921.

Published by Authority. *Report on the Administration of the Delhi Crown Lands*. Lahore: Civil and Military Gazette Press by Samuel T. Weston, 1910.

Punjab Government Press. *Records of the Delhi Residency and Agency: 1807–1857*. Lahore: Sang-E-Meel Publications, 2006.

Roberts, Emma. *Scenes and Characteristics of Hindustan*. London: Allen Press, 1837.

Rose, H. A., D. Ibbetson and E. D. Maclagan. *Glossary of the Castes and Tribes of the Punjab and North West Frontier Province*. Lahore: Government Printing Press, Punjab, 1911.

Shekhar, Chander and Shama Mitra Chenoy. *Dargah Quli Khan, Muraqqa-e-Dehli: The Mughal Capital in Muhammad Shah's Time*. Delhi: Deputy Publication, 1989.

Smith, Daniel Boyes. *Report on Epidemic Cholera, as it Prevailed in the City of Delhi, at Goorgaon and the Surrounding Districts, During the Rainy Season of 1861*. Lahore: Government Press, 1861.

Stuart, C. M. Villiers. *Gardens of the Great Mughals*. London: Adam and Charles Black, 1913.

Trotter, Lionel J. *The Life of John Nicholson*. London: John Murray Publications, 1898.

Wyman, Fredrick F. *From Calcutta to the Snowy Range: Being the Narrative of a Trip through the Upper Provinces of India to the Himalayas Containing an Account of Monghyr, Benares, Allahabad, Cawnpore, Lucknow, Agra, Delhi and Simla*. London: Tinsley Brothers, 1866.

PRIVATE PAPERS

Lawrence Papers (Mss Eur F 90)

Vernon Smith Papers (Mss Eur F 231)

RECORDS OF PROCEEDINGS OF THE MUNICIPAL CORPORATION OF DELHI, TOWN HALL

General Meetings of the Municipal Committee

Ordinary Meetings of the Municipal Committee (Executive Committee)

SECONDARY SOURCES

Adas, Michael. *Machines as the Measure of Man*. Cornell: Cornell University Press, 1990.

Aguiar, Marian. *Tracking Modernity: India's Railway and the Culture of Mobility*. Minnesota: University of Minnesota Press, 2011.

Ali, M. Athar. 'Capital of the Sultans: Delhi during the Thirteenth and Fourteenth Centuries', in *Delhi Through the Ages: Selected Essays in Urban History, Culture and Society*, ed. R. E. Frykenberg. New Delhi: Oxford University Press, 1994.

Anderson, Clare. *Legible Bodies: Race Criminality and Colonialism in South Asia*. Oxford: Berg Publishers, 2004.

Andrew Johnson, David. *New Delhi: The Last Imperial City (Britain and the World)*. Basingstoke: Palgrave Macmillan, 2015.

Appadurai, Arjun. *Modernity at Large: Cultural Dimensions of Globalisation*. Minnesota: University of Minnesota Press, 1996.

Arnold, David. *Police Power and Colonial Rule: Madras, 1859–1947*. New Delhi: Oxford University Press, 1986.

———. *Colonising the Body: State Medicine and Epidemic Disease in Nineteenth-Century India*. Berkeley: University of California Press, 1993.

———. 'Agriculture and Improvement in Early Colonial India: A Pre-History of Development', *Journal of Agrarian Change* 5, no. 4, 2005a, 505–25.

———. *The Tropics and the Traveling Gaze: India, Landscapes and Science, 1800–1856*. New Delhi: Permanent Black, 2005b.

———. 'The Problem of Traffic: The Street Life of Modernity in Late Colonial India', *Modern Asian Studies* 46, no. 1, 2012, 119–41.

Arnold, David, and Ramachandra Guha (eds), *Nature, Culture and Imperialism: Essays on the Environmental History of South Asia*. New Delhi: Oxford University Press, 1996.

Asher, C. B. 'Delhi Walled: Changing Boundaries', in *The Urban Enceinte in Global Perspective*, ed. J. Tracy. Cambridge, Massachusetts: Cambridge University Press, 2000.

Barrow, Ian J. *Making History, Drawing Territory: British Mapping in India c. 1756–1905*. New Delhi: Oxford University Press, 2003.

Baviskar, Amita. 'Between Violence and Desire: Space, Power and Identity in the Making of Metropolitan Delhi', *International Journal of Social Science* 55, no. 175, 2003, 89–98.

Bayly, C. A. *Rulers, Townsmen and Bazaars: North Indian Society in the Age of British Expansion 1770–1870*. Cambridge, Massachusetts: Cambridge University Press, 1983.

————. 'Delhi and Other Cities of North India during the "Twilight"', in *Delhi Through the Ages*, ed. Frykenberg. New Delhi: Oxford University Press, 1994.

————. *Empire and Information: Intelligence Gathering and Social Communication in India, 1780–1870*. Cambridge: Cambridge University Press, 1996.

————. 'The Pre-History of "Communalism"? Religious Conflict in India, 1700–1860', in *Origins of Nationalism in South Asia: Patriotism and Ethical Government in the Making of Modern India*, ed. C. A. Bayly. New Delhi: Oxford University Press, 1998.

Beattie, James. 'Imperial Landscapes of Health: Place, Plants, and People between India and Australia, 1800s–1900s', *Health and History* 14, no. 1, 2012, 100–20.

Bhan, Gautam. 'Planned Illegalities: Housing and the "Failure" of Planning in Delhi: 1947–2010', *Economic and Political Weekly* XLV III, no. 24, 2013, 58–70.

Bhasin, Gurpreet. *Public Spaces and Discursive Practices in Colonial Delhi, 1860–1915*, Unpublished PhD Thesis, The Open University, 2008.

Bhattacharya, Nandini. *Contagion and the Enclaves: Tropical Medicine in Colonial India (Postcolonialism Across the Disciplines)*. Liverpool: Liverpool University Press, 2012.

Birla, Ritu. *Stages of Capital: Law, Culture and Market Governance in Late Colonial India*. Durham: Duke University Press, 2009.

Blake, S. *Shahjahanabad: The Sovereign City in Mughal India, 1639–1739*. Cambridge: Cambridge University Press, 1991.

————. 'Cityscape of an Imperial Capital: Shahjahanabad in 1739', in *Delhi Through the Ages*, ed. Frykenberg. New Delhi: Oxford University Press, 1994.

Carrithers, Michael, and Caroline Humphrey (eds), *The Assembly of Listeners: Jain in Society*. Cambridge: Cambridge University Press, 1991.

Celik, Zeynep. *Urban Forms and Colonial Confrontations: Algiers Under French Rule*. London: University of California Press, 1997.

Chakrabarty, Dipesh. *Provincializing Europe: Postcolonial Thought and Historical Difference*. Princeton: Princeton University Press, 2000.

Chakravarty, Surajit, and Rohit Negi (eds), *Space, Planning and Everyday Contestations in Delhi (Exploring Urban Change in South Asia)*. New Delhi: Springer India, 2016.

Chandavarkar, Rajnarayan. *Imperial Power and Popular Politics: Class, Resistance and the State in India, c.1580–1950*. Cambridge, Massachusetts: Cambridge University Press, 1998.

Chatterjee, Partha. *The Nation and its Fragments: Colonial and Postcolonial Histories*. Princeton: Princeton University Press, 1993.

Chattopadhyay, Swati. *Representing Calcutta, Modernity, Nationalism and the Colonial Uncanny*. London: Routledge, 2005.

———. 'Introduction: The Historical Legacy of the Suburbs in South Asia', *Urban History* 39, no. 1, 2012, 51–55.

Chaturvedi, Bharati. *Finding Delhi: Loss and Renewal in the Megacity*. New Delhi: Penguin Books, 2010.

Chenoy, Shama Mitra. *Shahjahanabad: A City of Delhi 1638–1857*. New Delhi: Munshiram Manoharlal Publishers, 1998.

Chopra, Preeti. *A Joint Enterprise: Indian Elites and the Making of British Bombay*. Minneapolis: University of Minnesota Press, 2011.

———. 'Free to Move, Forced to Flee: The Formation and Dissolution of Suburbs in Colonial Bombay, 1750–1918', *Urban History* 39, no. 1, 2012, 83–107.

Cohn, Bernard. 'Representing Authority in Victorian India', in *The Invention of Tradition*, ed. Eric Hobsbawm and Terence Ranger. Cambridge, Massachusetts: Cambridge University Press, 1983.

Cooper, Fredrick, and Ann. L. Stoler (eds), *Tensions of Empire: Colonial Cultures in a Bourgeois World*. Berkeley: University of California Press, 1997.

Cort, John E. (ed.), *Open Boundaries: Jain Communities and Cultures in Indian History*. New York: State University of New York Press, 1998.

Crowe, Sylvia, Sheila Haywood, Susan Jellicoe and Gordon Patterson. *The Gardens of Mughal India*. London: Thames and Hudson, 1972.

Cunningham, Bissell William. *Urban Design, Chaos and Colonial Power in Zanzibar*. Indiana: Indiana University Press, 2011.

Daechsel, Marcus. 'Sovereignty, Governmentality and Development in Ayub's Pakistan: The Case of Korangi Township', *Modern Asian Studies* 45, no. 1, 2011, 131–57.

Dalrymple, William. *The Last Mughal*. New Delhi: Penguin Books, 2006.

Dalrymple, William, and Yuthika Sharma (eds), *Princes and Painters in Mughal Delhi, 1707–1857*. New York: Asia Society, 2012.

Das, Pallavi V. 'Railway Fuel and its Impact on the Forests in Colonial India: The Case of the Punjab, 1860–1884', *Modern Asian Studies* 47, no. 4, 2013, 1283–1309.

Davies, Phillip. *Splendours of the Raj: British Architecture in India, 1660–1947*. London: Penguin Books, 1985.

Dean, Mitchel. *Governmentality: Power and Rule in Modern Society*. Second Edition. London: SAGE Publications Ltd, 2010.

Derbyshire, Ian D. 'Competition and Adaptation: The Operation of Railways in Northern India: Uttar Pradesh 1860–1914', in *Our Indian Railway: Themes in India's Railway History*, ed. Roopa Srinivasan, Manish Tiwari and Sandeep Silas. New Delhi: Foundation Books, 2006.

Dirks, Nicholas. *Castes of Mind: Colonialism and the Making of Modern India*. Princeton: Princeton University Press, 2001.

Dossal, Mariam. *Imperial Designs and Indian Realities: The Planning of Bombay City, 1845–1875*. New Delhi: Oxford University Press, 1991.

Drayton, Richard H. *Nature's Government: Science, Imperial Britain and the 'Improvement' of the World*. Yale: Yale University Press, 2000.

Duncan, James S. *In the Shadows of the Tropics: Climate, Race and Biopower in Nineteenth Century Ceylon*. Aldershot: Ashgate, 2007.

Dundas, Paul. *The Jains*. London: Routledge, 1992.

Dupont, Veronique, Emma Tarlo and Denis Vital (eds), *Delhi: Urban Space and Human Destinies*. Delhi: Manohar Books, 2000.

Dutta, Partho. *Planning the City: Urbanisation and Reform in Calcutta, c. 1800– 1940*. New Delhi: Tulika Books, 2012.

Ehlers, E., and T. Krafft (eds), *Shahjahanabad/Old Delhi: Tradition and Social Change*. New Delhi: Manohar Books, 2003.

Evenson, Norma. *The Indian Metropolis: A View towards the West*. New Haven: Yale University Press, 1989.

Farooqui, Amar. *Zafar and the Raj: Anglo-Mughal Delhi, c. 1800–1850*. New Delhi: Primus Books, 2013.

Farooqui, Mahmood. *Besieged: Voices from Delhi, 1857, with Notes on the Rebellion Papers and Governance in Delhi 1857*. New Delhi: Viking Books, 2010.

Ferguson, James. *The Anti-politics Machine: 'Development', Depoliticisation and Bureaucratic Power in Lesotho*. Cambridge, Massachusetts: Cambridge University Press, 1990.

Foucault, Michel. 'Governmentality', in *The Foucault Effect: Studies in Governmentality with Two Lectures and an Interview with Michel Foucault*, ed. Graham Burchell, Colin Gordon and Peter Miller. Chicago: University of Chicago Press, 1991.

———. *Security, Territory, Population: Lectures at the College de France 1977–78*, ed. M. Senellart, trans. Graham Burchell. London: Palgrave Macmillan, 2007.

———. *The Birth of Biopolitics: Lectures at the Collège de France, 1978–79*, ed. M. Senellart. New York: Palgrave Macmillan, 2008.

Freitag, Sandria. *Collective Action and Community: Public Arenas and the Emergence of Communalism in North India*. Berkeley: University of California Press, 1989.

———. 'Contesting in Public: Colonial Legacies and Contemporary Communalism', in *Making India Hindu: Religion, Community and the Politics of Democracy in India*, ed. David Ludden. New Delhi: Oxford University Press, 1996.

Ghertner, David Asher. *Rule by Aesthetics: World-Class City Making in Delhi*. Oxford: Oxford University Press, 2015.

Gillion, Kenneth L. *Ahmedabad: A Study in Urban History*. Berkeley: University of California Press, 1968.

Glover, William J. 'Constructing Urban Space as Public in Colonial India: Some Notes from the Punjab', *Journal of Punjab Studies* 14, no. 2, 2007a, 211–24.

———. *Making Lahore Modern: Constructing and Imagining a Colonial City*. Minneapolis: University of Minnesota Press, 2007b.

Gooptu, Nandini. *The Politics of the Urban Poor in Early Twentieth-century India*. Cambridge, Massachusetts: Cambridge University Press, 2004.

Goswami, Manu. *Producing India: From Colonial Economy to National Space*. Chicago: University of Chicago Press, 2004.

Grant Irving, Robert. *Indian Summer: Lutyens, Baker and Imperial Delhi*. Yale: Yale University Press, 1982.

Guha, Ramachandra. 'Forestry in British and Post-British India: An Historical Analysis', *Economic and Political Weekly* 18, no. 44, 1983, 1882–96.

Guha, Ranajit. *A Rule of Property for Bengal: An Essay on the Idea of the Permanent Settlement*. Paris: Mouton & Co., 1963.

Guha, Sumit (ed.), *Growth, Stagnation and Decline?: Agricultural Productivity in British India*. New Delhi: Oxford University Press, 1992.

Gupta, Akhil. *Red Tape: Bureaucracy, Structural Violence and Poverty in India*. Durham: Duke University Press, 2012.

Gupta, Narayani. 'Military Security and Urban Development: A Case Study of Delhi 1857–1912', *Modern Asian Studies* 5, no. 1, 1971, 61–77.

———. *Delhi Between Two Empires: 1803–1931: Society, Government and Urban Growth*. New Delhi: Oxford University Press, 1981.

———. 'Delhi and its Hinterland: The Nineteenth and Early Twentieth Centuries', in *Delhi Through the Ages*, ed. Frykenberg. New Delhi: Oxford University Press, 1994.

———. 'The Management of Urban Public Spaces, Shahjahanabad, New Delhi, Greater Delhi, 1851–1997', in *Urban Governance: Britain and Beyond since 1750*, ed. Robert J. Morris and Richard H. Trainer. London: Ashgate, 2000.

Habib, Irfan. 'Notes on the Economic and Social Aspects of Mughal Gardens', in *Mughal Gardens: Sources, Places, Representations and Prospects*, ed. J. L. Wescoat Jr. and J. W. Bulmahn. Harvard: Harvard University Press, 1996.

Harcourt, Bernard E. *The Illusion of Free Markets: Punishment and the Myth of the Natural Order*. Cambridge: Harvard University Press, 2011.

Harrison, Mark. 'Tropical Medicine in Nineteenth Century India', *The British Journal for the History of Science* 25, no. 3, 1992, 299–318.

———. *Climates and Constitutions: Health, Race, Environment and British Imperialism in India, 1600–1850*. New Delhi: Oxford University Press, 1999.

Hasan, Farhat. *State and Locality in Mughal India: Power Relations in Western India, 1572–1730*. Cambridge, Massachusetts: Cambridge University Press, 2004.

Harvey, David. *Paris, Capital of Modernity*. London: Routledge, 2006.

Haynes, Douglas. *Rhetoric and Ritual in Colonial India: The Shaping of a Public Culture in Surat City, 1852–1928*. Berkeley: University of California Press, 1991.

Hazareesingh, Sandip. *The Colonial City and the Challenge of Modernity: Urban Hegemonies and Civic Contestations in Bombay City 1900–1925*. New Delhi: Orient BlackSwan, 2007.

Herbert, Eugenia W. *Flora's Empire: British Gardens in India*. Pennsylvania: University of Pennsylvania Press, 2011.

Hosagrahar, Jyoti. *Indigenous Modernities: Negotiating Architecture and Urbanism*. London: Routledge, 2005.

Huber, Valeska. *Channelling Mobilities, Migration and Mobilisation in the Suez Canal Region and Beyond, 1869–1914*. Cambridge, Massachusetts: Cambridge University Press, 2013.

Inden, Ronald. *Imagining India*. Oxford: Basil Blackwell, 1990.

Islam, Khurshidul, and Ralph Russell. *Three Mughal Poets: Mir, Sauda, Mir Hasan*. New Delhi: Oxford University Press, 2012.

Islamoglu-Inan, Huri (ed.), *Constituting Modernity: Private Property in the East and West*. New York: I. B. Tauris, 2004.

Jalal, A., and S. Bose. *Modern South Asia: History, Culture, Political Economy*. New York: Routledge, 2004.

Joyce, Patrick. *The Rule of Freedom: Liberalism and the Modern City*. London: Verso Books, 2003.

Kaviraj, Sudipta. 'Filth and the Public Sphere: Concepts and Practices about Space in Calcutta', *Public Culture* 10, no. 1, 1997, 83–113.

Kennedy, Dane. *The Magic Mountains: Hill Stations and the British Raj*. Berkeley: University of California Press, 1996.

Kerr, Ian J. (ed.), *27 Down: New Departures in Indian Railway Studies*. New Delhi: Orient BlackSwan, 2007.

Kidambi, Prashant. 'Housing the Poor in a Colonial City: The Bombay Improvement Trust, 1898–1918', *Studies in History* 17, no. 57, 2001, 57–79.

———. *The Making of an Indian Metropolis: Colonial Governance and Public Culture in Bombay, 1890–1920*. Aldershot: Ashgate, 2007.

King, Anthony. *Colonial Urban Development: Culture Social Power and the Environment*. London: Routledge, 1976.

Koch, Ebba. 'The Mughal Waterfront Garden', in *Gardens in the Time of the Great Muslim Empires*, ed. Attilio Petruccioli. Leiden: Brill Publishers, 1997.

———. *The Complete Taj Mahal and Riverfront Gardens of Agra*. London: Thames and Hudson Ltd, 2006.

Lahiri, Nayanjot. 'Commemorating and Remembering 1857: The Revolt in Delhi and Its Afterlife', *World Archaeology* 35, no.1, 2003, 35–60.

Laidlaw, James. *Riches and Renunciation: Religion, Economy and Society Among the Jains*. Oxford: Clarendon Press, 1995.

Lefebvre, Henri. *The Production of Space*, trans. Donald Nicholson-Smith. Oxford: Wiley-Blackwell, 1991.

Legg, Stephen. 'Governmentality, Congestion and Calculation in Colonial Delhi', *Social and Cultural Geography* 7, no. 5, 2006a, 709–29.

———. 'Postcolonial Developmentalities from the Delhi Improvement Trust to the Delhi Development Authority', in *Colonial and Postcolonial Indian Geographies*, ed. S. Corbridge, S. Kumar and S. Raju. London: SAGE Publications, 2006b.

———. *Spaces of Colonialism: Delhi's Urban Governmentalities*. New Delhi: Wiley-Blackwell, 2007.

———. *Prostitution and the Ends of Empire: Scale, Governmentalities and Interwar India*. Durham: Duke University Press, 2014.

Leonard, John G. 'Urban Government under the Raj: A Case Study of Municipal Administration in South India', *Modern South Asian Studies* 7, no. 2, 1973, 227–51.

Macdonald Gumprez, Ellen. 'City-Hinterland Relations and the Development of a Regional Elite in Nineteenth Century Bombay', in *Railways in Modern India*, ed. Ian J. Kerr. New Delhi: Oxford University Press, 2001.

Mann, Michael. 'Torchbearers Upon the Path of Progress: Britain's Ideology of Moral and Material Progress in India: An Introductory Essay', in *Colonialism as Civilising Mission: Cultural Ideology in British India*, ed. Harald Fischer-Tiné and Michael Mann. London: Anthem Press, 2004.

———. 'Turbulent Delhi: Religious Strife, Social Tension and Political Conflicts, 1803–1857', *Journal of South Asian Studies* XXVIII, no. 1, 2005, 5–34.

———. 'Delhi's Belly: The Management of Water, Sewage and Excreta in a Changing Urban Environment during the Nineteenth Century', *Studies in History* 1, no. 23, 2007, 1–31.

Mann, Michael, and Samiksha Sehrawat. 'A City with a View: The Afforestation of the Delhi Ridge, 1883–1913', *Modern Asian Studies* 2, no. 43, 2009, 543–70.

Masselos, Jim. 'Jobs and Jobbery: The Sweeper in Bombay Under the Raj', *Indian Economic and Social History Review* XIX, no. 2, 1982, 101–39.

———. 'Appropriating Urban Space: Social Constructs of Bombay in the Time of the Raj', in *The City in Action: Bombay Struggles for Power*, ed. Jim Masselos. New Delhi: Oxford University Press, 2007.

Mehra, Diya. 'Planning Delhi ca. 1936–1959', *South Asia: Journal of South Asian Studies* 36, no. 3, 2013, 354–74.

Mehta, Uday S. *Liberalism and Empire: A Study in Nineteenth-Century British Liberal Thought.* Chicago: University of Chicago Press, 1999.

Metcalf, Thomas R. *An Imperial Vision: Indian Architecture and Britain's Raj.* London: Faber and Faber, 1989.

———. *Ideologies of the Raj.* Cambridge, Massachusetts: Cambridge University Press, 1994.

———. 'Past and Present: Towards and Aesthetics of Colonialism', in *Paradigms of Indian Architecture: Space and Time in Representation and Design*, ed. G. H. R. Tillotson. London: Curzon Press, 1998.

Miller, Peter, and Nikolas Rose. *Governing the Present: Administering Economic, Social and Personal Life.* Cambridge, Massachusetts: Polity Press, 2008.

Mitchell, Timothy. 'The Limits of the State: Beyond Statist Approaches and their Critics', *The American Political Science Review* 85, no. 1, 1991, 77–96.

———. *Rule of Experts: Egypt, Techno-Politics, Modernity.* Berkeley: University of California Press, 2002.

Morris, Jan. *Stones of Empire: Buildings of the Raj.* Oxford: Oxford University Press, 1983.

Murray, Tania L. *The Will to Improve: Governmentality, Development and the Practice of Politics.* Durham: Duke University Press, 2007.

Myers, Garth A. *Verandahs of Power: Colonialism and Space in Urban Africa.* Syracuse: Syracuse University Press, 2003.

Naim, C. M. 'Ghalib's Delhi: A Shamelessly Revisionist Look at Two Popular Metaphors', in *Urdu Texts and Contexts: The Selected Essays of C. M. Naim*, ed. C.M. Naim. New Delhi: Permanent Black, 2004.

Nair, Janaki. *The Promise of the Metropolis: Bangalore's Twentieth Century.* New Delhi: Oxford University Press, 2005.

———. 'Beyond Nationalism: Modernity, Governance and a New Urban History for India', *Urban History* 36, no. 2, 2009, 327–41.

Naqvi, Hamida Khatoon. 'Shahjahanabad, The Mughal Delhi, 1638–1803: An Introduction', in *Delhi Through the Ages*, ed. Frykenberg. New Delhi: Oxford University Press, 1994.

Oldenburg, Veena T. *The Making of Colonial Lucknow, 1856–77*. Princeton: Princeton University Press, 1984.

Otter, Christopher. 'Cleansing and Clarifying: Technology and Perception in Nineteenth-Century London', *Journal of British Studies* 43, no. 1, 2004, 40–64.

———. 'Locating Matter: The Place of Materiality in Urban History', in *Material Powers: Cultural Studies, History and the Material Turn*, ed. Tony Bennett and Patrick Joyce. New York: Routledge, 2010.

Pandey, Gyanenedra. *The Construction of Communalism in Colonial North India*. New Delhi: Oxford University Press, 1990.

Pernau, Margit (ed.), *The Delhi College: Traditional Elites, the Colonial State, and Education Before 1857*. Oxford: Oxford University Press, 2006.

———. *Ashraf into Middle Class: Muslims in Nineteenth-century Delhi*. New Delhi: Oxford University Press, 2013.

Pothen, Nayantara, *Glittering Decades: New Delhi in Love and War*. New Delhi: Viking Books, 2012.

Prakash, Gyan. *Another Reason: Science and the Imagination of Modern India*. Princeton: Princeton University Press, 1999.

———. 'The Urban Turn', in *The Cities of Everyday Life, Sarai Reader II*. New Delhi: Sarai: The New Media Initiative, 2002.

———. *Mumbai Fables: A History of an Enchanted City*. Princeton: Princeton University Press, 2011.

Prakash, Vikramaditya, and Peter Scriver. *Colonial Modernities: Building, Dwelling, Architecture in British India and Ceylon*. London: Routledge, 2007.

Prashad, Vijay. 'The Technology of Sanitation in Colonial Delhi', *Modern Asian Studies* 1, no. 35, 2001, 113–55.

Prior, Katherine. 'The State's Intervention in Urban Religious Disputes in the North-Western Provinces in the Early Nineteenth Century', *Modern Asian Studies* 27, no. 1, 1993, 173–203.

Rabinow, Paul. *French Modern: Norms and Forms of the Social Environment*. Massachusetts: MIT Press, 1989.

Rajagopalan, Mrinalni. *Building Histories: The Archival and Affective Lives of Five Monument in Modern Delhi*. Chicago: University of Chicago Press, 2017.

Rajan, Ravi. 'Imperial Environmentalism or Environmental Imperialism? European Forestry, Colonial Foresters and the Agendas of Forest Management in British India 1800–1900', in *Nature and the Orient: The Environmental History of*

South and Southeast Asia, ed. Richard Grove, Vinita Damodran and Satpal Sangwan. New Delhi: Oxford University Press, 1998.

Rao, Nikhil. *House but No Garden: Apartment Living in Bombay, 1898–1948,* PhD Thesis, University of Chicago, 2007.

———. *House but No Garden: Apartment Living in Bombay's Suburbs, 1898–1964.* Minneapolis: University of Minnesota Press, 2012.

———. 'Uncertain Ground: "Ownership Flat" and Urban Property in Twentieth Century Bombay', *South Asian History and Culture* 3, no. 1, 2013, 1–25.

Richards, J. F. 'The Historiography of Mughal Gardens', in *Mughal Gardens,* ed. Wescoat Jr. and Bulmahn. Harvard: Harvard University Press, 1996.

Robb, Peter G. *Ancient Rights and Future Comforts: Bihar, the Bengal Tenancy Act of 1885 and British Rule in India.* London: Curzon Press, 1997.

Roy, Ananya, and Aihwa Ong (eds), *Worlding Cities: Asian Experiments and the Art of Being Global.* Malden, MA: Wiley-Blackwell, 2011.

Russell, Ralph, and Khurshidul Islam. 'Ghalib: Life and Letters', in *The Oxford India Ghalib: Life, Letters and Ghalzals,* ed. Ralph Russell. New Delhi: Oxford University Press, 2003.

Scott, David. 'Colonial Governmentality', *Social Text,* no. 43, 1995, 191–220.

Scott, James C. *Seeing Like a State: How Certain Schemes to Improve the Human Condition Have Failed.* Yale: Yale University Press, 1998.

Sengupta, Tania. 'Between City and Country: Fluid Spaces of City and Provincial Administrative Towns in Nineteenth-century Bengal', *Urban History* 39, no. 1, 2012, 56–82.

Sharan, Awadhendra. 'In the City, Out of Place: Environment and Modernity, Delhi 1860s to 1960s', *Economic and Political Weekly* 41, no. 47, 2006, 4905–11.

———. 'From Source to Sink, "Official" and "Improved" Water in Delhi, 1868–1956', *Indian Economic and Social History Review* 48, no. 3, 2011, 425–62.

———. *In the City, Out of Place: Nuisance, Pollution, and Dwelling in Delhi, c. 1850–2000.* New Delhi: Oxford University Press, 2014.

Shorto, Sylvia. *British Houses in Late Mughal Delhi.* London: Boydell and Brewer Publishers, 2018.

Singha, Radhika. *A Despotism of Law: Crime and Justice in Early Colonial India.* New Delhi: Oxford University Press, 1998.

Sivaramakrishnan, K. *Modern Forests: Statemaking and Environmental Change in Colonial Eastern India.* Stanford, California: Stanford University Press, 1999.

Spear, Percival. *Twilight of the Mughals: Studies in Late Mughal Delhi.* Cambridge, Massachusetts: Cambridge University Press, 1951.

Spodek, Howard. *Ahmedabad: Shock City of Twentieth-Century India*. New Delhi: Orient BlackSwan, 2012.

Taneja, Anand. *Jinnealogy: Time, Islam and Ecological Thought in the Medieval Ruins of Delhi*. Stanford, California: Stanford University Press, 2017.

Tinker, Hugh. *The Foundations of Local Self-Government in India, Pakistan, and Burma*. London: Athlone Press, 1954.

Tomlinson, B. R. *The Economy of Modern India, 1860–1970*. Cambridge, Massachusetts: Cambridge University Press, 1993.

Vanaik, Anish. *Changing the Plot: Modern Property Relations in Colonial Delhi, 1857–1920*, Unpublished MPhil Thesis, Jawaharlal Nehru University, New Delhi, 2008.

———. 'Representing Commodified Space: Maps, Leases, Auctions and "Narrations" of Property in Delhi, c. 1900–47', *Historical Research* 88, no. 240, 2014, 314–32.

Walters, William. *Governmentality: Critical Encounters*. London: Routledge, 2012.

Washbrook, David. 'Sovereignty, Property, Land and Labour in Colonial South India', in *Constituting Modernity: Private Property in the East and West*, ed. Huri Islamoglu-Inan. New York: I. B. Tauris, 2004.

Wescoat Jr., J. L., and J. W. Bulmahn (eds), *Mughal Gardens: Sources, Places, Representations and Prospects*. Harvard: Harvard University Press, 1996.

Whitcombe, Elizabeth. 'The Environmental Costs of Irrigation in British India, Waterlogging, Salinity, Malaria', in *Nature Culture and Imperialism: Essays on the Environmental History of South Asia*, ed. David Arnold and Ramachandra Guha. New Delhi: Oxford University Press, 1995.

Wright, Gwendolyn. *The Politics of Design in French Colonial Urbanism*. Chicago: University of Chicago Press, 1991.

Yeoh, Brenda S. A. *Contesting Space in Colonial Singapore: Power Relations and the Urban Built Environment*. Singapore: Singapore University Press, 2003.

Index